SCIENCE
— for the —
EARTH

SCIENCE
for the
EARTH

Can Science Make the World a Better Place?

Edited by Tom Wakeford *and* Martin Walters

Foreword by Professor Stephen Hawking

JOHN WILEY & SONS
Chichester · New York · Brisbane · Toronto · Singapore

Published by John Wiley & Sons Ltd,
Baffins Lane, Chichester,
West Sussex PO19 1UD, England
Telephone National 01243 779777
International (+44) 1243 779777

Reprinted August 1995, November 1995

Other Wiley Editorial Offices

John Wiley & Sons, Inc., 605 Third Avenue,
New York, NY 10158-0012, USA

Jacaranda Wiley Ltd, 33 Park Road, Milton
Queensland 4064, Australia

John Wiley & Sons (Canada) Ltd, 22 Worcester Road,
Rexdale, Ontario M9W 1L1, Canada

John Wiley & Sons (SEA) Pte Ltd, 37 Jalan Pemimpin #05-04,
Block B, Union Industrial Building, Singapore 2057

Library of Congress Cataloging-in-Publication Data
Science for the earth: can science make the world a better place?/
edited by Tom Wakeford and Martin Walters.
p. cm.
includes bibliographical references and index.
ISBN 0-471-95283-4 ISBN 0-471-95284-2
1. Science—Social aspects—Popular works. 2. Science—Environmental
aspects—Popular works. 3. Environmental sciences—Popular works.
I. Wakeford, Tom. II. Walters, Martin.
Q175.5.S362   1995   94–43583
                                                      CIP

British Library Cataloguing in Publication Data
A catalogue record for this book is available from the British Library

ISBN 0-471-95283-4 (ppc)
ISBN 0-471-95284-2 (pbk)

Typeset in 11/13 pt Times by Dobbie Typesetting Limited, Tavistock, Devon
Printed and bound in Great Britain by Biddles Limited, Guildford and King's Lynn

This book is printed on acid-free paper responsibly manufactured from sustainable
forestation, for which at least two trees are planted for each one used for paper
production.

Contents

Foreword

Stephen Hawking

WHETHER we like it or not, science has changed the world a great deal since the start of the Industrial Revolution. Some people may deplore this, but there is no practical possibility of putting back the clock and returning to how we were in 1800. Not that many people would want to go back.

Although we cannot go back, we have to think very seriously about how we go forward from here. We know about the population explosion and global warming. These are grave problems that we will have to face in the next century. More worrying to me are developments that threaten the very survival of the human race. An all-out nuclear war was one of these dangers. The chances of such a war have decreased since the collapse of the Soviet Union, but most of the Cold War weapons are still around. It is very important that the vast majority of these weapons, American, British, French and Chinese, as well as Soviet, should be dismantled and their fissile material made unusable. There is now no Great Enemy to justify maintaining a large nuclear arsenal.

Even if we manage to avoid killing ourselves in a war, or poisoning ourselves with pollution, there will still be great dangers for the human race. The development of genetic engineering can bring great benefits, but also opens the doors to frightening possibilities. Imagine a virus appearing that is as deadly as the AIDS virus, but which is spread by airborne infection like the common cold. It could wipe out most of the human race. It is no good banning research on genetic engineering. People would still do it in secret because it can pay.

As scientists, it is our duty to educate ourselves, and the public, about both the opportunities and the dangers that science offers. The human race cannot turn its back on science, but it needs to be taught how to use it responsibly.

Stephen Hawking

Introduction

HOW can science be 'for the Earth'? Throughout the 20th century most scientists and many others have denied that the practice of science can be 'for' anything other than the dispassionate pursuit of 'objective' truth. Until recently, the implication of the title of this book would have been treated with derision. Only a revolution over the past 10 years in attitudes both to the human impact on the environment and to the nature of scientific endeavor has made this book possible.

Crossing traditional academic boundaries to bring together scientists, social scientists, diplomats, environmentalists and human rights campaigners, this collection draws together a rich and diverse selection of critical reflections on science. Yet the book is not 'anti-science', nor 'against scientists'. Rather, the authors seek to explore the ways in which the dominant cultural ethos that promotes belief in science's exclusivity, distance and elitism undermines humanity's ability to engage with many of its most pressing problems.

The contributors to this book all believe that science can and must radically reform itself to be able to contribute to the solution of social and environmental problems. Almost every contribution has been written specially for this book. The chapters have been divided into three parts, but can be read in any order.

Part I takes a critical overview of current scientific practice. Why don't scientists think philosophically? Is scientific truth independent of culture? Does the present technological society offer 'progress'? Where do indigenous peoples fit in? Why are there so many disciplines in science that seem unable to communicate with one another, let alone be understood by other audiences? All these questions are posed, and answers suggested, in the context of an environmental crisis.

In the first chapter, David Suzuki, best known as a geneticist and broadcaster, uses the insights drawn from this work to identify industrial society's 'sacred truths'. He believes that we cling to these truths because of perceptual filters through which we perceive the world. The truths are taken for granted, yet are the cause of many of our problems. Suzuki challenges us with seven sacred truths that touch on issues relating to nature, economic growth, human intelligence and democracy. He concludes that only by educating ourselves out of these and other disastrous beliefs can we reach a sustainable future.

Lynn Margulis, distinguished by her work in cell biology and global ecology, confronts scientists with their discouraging attitude to philosophy and other 'ways of knowing'. She feels her scientist colleagues have been driven to promote implausible ideas because of their tightly circumscribed experiences and closed-minded obstinacy. She uses the insights of astronauts to take us outside the Earth and look from outside in, while also drawing attention to the elaborate systems of knowledge of indigenous peoples and their relationship with local problems, resources and the pressing needs of their societies.

In Chapter 3, James Lovelock accuses science today of being fat, lazy and corrupt—a comfortable career for the mediocre. He feels that the revulsion of the Green movement towards modern science is justified. Lovelock, creator with Lynn Margulis of the Gaia hypothesis, atmospheric chemist and inventor, charts the rise of reductionism, publication rates and pseudo-certainty at the expense of true discovery and wonder. Above all, Lovelock deplores 'scientific correctness', which he sees as a new form of censorship. He also believes that there is an urgent need for more generalist scientists—he calls them 'planetary physicians'. Lovelock's contribution gives several insights and some urgent warnings from this new perspective.

From the very moment of its independence, India's rulers, beginning with Nehru, trusted that science alone 'could solve the problems of hunger and poverty, of insanitation and illiteracy, of superstition and deadening custom and tradition of vast resources running to waste'. So said Nehru. Writer and scholar Claude Alvares turns this argument on its head and instead charts the decline of science in his native India. Science, he claims, has made hunger and poverty worse, deprived people of their literacy of the natural world, brought its own superstitions and violent customs and wasted the energies of a nation. Drawing on the little-known writings on science by Mahatma Gandhi, a key player in ending colonial rule, Alvares suggests that decolonization will only be complete when 'modern' science has also been expelled.

Part II looks at some ways in which science, society and environment interact in particular contexts. Can scientific principles help the less developed world? Why do academic disciplines manage to encompass research that has huge implications for human society, yet apparently do not feel the need to address the risks inherent in the application of their knowledge? How can we know whether technology that is promoted in the name of science as 'progress' really is 'progress'? Is science teaching a tool for change or merely a mirror of present culture?

George Monbiot uses his experience of rural development in the less developed world to develop a critique of Garrett Hardin's *The Tragedy of the Commons*, which advocated the enclosure of common land as the only means of sustainable management. Monbiot's intimate knowledge of the human ecology of communities in both temperate and tropical regions enables him to challenge Hardin's arguments which, he points out, reflected the prevailing Western economic orthodoxy (at a time of panic about growing famine) more than any deep knowledge of native peoples. International eco-tourists appear to be among few groups that gain from the destruction of indigenous homelands. Monbiot's arguments are illustrated by a stunning photographic essay by his companion and photographer, Adrian Arbib.

For years John Whitelegg was a leading academic geographer in the UK and Germany. He now acts as an independent adviser and consultant on environmental and transport issues, and takes a critical look at society's use of technology to 'save time'. Using studies of transport and society, Whitelegg shows that time-saving, justified by 'scientific' reasoning, actually causes extra pollution. Tourism, even of the 'eco' variety, is no more than time-compressed virtual reality in an exotic location for Whitelegg, who goes on to outline a scenario where society could use time sustainably.

Crispin Tickell, now Warden of an Oxford University college, and previously British Permanent Representative at the United Nations, looks at the impact of climate change on cities, which he sees as a kind of collective organism sucking in resources and spewing out wastes. After surveying the factors making cities vulnerable to climate change, he looks at the general symptoms of distress which they may experience in the next century, emphasizing that the effects of climate change cannot be isolated from those of population increase, pollution and degradation of habitats and ecosystems.

The possible effects of global climate change discussed by Tickell have led to international climate negotiations which provide an example of the increasing use of 'green' economics, analyzed by Tony Cooper and Aubrey Meyer. Paralleling Margulis' description of natural scientists, they suggest that economists often have a conveniently narrow perspective on important problems. Yet, though our trust in crude economic reasoning should be less and less, such principles are used more and more, as in the global climate change negotiations described by Cooper and Meyer. They introduce the concept of the 'global commons' a concept premised upon limited natural resources and social justice.

Nigel Woodcock, an environmental geologist, analyzes the lack of communication between geologists and society, providing a case study of Lovelock's argument in Chapter 3. Woodcock reveals the paradox that the geological profession, who claim to be experts in the science of global change, are deeply involved in exploiting fossil fuels whose effluents most threaten the Earth's stability. He advocates an 'Earth system science' which embraces all Earth processes and parallels Margulis and Lovelock's Gaia hypothesis. Woodcock associates the low general awareness of resource issues with a failure in communication between geologists and society that has led not only to contradictory policy recommendations by scientists, but also to policy-makers too ill-informed to question them.

The precautionary principle is a phrase which has only recently entered public debate, but already it appears in government and industry's policy statements. What does it mean? Richard Lindsay tries to answer this question, drawing on his practical experience in nature conservation, but also drawing examples from the physical sciences and engineering. He concentrates on the increasingly widespread use of environmental impact assessments and explores the implications of uncertainty for decisions regarding humanity's relationship with its environment.

Darrell Posey, ethnobiologist and campaigner for the rights of indigenous peoples, uses his first-hand knowledge of the native peoples of the Amazon and other regions to examine whether green consumerism is the enemy or friend of the Amazonian Indians. Considering the wealth of indigenous knowledge of biology, pharmacy and ecology, and the reliance on such knowledge by pharmaceutical transnationals, Posey asks whether the controlled exploitation of these resources will lead to the saving of the region from logging, or the loss of the very culture which contains the priceless knowledge.

Drawing on his detailed knowledge of science education, Stephen Tomkins examines the role of schools in formulating an environmental ethic that will alter human behavior towards the environment. He sees schools as largely reflecting society, but yet slowly changing it for the better. Can we rely on teachers to deliver an environmental ethic to children? Despite the urgency for action he warns that over-centralized dictats are not the ideal solution. Tomkins calls for a greater awareness, in school, of the place of humans in evolution and ecology. A confidence in higher quality science teaching and a greater freedom for teacher-directed curriculum development may together be expected to produce a new holism in cross-curricular thinking about the environment, and a whole society with a more ecological thought-frame.

Part III offers insights into more general aspects of Western science and their relevance to our relationship with the Earth. What is 'reductionism' and is it the right approach to all science? Has the mechanist approach to scientific research been extended too far? Does ecology, perhaps the youngest science, have any lessons for the rest of society? Can there be science without the idea of progress? Do experts exist? Can science still be viewed as a unified project? Is science just a myth particular to our age? These are philosophical and sociological questions, yet all three authors believe that they are relevant to the reform of science.

As the first woman in black Africa to be awarded a PhD and the first female professor at the University of Nairobi, Wangari Maathai gives a unique personal overview of the relationship between science and the environment in nonindustrialized countries. She sees the world's population as a pyramid of financial wealth. Many of those at the bottom of the pyramid do not have enough resources to meet their own needs and those at the top are blinded, she suggests, by insatiable appetites backed by scientific knowledge and industrial power, the need to acquire, accumulate and over-consume. For Maathai, those at the bottom are as much the symptom of environmental degradation caused by others as the cause themselves.

Brian Moss compares science to Hans Christian Andersen's *Emperor*. From the viewpoint of a head of a large university biology department, Moss observes how scientific research and education are carried out in the context of Western capitalism. He also uses his unique insights from freshwater ecology to suggest the presence of alternative stable states in societies. Given the failure of even the most eminent scientific bodies to rise to the challenge of a science for the Earth, it may be, suggests Moss, that school students, seeing the Emperor to be without clothes, choose to study alternative subjects.

Harmke Kamminga, historian and philosopher of science, challenges the notion of an objective universal method which gives scientists privileged access to the truths about the world. She draws attention to the historical contingency of our criteria of scientific knowledge and to the 19th century legacy of a strong coupling between science and political power. Arguing that the privileged status that scientific knowledge has come to enjoy needs to be questioned to create a more socially responsible science, she suggests that scientists might consider how attributions of expertise are made and why. A 'science for the people' needs to acknowledge that all humans need to produce knowledge about the world in their interactions with the world, and that rational decisions about the kind of world in which we want to live are not—and should not be—the prerogative of scientific experts.

In the final chapter, biologist Tom Wakeford argues that practicing scientists need to shed their mantle of exclusivity and work to transform research into an open and inter-disciplinary enterprise. Only in this way can they stem the growing ambivalence to science and technology among the general public, and contribute to improving human welfare. He concludes that to deal with the environmental and other crises faced by humanity we must develop a 'research' paradigm that bridges the two cultures—not by giving scientists more authority and status, but by bringing science down to Earth.

Unified by their diversity of approaches, the contributors to this book have begun a new dialogue, one which must continue if science really is to be 'for the Earth'.

Acknowledgements

THIS book owes its origins to a chance encounter between its two editors, one a biologist, the other a writer and editor specializing in natural history and the environment. This only came about because of their mutual connection with two wonderful scientists, S. Max Walters and Norman W. Moore, to whom this book is dedicated. Tom Crompton and Tim Lenton have been involved in the *Science for the Earth* project ever since its first meeting in Cambridge, England, in 1992, which has now become an annual event.

It has been a pleasure to work with the contributors who were patient and helpful throughout the book's protracted gestation. Amongst the many others to whom we owe thanks for helping bring this project to fruition are: Tariq Ali, Tess Adkins, Patrick Bateson, Emm Birnie, Su Bowman, Caroline van den Brul, Bob Carling, Sarah Corbet, Alan Cottey, Lesli and Roger Day, Jan Dean, Ron Dimant, Michael Dolan, Rachel Duncan, The Ecological Foundation, Harriet Elson, Zak Erzinclioglu, Anita Gordon, Flora Hardy, Sheila Hargreaves, Caspar Henderson, Joyce Henderson, Jeremy Leggett, Sandy Lovelock, Paco Martinez-Murillo, Sue Mayer, Kate Maloney, Sue Masey, Audrey Mitton, Jenny Nelson, Ian Prestt, Frances Price, Donna Reppard, Miriam Rothschild, Jonathon Sinclair-Wilson, John Stolz, Landi Stone, Maggie Thurgood, Oliver Tickell, Helga Tomkins,

Gail Vines, John Wakeford, WARMER Campaign, Phillip Webber, Deena Weinstein, Steven Yearley. We also thank Geoff Farrell, Iain Stevenson, Abi Hudlass and Claire Walker, and all those at John Wiley who brought about the efficient synthesis of the final product.

Royalties from sales of this book are being donated to Scientists for Global Responsibility (U.K.), the Union of Concerned Scientists (U.S.A.), and their affiliates.

Part I

OVERVIEW

David Suzuki.
Credit: Fred Phipps/CBC Television

Author biography

Unesco Prize-winning geneticist David Suzuki has felt increasingly drawn during his life to the social impacts of his science, from eugenics to rainforest destruction. Best known to biologists for his classic text *Introduction to Genetic Analysis*, he is more popularly known as a writer, radio and television journalist on scientific and environmental issues. He is host of the long-running Canadian TV series *The Nature of Things* as well as the BBC series *Cracking the Code*.

Chapter 1

David Suzuki

Blinded by Our Minds

IT HAS been my fortune to participate in two disciplines: in science as a geneticist and in journalism as a television host and writer. It is interesting to see the beliefs and values held by professionals in these two areas. The great boast of journalism is to aspire to reporting that is balanced and objective, whereas scientists perpetuate the image of objective seekers of truth who follow where the facts lead. In both cases, the reality is a long way from the ideals.

This is because, however seriously we espouse the model of objectivity, the inescapable fact is that each of us, regardless of profession, is first and foremost a human being with beliefs, values and attitudes which are shaped by our personal experiences. The way we perceive the world is conditioned by the cultural, social, economic and political milieu in which we grow up. Gender, religion, race, socioeconomic position and physical appearance all affect the kinds of experiences we have and thus the way we think.

That is why in both journalism and in science, despite the claims of simply reporting the facts, it does matter whether women and people of many races participate.

I was struck by how different perspectives may be when I became involved in a battle over the fate of the last untouched watershed in the southwestern corner of British Columbia. The Stein Valley is sacred to the area's aboriginal people who recruited environmentalists to help them oppose proposed logging of the forest. In the early 1980s, a native elder and I were flown by helicopter over the Stein Valley. He pointed out his people's sacred burial sites, the salmon spawning grounds, the grizzly bear feeding area and the site of a great battle between rival tribes centuries ago. The pilot chimed in: 'Last week I flew a group of forest industry people and politicians along the same route and all they talked about was jobs, board, feet and profit.' It was a striking illustration of how two groups of people could look down at the same watershed and forest, yet see profoundly different things. We encounter the same thing in the perspectives of Catholics and Protestants in Northern Ireland, of blacks and whites in South Africa, of Jews and Arabs in the Middle East—people sharing the same territory, but 'seeing' very different realities.

I dwell on this because these *perceptual filters* underlie our apparent inability to respond seriously to the global ecological crisis. Organizations ranging from Greenpeace to the Worldwatch Institute and the Union of Concerned Scientists have warned about the catastrophic degradation of the planet's life support systems. From the explosion in human numbers to decline in food production, deforestation, toxic pollution, atmospheric changes and species extinction, the facts are horrifying and undeniable. Yet the destruction continues.

In Rio de Janeiro in June 1992, the largest group of world leaders in history assembled for the Earth Summit.

4

It was meant to signal global concern for the degrading biosphere and the political commitment to act on it. Yet two weeks later, the heads of the Group of Seven leading industrial countries met in Munich and did not mention a word about Rio or the environment. And now, several years later, the urgency and will to act are not evident as governments scramble with their economies. The question is why, if the world is in such a desperate state, are we not responding as forcefully as we did in the Second World War, and more recently against Iraq?

In 1988, the US Presidential candidate, George Bush, promised to be an 'environmental president'. Once elected, he quickly showed that his statements were crass political opportunism. At the same time, Canadian Prime Minister Brian Mulroney suddenly discovered the environment as a priority. When he was re-elected in 1988, he appointed a high-profile man, Lucien Bouchard, as Minister of the Environment. I interviewed Bouchard shortly after his appointment and asked him what he felt was his most serious challenge. He answered immediately 'global warming'. Impressed, I asked how serious it was. 'We're talking about the survival of our species. If we don't act now, we face a catastrophe', he said. I was ecstatic and went on: 'So does that mean your government will cancel all megaprojects to develop oil and gas and concentrate on conservation and energy alternatives?' His response was a shock: 'We can't annihilate the past. We made political promises that we have to carry out.' So here was an intelligent, well-meaning person who articulated an understanding that global warming threatened our very survival, yet failed to integrate that crisis into his political priorities.

Bouchard's ability to defend completely contradictory demands illustrates the way we compartmentalize our lives so we see the world as disconnected fragments. During a heated argument with the president of one of Canada's largest forest companies over the environmental pollution by one of his company's pulp mills, he said with absolute sincerity 'I'm an environmentalist too. I have seven children and I care about the future.' Somehow, he too had failed to connect what his company was doing with the future of his children.

Try analyzing a typical 10 minute news report on radio or television. Items ranging from 10 to 40 seconds are strung together as completely separate reports. Each story is too brief to provide any of the historical context within which it matters, or what the broad implications are. So, like the increasingly fragmented way we live our lives, the media also shatter the world around us.

We have another very different problem: the great survival strategy of our species was adaptability, but that now blinds us to what is going on. Our species' plasticity enabled us to use our brains to recognize patterns of regularity in our surroundings and to exploit those patterns to our advantage. As we acquired a measure of control over the factors impinging on our lives, we adapted to a variety of habitats ranging from the Amazon rainforest to the deserts of Australia, the plains of Africa and the Arctic tundra. (Some of us even manage to adapt to New York or Los Angeles.) This cultural and social change was far faster than genetic change within a species, but still took place over centuries or even millennia. Today, change has become a normal part of the way we live. We have come to expect and even to welcome almost all change, and regard it as a measure of progress. In our ability to adapt to rapid change, we have lost the perspective of time and speed. Thus, although aboriginal people in North America still think in time-frames extending seven generations into the past and seven generations into the future, our priorities are often driven by annual car models or clothes fashions, quarterly stock dividends or the next pay check. In other words, we soon forget how things were and thus have no reference against which to compare the present.

One of the important lessons aboriginal people have taught me is to listen to my elders, whose knowledge and experience are priceless. As I've traveled across North America, I've talked to non-aboriginal elders from Newfoundland to Vancouver Island about what things were like 60 and 70 years ago. All across the country, my elders inform me that Canada and the United States have changed beyond recognition. Our elders are a living record of the enormous changes that have happened within the span of a single human life. By projecting the changes that they have experienced into the future, it becomes clear that our children already live in a radically diminished world and that the planet cannot sustain a continuation of this change into the next millennium. In the past, people would say 'There's plenty more where that came from'. There isn't plenty more today—all over the planet wilderness is disappearing and taking with it up to 50 000 species a year. In the past, others would shrug their shoulders and say 'That's the price of progress'. But it is not progress to use up now what should be the legacy for our children and for all future generations.

The greatest hurdles we face in convincing people of the severity of the eco-crisis are the psychic filters through which we perceive reality. I call these filters 'sacred truths', notions that are so deeply held that they are taken for granted and never questioned, yet are often the very cause of the problems we are trying to resolve. Let me show you what I mean.

(1) *We believe that human beings are superior to other life forms and because our intelligence enables us to understand and control our surroundings, we lie outside the natural world*

It is easy to understand why we have come to believe this. Eighty percent of North Americans live in cities and towns. We live in a human-created environment that gives the illusion that we can 'manage' our surroundings. Furthermore, the very notion of wildness or our biological roots has become a pejorative. Foresters speak of old growth forests as 'wild' forests and the tree plantations that replace them as 'normal' forests. If we refer to someone as an 'animal' or being 'wild', we insult them, just as we do by calling them 'pigs', 'apes', 'chickens', 'asses', etc.

Very few urban dwellers understand that as biological beings we continue to depend on the natural world for our very lives. We have an absolute requirement for air, water and soil through the food we eat. These are part of a global common that we neither fully comprehend nor control, and they are the very underpinnings of global economies. It is the interdependence of all life on Earth and the physical environment that make the planet hospitable for human life. By disconnecting ourselves from the natural world we can continue to believe that even though the birds nesting around Lake Ontario and the fish that live in it have a high frequency of developmental abnormalities and tumors, human beings can continue to drink its water and pollute it. We believe that we can get rid of vast quantities of toxic chemicals by diluting them in the air, water or soil, or foisting them on the poor in our own countries and abroad. We fail to recognize the signals—beluga whales that are too toxic to touch, thousands of seals dying in the North Sea, species' disappearance—as warnings because we no longer feel connected to them. Not long ago, coal miners took canaries into the pits with them to warn them of dangerous gases. Today, 'canaries' are collapsing all around us, but we fail to recognize the signs because we believe so strongly that we are different.

(2) *We believe that science provides us with the insights upon which our control is based*

Anyone who understands how science differs from other ways of knowing recognizes that this assumption is wrong. The essence of the scientific method is that we focus on a part of nature, attempt to bring it into the laboratory or under the microscope and control factors impinging on it and emanating from it. In this way, we gain knowledge about that isolated bit of nature. Ever since Newton's time it has been our belief that by focusing on the smallest fragments of nature, eventually we can understand the whole by piecing the parts together. Twentieth century physicists have understood that such reductionism simply does not work at the most elementary levels of matter. As Nobel laureate Roger Sperry has said, 'There are properties that emerge from the whole that cannot be predicted on the basis of the properties of the individual parts.' Unfortunately, most medical doctors, biologists, business people and politicians continue to operate on Newtonian assumptions.

Even if scientists were able to come up with principles that govern higher levels of organization and provide some measure of predictability and control, how much do we know? Although the growth of science has exploded in the 20th century, especially since the Second World War, the amount that we do not know is still far more impressive than the amount that we do, especially in the biological sciences. To take as one simple example: how many species are there on Earth? We do not know. There are ways of estimating, and these estimates vary from 5 to 30 million. To date, biologists have identified 1.4 million species. That merely means that a dead specimen has been given a name. It does not mean we know anything about its basic biology, habitat, food needs, reproduction, interaction with other species, geographic distribution, and so on. I spoke to the eminent entomologist, Tom Eisner of Cornell, who has done more to interest people in insects than anyone I know, and he said he knows perhaps five or six insects 'very well'. And he is a world expert on insects. I reckon that hundreds of billions of dollars have been spent on studying *Drosophila melanogaster*, the fruit fly, and yet we still do not even know how it survives the winter in Canada or what its natural distribution is. It is simply erroneous to put so much faith in science as the means of our long-term environmental salvation.

(3) *We believe we can manage new technologies so their hazards can be minimized*

In the past, new technologies have rapidly become a part of our lives, so that their social, medical and environmental 'costs' only become apparent later. But can we do proper cost–benefit analyses of new technologies beforehand? History informs us that we cannot. We are so ignorant about the biophysical nature of the planet that we cannot anticipate the long-term consequences of most things. Take two examples. When the atomic bomb was first built, what would a cost–benefit study have come up with? The advantages were that the bombs might hasten the end of a nasty war and thereby save countless lives. There was some knowledge that radiation caused mutations. Perhaps a wild-eyed futurist might have foreseen a worldwide arms race, although the Soviet Union had not yet become the West's enemy. But no-one could have anticipated radioactive fallout (which was discovered at Bikini), hydrogen bombs, electromagnetic pulses of gamma rays or nuclear winter because these were all discovered after the end of the war.

Consider pesticides. If at the time DDT was first being used as a pesticide there had been a cost–benefit analysis, the benefits of killing agropests, disease vectors or just plain nuisance insects were obvious. Geneticists could have suggested that by selecting resistance genes, the pesticides would quickly lose their effectiveness and ecologists might have pointed out that as insects are over 90% of all animal species, they are the most ubiquitous and arguably the most important group of animals on Earth. When only one in a thousand insect species is a pest to human beings, spraying with chemicals that kill all insects just to get at the one or two that annoy us does not make much ecological sense. But no-one would have mentioned biomagnification, the process whereby trace levels of molecules are concentrated hundreds of thousands, or even millions, of times up the food chain. That is because we only learned of the phenomenon of biomagnification when birds such as eagles began to disappear because of high levels of DDT. The lesson that history provides is that the benefits of new technologies are immediate and obvious, that is why we love novelty. But the costs—and every technology, however beneficial, has costs—cannot be predicted beforehand because we know so little.

(4) *We believe that through environmental assessments we can avoid environmental problems from new developments such as dams, clear-cut logging, factories, etc.*

This sacred truth must be dropped for the same reasons that number 3 is wrong. But there is an additional point. Human beings will continue to cut forests, build dams and develop housing, and one way of trying to anticipate the ecological consequences is by having environmental impact assessments. The problem is that the enormity of our ignorance precludes making even educated guesses.

Environmental assessments, for example, of drilling for oil in the high Arctic, are made on the basis of seasonal studies carried out over perhaps two or three years. In the Arctic, where water is frozen for nine months of the year, it is completely dark for four to five months and conditions are hostile for human beings, research conditions are, to say the least, difficult. Generally studies are carried out by summer students (often under the direction of the companies wanting to drill) looking at a few species. Now, in the Arctic, populations of different animals and plants are exquisitely adapted to this unforgiving environment and may fluctuate in cycles covering 15 or 20 years or more. The notion that a short summer assessment of a select group of organisms over a limited range tells us anything at all about the complexity of Arctic communities is simply ludicrous. Such data are scientifically worthless because they are so limited in scale, scope and duration. These ideas are explored further in Richard Lindsay's chapter.

(5) *We believe the economy is the major priority that must occupy us and that all other areas make up a part of the economy*

The fundamentals underpinning all life on Earth are air, water, soil and biodiversity. Without these, we and most other creatures would not be here. So they must be considered a sacred truth that comes before all else. Everything we have in our homes and workplaces, whether plastic, glass, metal, energy, cloth, wood, etc., comes from the Earth. The planet is finite, so our economy is founded on limited resources. Some are renewable (thank goodness), but must be exploited in a way that allows their sustainability.

Economics is a human construct that is now completely out of touch with the real world. For one thing, mainstream economists do not speak of limits to growth or of resources. As they believe the human mind is the greatest resource and is limitless in its potential, the faith is that we will discover new sources when resources run out, invent new alternatives or travel to other places in the universe. Even more pernicious, air, water, soil and biodiversity are classified as 'externalities' to economics; they are not even a central part of this construct. This enables economists to build a system of values on the basis of human utility. If something has a use for us, then it is worth something. If it does not, then it is worthless. This is species chauvinism of the highest order that lets us—one species out of perhaps 30 million—set a value on everything. The Premier of Quebec, Robert Bourassa, has a grand scheme to dam every major river flowing into James and Hudson's bays for electricity. He speaks of millions of kilowatts 'wasted every day' in an area that is an 'empty wasteland.' Yet to the thousands of aboriginal people and the countless indigenous plants and animals, the area is fully occupied and fully developed. But the economic mentality does not see it the same way.

Global economics now afflicts countries around the world, seeming to be the key to their future prosperity and progress. But because money is no longer based on reality, it has come solely to represent itself and can now be multiplied without any relation to the real world. The recent struggle of governments and banks to bring currency values under control exposed the horrible fact that currency speculators today spend 600 billion dollars a day on the markets, dwarfing most government economies, yet contributing absolutely nothing to the planet except the making of more money.

Globalization of the economy and the market means that national boundaries become porous to money. Money grows faster than biological organisms, so, for example,

British Colombian temperate rainforests 'add fiber' at the rate of 1–2% per year. Clearly, if only 1 or 2% of the trees were cut down annually in any one area, the forests could be maintained forever, but it makes no 'economic sense' to recover only 1 or 2% of an investment when, by clear-cutting the entire forest, the money can provide 7–8% on interest alone. If the money was invested in forests in Papua New Guinea or Malaysia, it could bring in 20%. Once the forests are gone, the companies can invest in fish, and when the fish are gone, the money can be put into computers or into biotechnology. Thus, global economics, as described in Cooper and Meyer's chapter, drives the destruction of the planet.

(6) *We believe that growth is the criterion of 'progress'*

This is a corollary of truth number 5. In our society, progress has become synonymous with growth. We measure the performance of a company or government by its profit margin or growth in the economy. But as everyone wants progress, when that is measured by growth, there is no end to it. No country on Earth has decided that it has enough and wishes to stay at that level of income and consumption. Because when growth is progress, then stasis or balance becomes a kind of death. No company can afford to stay at the same level of income or profit or market share in the topsy-turvy world of economics.

The Brundtland Commission coined the phrase 'sustainable development' as the means of our ecological salvation. However, in most parts of the developed world, development does not refer to personal or spiritual development, but to growth. In a finite world, this is simply an impossible goal. There *are* limits to growth, and many of us believe we have already overshot the carrying capacity of the planet. The depredations are not just from population growth in the developing countries, but are far greater from the consumptive demands of the developed world. The challenge is twofold: to make a greater share of the planet's resources accessible to the poor countries so that they will bring their reproductive rate down, while drastically cutting back on consumption and pollution by the developed nations.

(7) *We believe that, in a democracy, we elect people to represent us and lead us into the future*

There are two points to make about this notion. The first is that politicians clearly do not 'represent' us. If they did, over half would be women and there would be those from visible minorities, from white collar workers, full-time homemakers, etc., in direct proportion to their numbers. In fact, politicians come disproportionately from law and business because its practitioners have the means to handle the costs of running for office and of defeat. This skews government priorities towards issues of jurisdiction and economics.

We live in a world in which the dominant issues of our time—genetic engineering, computers, telecommunications, ecological destruction—are caused and will be solved by applications of science and technology. Yet most politicians, especially lawyers and business people, are scientifically 'illiterate' and incapable of assessing the scientific and technological recommendations of their advisers. We are not led into the future, we back into it.

The second point to make is that the way we establish human bureaucratic subdivisions to run our affairs does not make ecological sense. Our national, provincial and municipal borders are generally geometric—shapes that have little to do with the geophysical boundaries of watersheds, lake and river systems, foothills, mountain tops and so on. It is simply not possible to regulate water, air or living organisms as if they conform to human jurisdictions. The greatest body of freshwater in the world, the Great Lakes, supports about 35 million people. We use the waters for transportation, fishing, recreation, industry, agriculture, sewage disposal and drinking water. Water regulations are administered by different departments corresponding to these human uses, each of which has its own requirements and priorities. Thus the water is not dealt with as a single ecological system. Furthermore, the jurisdictional turf wars encourage jealousy and mistrust. Two countries, Canada and the USA, impinge on the Great Lakes and so there is an International Joint Commission. However, two provinces and eight states also border the Great Lakes, and dozens of municipalities, ranging from cities such as Chicago, Detroit and Toronto. These human bureaucratic fiefdoms prevent the cooperation and sharing that is needed for a comprehensive strategy of protecting the Great Lakes.

These are just a few sacred truths. Others can no doubt come up with their own list that illustrate other fallacious beliefs. If we are to come to grips with the magnitude and severity of the global eco-crisis and the need for profound change, we must recognize the fallacies of our beliefs so that we can then see the world through completely different eyes. Only then can we begin to reassess our place in the natural world and formulate the best strategies to reach a truly sustainable future.

Annotated List of Further Reading

Manufacturing Consent: Thought Control in Democratic Societies, Noam Chomsky, Boston: Beacon Press, 1991.

Ironically called 'One of the most important intellectuals alive' by the book review of the *New York Times*, a newspaper he has condemned, Noam Chomsky has written extensively on the way capitalist democracies manufacture the consent of the public rather than engendering understanding. Why do we remember Vietnam when more people were dying at the same time in East Timor?

Global Ecology: Conflicts and Contradictions, Wolfgang Sachs (Ed.), London: Zed Books, 1992.

A radical critique of the 'globalization' of western knowledge under the banner of environmentalism. Many environmentalists now support the global empowerment of government, corporations and science rather than more democracy and local self-reliance. Once they strove for cultural diversity, now they see no other choice than to push for a world-wide rationalization of lifestyles. This book offers elements of an alternative vision.

Biology as Ideology/The Doctrine of DNA, Richard Lewontin, New York: HarperCollins and London: Penguin, 1992.

Takes a close and informed look at the tidy and showmanlike packaging of science, especially new genetic techniques, as the panacea to human problems, persuasively demonstrating how science and scientists are moulded by society. By admitting the shadings and limitations within science, a leading geneticist here helps us rediscover both the richness of human nature and the value of science.

Lynn Margulis.
Credit: University of Massachusetts Photo Service

Author biography

Lynn Margulis engages in research spanning the smallest living systems, bacteria, to possibly the largest, Gaia; ranging from the technical minutiae of microbiology to the thrill of the communication, history and philosophy of science. Though now a member of the National Academy of Sciences, her 1960s investigations into the possible symbiotic origin of chloroplasts and mitochondria went without recognition and often even lacked official funding. Within the past 20 years genetic techniques have vindicated her early ideas, as set out in the second edition of her book, *Symbiosis in Cell Evolution*. The symbiotic origin of cilia from spirochete bacteria, which she is currently investigating, has so far been either ignored or rejected, but the theory that the cell organelles responsible for respiration and photosynthesis in animals and plants originated as bacteria is now accepted as scientific fact.

Chapter 2

Lynn Margulis

'A Pox Called Man'

MY TITLE is from Nietzsche, who said 100 years ago that 'The Earth is a beautiful place, but it has a pox called man.'

Firstly, I would like to consider philosophy and philosophers. Scientists resent philosophy. I think this is because they are afraid that philosophers will reveal what scientists really do. I agree with Kierkegaard's assertion

The less support an idea has, the more fervently it must be believed. A totally preposterous idea requires absolute unflinching faith.

I suggest that our culture is teeming with preposterous ideas, believed with unflinching faith by scientists and everyone else, and that some of these actually corrupt our potential concern for the Earth.

Modern science has given very important insights about life, but our culture prevents us from accepting and utilizing those insights. I use four main examples: the Earth from space; the Chewong peoples of the forested regions of Malaysia; the organisms of the microcosm, most of which are ignored by biologists; and lessons from Gaia, the Vernadsky/Lovelock view of life beyond biology.

Nietzsche understood by philosophy 'a terrible explosive in the presence of which everything is in danger'. Scientists are terrified both by philosophy and philosophers. They tend to denounce philosophy as 'soft' or deny its relevance, when in fact it has much to say about what scientists do.

The Earth from space

The image of the Earth from space (Figure 2.1) transformed all the cosmonauts and astronauts. They have tried to explain their philosophical shift to the public, but feel they are not listened to. Frank White published a book

Figure 2.1. The Earth from space, courtesy of NASA

containing interviews with all living cosmonauts and astronauts, which takes us with them out into space, looking in. For example, Eugene Cernan, the last person to walk on the Moon, says

When you are in Earth orbit, looking down, you see lakes, rivers, and peninsulas such as Florida or Baja California. You quickly fly over the changes in topography like snow-covered mountains or deserts or tropical belts—all very visible. You pass through sunrise and sunset every ninety minutes.

When you are in Earth orbit you get a new perspective. One minute you are over the United States, the next minute, you are over another area of the world. You can see from pole to pole and ocean to ocean without even turning your head. You literally see North and South America go around the corner as the Earth turns on an axis you can't see and then miraculously Australia, then Asia, then all of America comes up to replace them. You ask yourself the question, 'Where really am I in space and time?'

You don't see the barriers of color and religion and politics that divide this world. You wonder, if you could get everyone in the world up there, wouldn't they have a different feeling—a new perspective?

The cosmonauts and astronauts are all trying to convey that same message. Scientists studying other planets, Mars, Jupiter, Venus, study them as wholes, but we who study the Earth do not. Why don't we? We don't because we are children of a Judaeo-Christian, Muslim, Neo-Darwinist or some other kind of religion. These religions are absurdities in that not only are they muddled, but they are dangerous for our relationship with the Earth and our non-human planetmates. The cultural background in which we have been brought up precludes our learning about the

Earth as a whole planet. When scientific results clash with cultural and religious unstated 'truths', science demurs.

Remote sensing capabilities, for example, tell us a good deal about the scale of the macrocosm. Figure 2.2 is a remarkable Landsat image of an Amazonian river (running from right to left) near Rondonia, Brazil. What are these lines? A variant of crop circles? A dehumanizing housing estate? At ground level we can see that these lines are actually roads surrounded on each side by destroyed strips of forest (Figure 2.3). The enormous rate of forest clearing makes it a global phenomenon.

We feel no pain as we saw off our noses to spite our faces because the tree carnage is done in the name of progress, saleable forest products and more 'Lebensraum' for desperate Brazilians.

The Elders

David Suzuki and Peter Knudtson's wonderful book, *Wisdom of the Elders*, shows that the pattern in many

Figure 2.2. Satellite image of stripes in the Amazon rain forest, courtesy of C. J. Tucker, NASA

Figure 2.3. One stripe of the Rondonia Amazon rain forest at ground level

traditional cultures is more conducive to learning about biology than is ours. An example is the *med mesign* concept of the Chewong peoples of Malaysia. *Med mesign* means 'different eye'. Each type of creature sees the world through its own eyes. There is a tiger way, a water-snail way, a monitor lizard way and a people way. *Med mesign* refers to the way each sees the world through his or her own perception. The Chewong identify with fellow life forms, illuminating their moral obligations in their attitudes and daily activities.

In one Chewong tale, a family is relentlessly pursued by a ravenous tiger. Bongso is the Chewong spiritual leader and hero. He is gifted with the ability to see in every other creature's world without losing the perspective of his own. He eventually succeeds in saving the terrified family by impaling the tiger with a trap made of sharp spears deep in the forest. As the villagers look on, he blows sacred smoke on the slain beast's head and asks it, 'Why did you want to eat us?'

And the tiger looks up, and with his last breath replies, 'All I saw was meat. All I saw was meat. All I saw was meat'. The tiger saw the fleeing family with *med mesign*. Indeed, each creature sees the truth looked at through its own eyes. The Chewong see meat as the wild game that they stalk in the forest. The man-eating tiger looked at mothers and babies, and all it saw was meat. All our culture sees is cash. All we see is cash. We only see cash. In the meantime, the forests are burned down, the rivers and oceans are polluted, children are neglected and people starve.

The organisms of the microcosm

What insights can we garner from biology? From science? What new insights do we get from studying the subvisible organisms of the microcosm?

The only ultimately productive beings are the cyanobacteria. These green geniuses convert sunlight into organic matter and release gases to the atmosphere. Many of them happen to be trapped inside plants. Productivity is a bacterial, especially cyanobacterial, virtuosity now, and it always has been. Ultimately, a nation's gross national product can only be biological, not industrial.

From school biology we know about biological variation, character changes, DNA changes and symbiogenesis. We know about the inheritance of variation and biotic potential—more individuals are produced than can possibly survive in the populations of all creatures at all times. We know that the most efficient way of getting rid of organisms, cockroaches for example, is not to kill them one by one, but to completely alter their habitat: to promote them, give them more habitat. We know about the effects of crowding. We know that the garbage never goes out, it just goes round and round. We know that matter is not lost, rather it circulates. We know that people's cells do not harbour former free-living photosynthetic bacteria, but those of plants do.

We know that there are natural limits to all population growth. This cannot be taught because our culture tells us that humans dominate the Earth. And the culture only sees cash. We know that crowding causes destruction. We know it causes fighting and other extremes of behavior. Whenever mammals are crowded, aggressive behavior results: even herbivores cannibalize their fellows if severely crowded and starved. We know these things. Why can we not do something about it? Because our cultural presumptions contradict this knowledge.

Other lessons come from the microcosm. We know that the living world is not just inhabited by animals and plants. Plants are virtually identical to animals from the view of microbiology. This divides life into the bacterial world and everything else. We know that life began three and a half billion years ago, whereas animals appeared fewer than 700 million years ago. Most evolution has not involved animals at all, and yet nearly all our studies of evolution are of animals (Figure 2.4).

The protoctists, about 250 000 species, are mute and powerless. Yet they invented nearly everything of interest to evolutionists. Development of sexes, cell fusion and intracellular motility are protoctist phenomena. The Protoctista constitute a fifth kingdom alongside plants, animals, fungi and bacteria (Figure 2.5). Protoctists consist of the nucleated cells (eukaryotes) lying outside the fungi, plants and animals. Symbiogenesis, my favorite subject, is involved in the speciation of all protoctists and many other eukaryotic organisms. Our cultural world is divided into 'plants, animals and germs', all presaging continued powerlessness for protoctists.

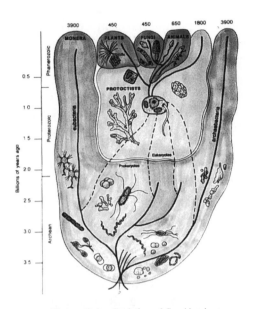

Figure 2.4. Evolution of five kingdoms

Figure 2.5. The five kingdom hand, representing the major types of life: bacteria, protoctists, fungi, animals and plants

In Western Australia, in Shark Bay, there are cyanobacterial ecosystems still in existence in areas too hypersaline for most other organisms. On this Australian coast, fascinating structures have been created by communities of cyanobacteria (Figure 2.6). Their counterparts have been studied in fossils which are at least 2000 million years old. Looking underwater, the oxygen bubbles, the waste of cyanobacteria, can be observed to be released, breaking towards the surface. In deserts, microorganisms, unlike humans, can survive for days, months, or even years. As soon as water comes, many types resume photosynthesizing. They convert sunlight into organic matter, leak oxygen and form communities. These microscopic communities are relatively stable, unlike those formed by humans. Studies of marine mud communities suggest that cyanobacteria and other accompanying microorganisms stabilize sediment to form community structures which allow the growth of many larger organisms.

Figure 2.6. Stromatolites of Shark Bay

It is now the 1990s and we still have not completed the 18th century Linnaean task of describing the species of life on Earth. This deficiency is especially evident in the three kingdoms which include microorganisms. My laboratory has spent 18 years studying 2 mm of what looks like dirty sand to most scientists. The microorganisms inhabiting the sand illuminate features of other beings. They grow, produce gaseous waste and alter their environment. Predation occurs even in bacteria. Symbiogenesis leads to new forms. Great sensitivity to environmental changes abounds.

Bacteria and protoctists are not primitive, nor necessarily unicellular or simple. Bacteria can carry out every biological process known in the biosphere, except talk. We feel we are independent of microorganisms and that they should be eradicated, but this view is just part of our inflated human arrogance. Ralph Waldo Emerson, the 19th century poet, summed up the view most people still retain of the evolutionary process

Striving to be man, the worm
Mounts through all the spires of form

Nearly everyone believes what our culture teaches: evolution has clearly come to its final summit, namely man.

Lessons from Gaia

Vernadsky is well known in Russia, but virtually unknown outside. He was a cartographer, crystallographer and a fine scientist. He gives us an insight into ideas behind biology. His book *The Biosphere*, was first published in 1926, but has yet to be fully translated into English. Vernadsky viewed life as a complex organic mineral, animated water.

He avoided the word 'life' and used 'living matter' instead. Gravity pulls things down, but living matter gradually pulls things across the Earth, he said. The biosphere is as much a manifestation of the Sun as it is of earthly properties.

> *Ancient religious institutions which regarded terrestrial creatures, especially human beings, as 'children of the sun', were much nearer the truth than those which looked upon them as a mere ephemeral creation, a blind and accidental product of matter and earth forces.*

Vernadsky wrote this in 1944, in English, but he still has been magnificently ignored. Why? Because his insights are at odds with our cultural unstated assumptions.

The Gaia hypothesis of J.E. Lovelock, originally developed independently of Vernadsky, holds that the surface temperature, chemistry of the reactive gases, redox state and pH of the Earth's atmosphere are homeorrhetically maintained by the metabolism, behavior, growth and reproduction of living organisms. Homeostasis is a physiological regulation around a fixed point, like the control of adult mammalian body temperature around $37°$ C, whereas homeorrhesis, a parallel concept, refers to a regulation around a changing set point, like temperature regulation in a developing mammalian embryo. The term 'Gaia', the name of a daunting Greek goddess, is, in Lovelock's view, simply 'a good four-letter word referring to the Earth.' She is also 'Ge' or 'Gaea' as in the continent Pan*gea*, the *Geos* satellite, *geo*logy, or *geo*graphy.

Gaian environmental regulation is achieved largely by the origin, exponential growth and extinction of organisms. All life is related by ancestry and physically connected by proximity to the fluid phases (water and air) at the Earth's surface. Organisms in communities form changing ecosystems that have persisted since the Archean period

29

(3900 to 2500 million years ago). The interactions of organisms, driven by solar energy, produce and remove gases such that the chemistry of non-noble gases, temperature and alkalinity are actively maintained within limits tolerable to life.

Within this conceptual framework, biological as well as physical sciences become appropriate to the analysis of the Earth's atmosphere and geologic history. Especially pertinent is the role of the microbiota—bacteria, protoctista and fungi—in Earth's surface gaseous exchange that involves the recycling of those chemical elements (e.g. H, C, O, N, P, S) absolutely required by life.

The product of the lively imagination of a British atmospheric chemist and the international space program, the Gaia idea has come of age. The atmospheric composition of the Earth signals unmistakably that the third planet is living: flanked by the dry carbon dioxide-rich worlds of Mars and Venus. One invokes either physiological science or magic to explain Earth's wildly improbable, combustive, thoroughly drenched troposphere (when compared with Mars and Venus). The Gaia hypothesis, in acknowledging this atmospheric disequilibrium, has opted for physiology over miracles.

Many scientists are unaware of the 25 years' worth of serious scientific Gaia literature and the potential contribution of the Gaia idea for integrating evolutionary, meteorological, sedimentological and climatological data. Unfortunately, some other Gaia literature, and the hysterically-toned 'New Age' commentary which accompanies it, has received so much press attention and contentious comment that much of the primary science remains unknown.

Despite the fact that an 'Earth system science' approach is vigorously encouraged for the solid earth sciences (see Woodcock, this volume), mention of the G-word (Gaia) still causes apoplexy in some scientific circles. This is remarkable, considering the broad parallelism of these approaches to understanding Earth processes. Despite avoidance of the term, a Gaian approach is advocated by the US National Academy of Sciences

> *A new approach to studying Earth processes [is needed], in which the Earth is viewed as an integrated, dynamic system, rather than a collection of isolated components.*

The Gaia hypothesis, rejected by some as the fantasy of New Age crystal-swingers, has largely been misunderstood by the scientific community, yet it demonstrates how life sciences are essential to understanding the Earth. Part of its failure to be accepted comes from its revelation of the inadequacy of evolutionary theory developed in the absence of climatologic and geologic knowledge. The Gaian viewpoint is not popular because so many scientists, wishing to continue business as usual, are loath to venture outside their respective disciplines. At least a generation may be needed before an understanding of the Gaia hypothesis leads to adequate research.

Gaia has been called 'Goddess of the Earth' or the 'Earth as a single living being'. These are misleading phrases.

I reject the analogy that Gaia is a single organism, primarily because no single being feeds on its own waste nor, by itself, recycles its own food. Much more appropriate is the claim that Gaia is a huge ecosystem, an interacting system, major components of which are organisms. Nowhere is this more evident than in examples of biotic influence on important geological processes, as described in Peter Westbroek's charming book *Life as a Geological Force*.

Gaia is noisy. If we listened carefully we could hear as our 30 million different species of planetmates sing to us.

Can you make out the words of the song? 'Got along without you before I met you, gonna get along without you now.'

Many species, especially those in the four non-animal kingdoms, do not need humans to take care of them and would not blink if we drove ourselves to extinction tomorrow. The assertion made by some politicians and propagandists that by preserving biodiversity we can somehow preserve the whole planet's life is just a further example of unabated human arrogance. Species conservation, as Niles Eldredge suggests, is primarily a matter of aesthetics and always has been

> It is essential for our survival to conserve the global ecosystem, which translates into conserving as much as possible of the natural ecosystems of the world. It isn't really a question of species survival at all (except in our case). It is quite true that only those of us who love nature will be hurt if the spotted owl of the old forests of the Pacific Northwest is really driven to extinction through destruction of its habitat. Targeting individual species for survival is, in part, an act derived more from aesthetics than economics. But logging interests are quite right when they accuse conservationists of not wanting to save the owl so much as they want to save the forest itself. The forest—those magnificent stands of Douglas firs and other tree species—stands for the habitat, the ecosystem, itself.

Biodiversity of microbes is essential to nutrient cycling and therefore to plant life, but the Earth could survive perfectly well a return to the pre-Phanerozoic microbial scum. Although mammalian aesthetics would be devastated, indeed survival would be undermined, were large forms of life to be permanently extinguished, Gaia would continue to prosper as she did 'before she met us'.

Culture

Every scientist does research in a cultural context. We cannot help it and it is very hard for investigators of today to see the extent to which our research is culturally dictated. But if we go back more than a hundred years, aided by Charles Gillespie's book *Genesis and Geology*, we see more clearly. In 1829 the Earl of Bridgewater pledged £8000 in his will to any great man who would study 'the Power, the Wisdom and the Goodness of God, as manifested in the Creation'. The eight works thus produced became known as the Bridgewater Treatises. Of the fortunate recipients, four were clergymen, four were physicians. Three of the eight had concerns about the Earth. I want to talk about one of these three.

Professor William Buckland, one of the first to lecture formally on geology in the 19th century, was entrusted with the sixth Treatise. Buckland introduced his Oxford University course with these words: that 'the indications of the power, wisdom and goodness of the Divinity will be demonstrated from the evidence of design in His works, and, particularly from the happy dispensation of coal, iron and limestone, by which the Omnipotent Architect or Divine Engineer has assured manufacturing primacy to his British creations.' In his treatise he went on to describe how 'a system of perpetual destruction, followed by continual renovation, has at all times tended to increase the aggregate of animal enjoyment, over the entire surface of the terraqueous globe'. The Earl's money had been made available to those who would study 'the Power, the Wisdom and the Goodness of God . . .', exactly what Buckland was doing.

We laugh at Buckland's contribution, yet he was merely working within his cultural context. He was pleasing the equivalent of his granting agency. Now let us laugh again at the National Science Foundation (NSF), which funds much of the scientific research carried out in the United States. If an investigator does what they, or other similar institutions around the world want, his loyalty cannot be to the Earth and its 30 million or so inhabitant species, because they do not fit the goals of the national institutions. The bulletin of the NSF outlines some of the guidelines under which the grants are awarded.

> *'The science has intrinsic merit leading to the advance in that field.'*
> *'The probability that the research leads to new or improved technology.'*
> *'Will it improve the quality of this nation's man-power base?'*
> *'Will it integrate resources to contribute to society and to the nation?'*

Jingoism and field chauvinism prevail. For an example of another kind of nonsense, look at the geology section in any recent NSF bulletin. 'Will the research provide insight into the physical and chemical processes that produce such geological features as hydrocarbon deposits?' But hydrocarbon deposits are biogenic; in fact, as I describe below they are protoctistical. So there is no formal way for biologists to work in this area because of the ignorance of the NSF. They have never heard of protoctists. Just as the Earl of Bridgewater did, the NSF officers determine the kind of work that people do. Scientists, like everybody else, have their outlook blinkered both by their cultural context and by those who pay for research allotments. Is there another way?

I think science itself is just one way of knowing. The way in which it informs can be multiplicitous and widely used, to further the aims of the Earl of Bridgewater, the NSF, or for other goals. Science is simply a non-dictatorial way of directing interactions with the material and energetic world. Science is a way of enhancing sensory experience with other living organisms and the environment generally. Everything is observed by an observer, but that observer exists within a cultural context.

Our culture measures scientific activity in the workplace by the rate of cash flow per square foot. Investigators are rewarded when we bring in students or grants, build buildings, buy chemicals—all of which increase the rate of cash flow. Biologists, geologists and natural historians want to nurture the rest of the biospheric inhabitants. They see that there is something out there other than people and that the others are essential to the maintenance of human culture, maybe even human existence. So we are confronted by an ultimate contradiction: we want to nurture the 30 million species with which we share the planet, but our culture insists that the world is made for humans. The criterion for 'scientific' success is the rate at which we convert the rest of the biosphere to urban ecosystems. Many of the conclusions of biological science cannot be encompassed by a culture which puts humans at the center of all things and only values the conversion of the biosphere into human habitat, including new biology buildings.

Conclusions

Kierkegaard said that the less support an idea has, the more fervently it must be believed. Totally preposterous ideas require absolute unflinching faith, including those discussed here by David Suzuki (Chapter 1). Our beliefs are so fervently held, so intimately embedded in our perspective that we can't even explicitly acknowledge them. By now I hope you will agree that

Figure 2.7. *The Earth at Night*, compiled by Woodruff T. Sullivan and the Hansen Planetarium, University of Washington, USA. Credit: © 1985 W. T. Sullivan, III

we have a cultural system
that ignores the air and water
and our biological heritage.

We have a society
that believes garbage goes out,
not around;
mistakes linen paper and metal disks
for food, searching the world at their demand;
and rewards scholars as they increase the rate of cash flow.

We suffer a culture that wants to convert the whole Earth
into its own image of God; an angry urban landlord.
Of course our culture resists the lessons of life.
Of course our culture dismisses bacteria, protoctists, and
*   fungi as germs and disdains the stranger.*
It knows no other way.

The bright dots in the photograph (Figure 2.7) are cities full of people. 'The Earth is a beautiful place', said Nietzsche, 'but it has a pox called man.'

Annotated List of Further Reading

Gaia and the Colonization of Mars, Lynn Margulis and Oona West, *GSA Today*, November, pp. 278–291, 1993.

The latest formulation of the Gaia hypothesis and its relevance to life on other planets. Most importantly, the article includes a bibliography of the professional and popular literature on Gaia.

Wisdom of the Elders: Honouring Sacred Visions of Nature, David Suzuki and Peter Knudtson, London: Bantam Press, 1992.

David Suzuki and science writer Peter Knudtson have collected and preserved Native people's profound ecological wisdom about our universe, our planet, and our physical and spiritual lives. Each story is meticulously documented for authenticity, and each conveys a sense of both the diversity and unity of Native people's intellectual and experiential insights into the workings of nature.

Life as a Geological Force, Peter Westbroek, W. W. Norton, 1991.

A rare combination of geological and biological breadth of knowledge leads Peter Westbroek to the conclusion that the smallest living things can act, over geological time, as a powerful force in shaping the Earth because of their modulating influence on lithospheric and atmospheric processes.

The Overview Effect: Space Exploration and Human Evolution, Frank White, Houghton Mifflin, 1987.

Including interviews with almost every living cosmonaut and astronaut, Frank White's book gives the unique insights of those who have watched the Earth from space. Many found themselves drawn to the same conclusion as Jim Lovelock, that the Earth, better called Gaia, should be seen as a single living system.

Symbiosis in Cell Evolution, Second Edition, Lyn Margulis, New York: W. H. Freeman, 1993.

A modern account of the evolution of the five kingdoms of life.

Genesis and Geology, C. Gillespie, Cambridge: Harvard University Press, 1951.

A historian's examination of the relationship between scientists and those who fund them, especially in the case of the Earl of Bridgewater.

James Lovelock.
Credit: Sandy Lovelock

Author biography

An independent scientist for the past 25 years, James Lovelock is best known for his authorship of the Gaia hypothesis, developed in the 1970s and popularized through *Gaia: A New Look at Life on Earth*. He also developed the electron capture detector which led to the ability to monitor chemicals at very low concentrations in the environment. This led indirectly to the banning of pesticides such as DDT. A Fellow of the Royal Society, he has written two recent books, *The Ages of Gaia*, and *Healing Gaia: The Practical Science of Planetary Medicine*, as well as numerous scientific papers and articles.

Chapter 3

James Lovelock

The Greening of Science

I FIRMLY believe that science is badly in need of greening and that everyone, including the greens, need science, but not the kind of science we have now. We want science to return to natural philosophy and be once again its old familiar and welcome part of our culture. Science must abandon its genteel posturing and come down to Earth again quite literally. This is no easy task, it requires scientists to recognize that science has grown fat, lazy and corrupt and, like an obese atherosclerotic man, imagines that more rich food will cure his condition.

That science should be in this condition is disastrous at this time in history, when more than ever we need firm guidance and a clear understanding of the Earth. I will now try to show you how this has happened and put before you what I think should be done to make science green again.

In the 18th century science was a natural philosophy open to anyone interested in the world around them. Scientists such as Erasmus Darwin, Darwin's grandfather, were laying the foundations of the theory of evolution by natural selection, and the father of geology, James Hutton was already calling the Earth a superorganism whose proper study should be by physiology. He was indeed the first to recognize the existence of Gaia. These scientists talked to one another and shared a view of the world that we would now call 'top-down'. By this I mean it was a view of the whole system, a view that recognized that living organisms and complex systems were always something more than the mere addition of their parts. In recent times 'top-down' has an additional significance, for it is that view of the Earth from space we know so well. Science abandoned this enlightened view in the 19th century and began to look at the world and life from the bottom up. This is the reductionist approach and it followed naturally when science separated into a set of neat compartments where specialists and experts could ply their professions in complacency. We must not make the mistake of condemning reduction as wholly bad. It is a necessary way of examination; one that uses a microscope instead of a telescope. Its greatest triumph was the discovery of DNA and the genetic coding; its greatest shame was blood up to the elbows vivisection. What is inexcusable is the way that reductionism has dominated science right up until today, and justified the feudal separation of the sciences into rival baronies, each with its own arcane language and tribal customs. How many physicists are proud of their ignorance of what they call the 'soft sciences'? How many biochemists can name the wildflowers of their countryside? In such a climate of opinion it is not surprising that most scientists today regard Gaia, the theory of the Earth as a living organism, as naive. Yet few of them would be able to offer a satisfactory definition of life as an entity or a process. Life is a systems phenomenon and quite beyond their reductionist vision.

I think that the common revulsion among greens towards modern science is justified and arises because they recognize instinctively that the sense of wonder, the sacramental side of science, has all but vanished. They feel that it is no longer a vocation of benign natural philosophers, the practice of amiable professors and of Drs Who. They see science for what it is, a comfortable career for the mediocre, with the prospect of tenure and pension rights, protected by trade unions.

Complex social and cultural influences led science to move from the creative activity of a few talented individuals to become the unproductive career of middle management. The downfall encouraged, and was encouraged by, a disastrous decline of educational standards at both school and university. Let me illustrate by telling you of my experience as a student in 1938.

At the age of 18, I was about to leave school equipped with A levels in physics, chemistry and two mathematics. My headmaster said to me, 'Lovelock, you are a fool to want to do science. Science is only for those with genius or with ample private means, and I know you have neither of these. You may be keen now, but when you come to marry you will bitterly regret your decision.' He was right, of course. In the years after the depression of the 1930s, graduate scientists were employed by industry at zero salary for a year or more on the grounds that they were gaining industrial experience. But I was obstinate and determined to spend my life doing science and quite content to start by working by day as an apprentice to some consultant chemists and attending evening classes at Birkbeck College.

I have sympathy for those students reported in the *Sunday Times* as complaining that their degrees were too hard for them to attain. They should never have been sent to universities to sit them. I wish that the exams were harder still so that only those with a vocation for science would dare to take them. Then maybe we should not see science fragmented into a vast array of expertises, each of them a safe, secure haven for the mediocre or an empire in which the career-minded could satisfy their ambitions. This kind of science achieves little at vast cost and is obscure both to itself and to the public. It will be useless in the battles soon to come.

Generations of unfortunate students have been led to believe the falsehood that only by spending vast sums of money, and by employing them in their thousands and calling them scientists, can we keep ahead. Older scientists who recruited them seem to have forgotten the story about an Astronomer Royal in the last century. The Queen of the Netherlands came to visit the Greenwich Observatory. As he showed her around she noticed that his clothes were very worn and asked him, 'What is your salary?' '50 Pounds a year, Ma'am,' he replied. 'But that is disgraceful', said the Queen, 'How can Her Majesty Queen Victoria pay her astronomer such a pittance of a wage? I will ask her to see if you cannot be supported in a manner fit for your important post.' The astronomer is said to have replied, 'Indeed, Ma'am, do no such thing. If this post were better paid no scientist would get it.'

He was right, of course. Scientific salaries increased in real terms in the early 1950s and from then on an increasing number of applicants for posts in science were those seeking a career in science. No longer was science the vocation of mad-men like me who could think of no other way of spending a life. In ceasing to be a vocation, science became increasingly divided into expertises. It is easy and much more secure, to be a specialist in cryptogamic biochemistry, or in mesopheric aeronomy, than to be a general practitioner of science. So much so, that as far as I know,

I am almost the only one in the United Kingdom. This is an absurd state of affairs. Who would run a health service with no general practitioners, only specialists? Just imagine expecting a gynaecologist to diagnose your father's swollen nose or an ophthalmologist the vague but real disturbances of the menopause. Yet, quite seriously for the health of the Earth, its current problems are all treated separately by specialists, each of whom considers his speciality the only one to be important.

It would be bad enough if the number of specialities stayed constant, but they do not, for the centripetal tendency of modern science is formidable. I once had the intriguing experience of translating between two Dutch electronics engineers. Both, like most, if not all, Dutchmen, spoke near-perfect English, but to each of them the electronic language of the other was incomprehensible. One had been trained in the electronics of analog communication systems and designed radio transmitters; the other was an engineer skilled in the digital electronics of computers.

An unfortunate event for the growth of both environmentalism and science after the Second World War was the establishment of the American hegemony. The war had vastly enriched the USA, whilst it had impoverished the nations of Europe. It is true that in amazing acts of generosity the USA did much to redress the balance in the post-war period. But the center of power had shifted, and with it the center for the growth of ideas and philosophy. Europe was too busy licking its wounds and trying to recover to exert any useful check on the innocent, but purely material, philosophy of the New World.

To illustrate what I mean: in the UK the Medical Research Council (MRC) was still deep in the older traditions, possibly because during the war physiologists were in the ascendant and physiology is one of the very few sciences still to have a top-down view. The MRC was still a flourishing and productive scientific enterprise. However, it was the practice of the MRC not to patent medical discoveries; they had come from research funded from public resources and should be freely available for the public good. This wonderfully innocent UK policy soon led American entrepreneurs to use the MRC as a feeding ground for free patentable ideas. They were astonished that such suckers could exist in the real, hard world they knew. In the most notorious example, we found ourselves paying royalties to American companies for inventions and discoveries, such as penicillin, that we had ourselves made.

The vigor and competitive sense of American life has much to recommend it, but it is disastrous for science. It has led to an ethic throughout the first world, where winning prizes, getting rich or powerful are the proper objectives of a life in science. In a vocation-oriented scientific life, cheating is pointless and rarely occurred. In the new, winner-takes-all science, cheating is fine so long as you are not caught out. Now science has become all too like the degraded charade of the Olympic Games.

The American domination also brought in the adversarial and the mission-oriented approaches to science. No longer was it sufficient to be curious, to have a go, to try out an idea. A clear-cut plan of action in a written proposal was needed before research could start. Scientists were expected to give firm yes or no answers when questioned by legislators, even when they were sure that no certainty was possible.

To anyone who is not a creative scientist this seems sensible, orderly and accountable. In practice, it is as foolish as expecting a composer, a painter or a novelist to produce worthwhile art under such conditions. The essence of creativity is intuition. The creative quite literally do not know how their inspiration arrives. There is no way a creative scientist could write a proposal explaining his next creation. What in practice he is forced to do is to lie and write a proposal for his previous creation.

Among the imports from the New World are crazy practices like judging scientists by the number of papers they write, regardless of quality, or by the number of citations of these papers. It would be hard to find a more effective way for making science second-rate.

To my mind the most malign influence on modern science is the peer review. This institution was born when science took over the role once played by the Church as the source of knowledge and guidance. But it took as a model the medieval Church with its dogma and authoritarianism. Like that Church, science is vastly divided and sectarian, and exists much more for the personal benefit of its practitioners than for the enrichment of knowledge and the enlightenment of us all. It even has an inquisition, and this is what they call the peer review. Before a scientist can be funded to do a piece of research, and before he can publish the results of his work, it must be examined and approved by an anonymous group of so-called peers. This inquisition cannot hang or burn heretics yet, but it can deny them the ability to publish their research, or to receive grants to pay for it. It has the full power to destroy the career of any scientist who rebels. It has a marginal value in sifting the wheat from the chaff in pedestrian research, particularly if it is technologically oriented. But it is a profound discouragement to creativity. Imagine what it would be like in the Arts if the critics were anonymous and had the power, if they did not approve, to stop a book being written and published. In such a world telephone directories and technical manuals would do well, but where would be *Lord of the Flies* or *Animal Farm*. Maybe science is merely the first victim of a new kind of censorship. A Poet Laureate once told me that it was usual for failed poets to become critics.

America itself is now mellowing, but it has not yet escaped its struggles with bureaucracy. Sometimes the battle is won for science. Consider, for example, those enthralling visions of our planets brought into our homes from the Voyager spacecraft on its amazing journey out into the universe; consider the landing on Mars of the Viking 12 years ago. A landing that for me confirmed a prediction of Gaia theory, namely that Mars was dead. These were and are the products of real science and of engineering exquisite in its perfection. Yet these great achievements represented a tiny fraction of NASA's expenditure and had to be hard bargained for. What costs money is humans in space. No-one would deny the thrill and achievement of the first astronauts and their capacity to let us share with them that stunning view of the Earth from space. Personally, however, I find it nauseating that the stunningly good engineering and science that the pioneers of space made for us should be now used for purposes of the utmost banality: to disseminate junk entertainment by satellite television, or to support the low-level human purpose of giving joy-rides in space to each sex and ethnic group of the numerous human tribes. Pointless, if we can afford it, but appalling when precious information gathered by Landsat and other satellites, essential in the understanding of our present predicament, now rots for lack of funds to store it properly.

I have just made a harsh criticism of my profession, science. You are right to ask, do I have a remedy? And I would have to reply that I know of no panacea for the ills of science. Even if it were practical to reorganize science and re-establish the creative kernel that existed in the past, there would be great resistance from the institutions and from vast hordes of graduates and PhDs in science, who would in effect be refugees from a kind of welfare state within the state.

The cure will come from the natural course of events. There will be pressure to provide accurate forecasts and to recommend sensible action in the adverse global changes soon to come. This may be enough to break the bonds and set science free again. My reason for hoping that this is so is because I have long thought there to be resemblances between the world of today and that period of our history 50 years ago, before the Second World War. In 1938 we all knew that war was inevitable; what we did not know was when it would come and what would happen when it did. Like now, there was a great deal of confusion over what to do. Many in those days thought Hitler to be a lesser threat than Stalin.

Today we face a different, but just as certain, threat: environmental disorder. Just as in 1938 there were confused voices calling for contradictory action, so there are now. There are those who see the environment in human terms only and seem to regard the science-based chemical and nuclear industries as the only enemy. Their behavior is as inconsistent and as negative as that of those of the left who, after Munich, called stridently for disarmament. Others see the preservation of wildlife, particularly cuddly animals and rare birds, as the main, if not the only, problem. They are limited in their vision like those of the right who saw Russia as the only threat. It took the invasion of Bohemia and of Poland to make it clear who was the enemy and what was the real cause. I suspect that it will take the first great surprises soon to come to awaken us, as did war 50 years ago.

Make no mistake. What we are now doing to the world by degrading the land surfaces and by adding greenhouse gases to the air at an unprecedented rate, is new in the experience of the Earth. The consequences are unpredictable, except to say that they will surely include surprises, some of which may be terrifying in human terms.

In the war of 1939, as good citizens, scientists willingly enlisted their knowledge, their experience and their lives. They did this even though they expected that war would be the end of good science, and that for the duration they would be employed on nothing but soulless, even amoral, military research and development. It is true there was plenty of this for those who were suited to it, but in general the pessimists were wrong, the pace of theorizing, of discovery and invention quickened and played its part in winning the war, but also unexpectedly expanded our capacity to view and understand the universe through radiotelescopes and our ability to understand life through deeper insight into its chemistry.

In the glamorizing of the battles and the dramatization of the pain and tragedy of war, it is easily forgotten that for most of the time the battlefield is a quiet place. A place where there is all the time needed to think, wonder and talk about the future of world peace. It is a place where the pressures of the peacetime routine of living no longer operate. Who there would worry about paying the rent or be a hypochondriac about an attack of indigestion. It was in quiet places and at quiet times during the war that the great plans for social and health services were drafted and the thoughts were sown that led in later years to a deeper understanding of the physical universe and its limits in space and time, and to the discovery of the double helix of DNA, the instructions of life itself.

What I hope will happen is that in between the more disastrous of the surprises soon to come, great storms and droughts and atmospheric phenomena never before seen, there will be time to think and the will to react. As Dr Johnson said, 'Nothing so concentrates the mind as the prospect of hanging.' I believe that soon the prospect of large and daunting change will be seen. Then we shall become aware of a larger need and science will cease its pettifogging and come together as it did under the lesser stress of war. It might even evolve to become like the science of 1940, a shining vocation, lean and fit and as tough in mind and heart as were the nurses of Florence Nightingale's time.

Let me digress for a moment to tell you about those days and why I feel so passionately that science has been betrayed and corrupted by wealth and power. I grew up in the string and sealing wax school of science that persisted until about 1960. It was an ecumenical science where biologists, chemists and physicists met and talked coherently and sparked ideas. In those long-gone days there was little money for science and yet, perversely, Britain was doing very well at science and was recognized globally as a key scientific center. Yet, strangely, we were so poorly equipped that if the interest was compelling we were obliged to spend a portion of our salaries on equipment. I well remember buying dusty war surplus electronic gear from shops in Lisle Street, near Leicester Square. Shops that existed in juxtaposition with massage parlors and displays of libidinous literature. I often wondered how the girls that roamed the streets knew so unerringly which of us were their potential customers. They never confused those in search of electronics with those in search of erotics.

It was with bits and pieces from Lisle Street that I made, in 1957, my first electron capture detector, the device that was destined to provide the data that enabled Rachel Carson to write *Silent Spring* and which first discovered chlorofluorocarbons (CFCs) in the atmosphere.

Now, if you enter a laboratory almost anywhere and ask the scientists if they know how their instruments work or if they could make or repair them, they will, if truthful, answer no. Using a scientific instrument now is rather like driving a car or switching on a television; all of us use these things, but have no idea how they work, nor could we make or repair them. This may be acceptable with cars and televisions, but in science it means that the scientists no longer know what they are doing.

An example of the damage done by doing science this way occurred in the late 1970s, when laboratories around the world were trying to measure CFCs in the atmosphere. Because of peer review and the need to submit proposals before money would be paid, the proposers were obliged to claim that they could measure CFCs accurately. They could not be honest and admit that they had no independent standard of calibration. Had they done so, the peer review would not have approved their funds. To make matters worse, the unwise among them set the stakes by claiming an accuracy of a few percent. Now at that time CFCs were present at about 150 and 300 parts per trillion. Good chemists know that to calibrate any instrument at the part per billion level is fraught with difficulty; to calibrate at the parts per trillion level is an heroic task. Yet 18 laboratories submitted proposals and were funded to measure CFCs in the atmosphere. Most of them used commercial gas chromatographs equipped with electron capture detectors for the measurements. The results they produced should, if their claims of accuracy were correct, have agreed to within a few percent. In fact, because they had no accurate standards to calibrate their instruments, the results were scattered over a range of 300 percent. Also, measurements that were supposed to be done independently showed strong evidence of collusion among the investigators.

It might have been years before we knew accurately how much of the CFCs were in the atmosphere. Accurate standards were unavailable until I turned an old barn where I lived in Devon into a dilution chamber and Dr Ray Weiss in the USA made them by an alternative method. In the CFC affair, with its high public profile, it seems that when the pressure is on, a high proportion of scientists will be driven to make claims they cannot sustain. Friends of the Earth, keep this in mind when the next claim for your time and cash are sought for some scientific venture. Be especially skeptical if the scientists claim that what they are doing will save all life on Earth.

You may be thinking: if all this is true, how on Earth does science continue to be successful and to achieve as much as it does. The thing that saves science from oblivion as an amazing cliché or outmoded philosophy is its internal self-correction. Science is always up for trial by experimental test. In the end, the truth usually comes out.

However, big science is ill-equipped to handle the environment. It badly needs a top-down unified view of the Earth, but because of the fragmentation of science it is unlikely to get one. The most prestigious international scientific program for the environment was first called the International Geosphere Biosphere Program, IGBP for short. The name chosen well illustrates my point. A dull, confused name for a serious attempt to deal with the global environment. I was told by Sir John Kendrew, who was in at the beginning, that the reason for choosing to call it by this hopelessly unattractive name was that the biologists on the planning committee felt that biology would be left out if some 'bio' subject was not included in the title. It is now thankfully called The Global Change Programme. Big science rejects Gaia; it even rejects geophysiology, but it has little to offer instead but the mixture as before.

Theologians talk of a proper concern for the environment as 'The Reintegration of Creation'. To them, the environment is Creation. Our task is easier. It is merely the reintegration of ecology and science. So what should we do? One approach is what I have called planetary medicine.

Planetary Medicine

Hans Johst once said 'Whenever I hear the word "culture", I release the safety catch of my Browning!' I don't know what in particular incensed Johst about culture, but I suspect that he knew the word prefaced a gush of hypocrisy. For me the same kind of anger comes when I hear that cliché 'the fragile Earth'. I get ready for a flood of words and a televisual presentation of cuddly animals and lush vegetation. The words may come from a prominent green presenter, but to me they will sound green only with the mildew of insincerity. In Victorian times that same word 'fragile' was used with a similar tendency to describe women, and to justify their domination. They were called fragile because it implied a feeble delicacy that needed male protection. Victorian women were not fragile, they were tough. They had to be to survive.

So it is with the Earth, and fortunately for us, it is very tough indeed. In the near four billion years of its existence as a live planet, it has survived at least 30 major impacts, each of them devastating enough to destroy more than half of the life present. In addition, solar output has increased by 25% and perturbations have occurred, such as the appearance of oxygen as the dominant chemical species. What we are doing now in the way of the pollution and destruction of natural ecosystems is by comparison a minor upset. Those who call the Earth fragile, or who say that some human act will destroy all life on Earth, are either ignorant of what the Earth really is or are using 'Earth' metaphorically as a synonym for humans. Either way, we use fragile as did those Victorian men about their women: applying to our planet a dependent status, almost as if it were a possession.

We still talk about the Earth as if the planet in our minds were a multicolored political sphere mapping the territories of tribes and nations. The real Earth, that stunning blue and white globe, has become just a visual cliché, no longer inspirational, a banal image advertizing soap on satellite television.

As the only organized intelligence, perhaps we have the duty as well as the right to take charge of the Earth and govern it responsibly. Maybe so, but first we must ask, what is the Earth? This may seem a trivial question—everyone knows what the Earth is—but unfortunately there seems to be no common view. Almost as if the Earth were an evolutionary inheritance, which we, like fleas on the back of a camel, just take for granted and never notice what it is. Even scientists differ about what the Earth is.

There are three scientific views of our planet. Firstly, a small minority which includes me, who call ourselves geophysiologists, see the Earth as a quasi-living system or, if you prefer, a planetary-sized ecosystem—something called Gaia. We postulate that this system automatically regulates such important properties as climate and atmospheric composition, so that they are always more or less comfortable for life.

A larger minority prefer what the climatologist Stephen Schneider has called co-evolution. They see life and its environment as only loosely coupled. They agree with geophysiologists that the composition of the air, the ocean and the rocks is affected by the presence of life, but they reject the idea that the Earth may be self-regulating so as to sustain a comfortable environment.

Co-evolution originated from the ideas of the Russian scientist Vernadsky. He was the man who first used the notion of the biosphere, in the familiar vague way we still use it. Co-evolutionists recognize the need for interdisciplinary research and are the force behind the global change and the international geosphere biosphere programs. It may be some time before we know whether co-evolution or Gaia is nearer the truth.

There are a few, mostly geographers, who see the Earth as a whole, but the majority of scientists, even if they give lip service to either Gaia or co-evolution, still act as if the Earth were a ball of white hot, partially melted rock with just a cool crust moistened by the oceans. On the surface they see a thin, green scum of life whose organisms have simply adapted to the material conditions of the planet. With such a view go metaphors like 'the space ship Earth'. As if humans were the crew and the passengers of a rocky ship forever traveling an inner circle around the Sun. As if the four billion years life has existed on Earth were just to serve as our life support system when we happened to come aboard. Seen this way, obviously the Earth might appear fragile, like one of those great greenhouses, called 'biospheres', in Arizona. Those who see it in this way must wonder how it has survived so long.

This is the conventional wisdom about the Earth and it is still taught in most schools and universities. It is almost certainly wrong and has arisen as an accidental consequence of the fragmentation of science, a fragmentation into a growing collection of independent scientific specialities. Practicing scientists are aware of the limitations of this diffuse conventional wisdom about the Earth, but even when they are specialists in some branch of earth or life science, they still seem to act as if it were true. If we as scientists want to know about life, the universe, or the Earth, we read about it in the *New Scientist* or *Scientific American*. Back in the laboratory, where serious science is done, we continue in our own speciality without concern for either the general wisdom or the intricate details of the specialities of our close colleagues.

If you think I exaggerate, try attending discussion meetings on the three closely related earth sciences. For example, on one day you could attend a discussion on the chemistry of stratospheric ozone; on another day, a discussion of the geophysics of fluid motion in the oceans; and on the third day, a discussion on the geochemistry of rock weathering. These are all earth science topics, but you would find little that was shared in common between them. More seriously, a considerable proportion of the scientists from each of the three discussions would be unaware of the discoveries of the others. Of course, no single scientific approach can lead to a complete understanding of the Earth; all are needed. We need the reductionist model of the Earth to understand details at the molecular level. A key example is the chemistry of the stratosphere. It was only through the application of classical atmospheric chemistry and physics that Rowland and Molina first made known the threat to ozone from CFCs. From biogeochemistry there came, through the work of G. E. Hutchinson, the recognition of the role of microorganisms in the soil and the oceans as the source of methane and nitrous oxide. From geophysiology came the recognition that atmospheric gases, like carbon dioxide, methane and dimethyl sulfide, may be part of a physiological climate regulation.

We are at a time when scientists as professionals seem to have lost sight of the Earth as a planet in the intricacies of detail. As a result, when confronted with environmental concerns, they tend to think about specific dangers to people, especially themselves, and ignore hazards that loom on a planetary scale. The foremost personal and public fear is that of cancer. Consequently, any environmental chemical or radiation thought to cause cancer is given attention out of all proportion to the real risk it poses. Nuclear power, ozone depletion and chemicals such as dioxin and polychlorinated biphenyls (PCBs) are regarded as the most serious of environmental hazards because of this fear, but also because nuclear radiation and halocarbons are so easy to measure. I think that the potential hazards of the gaseous greenhouse and land abuse have, until recently, been ignored because they perturb the planet, not necessarily individual people, and because they are much more difficult to quantify.

Environmental groups are right to be skeptical about the claims of big science. Yet the science advisers to the greens, who may feel objective, are in fact reflecting the needs and the prejudices of the scientific community to which they belong. The community itself is divided and uncertain in the face of a worldwide decline in funds. Also, it is not easy to be responsible where there is no accountability. A consequence is that the list of priorities often given by the leaders of the greens reflects the list of working priorities of the scientific community, rather than the priorities of people—still less the priorities of the planet.

This is why until fairly recently the greens appeared to list global dangers in order of priority as follows: first, all things nuclear, whether power stations, processing sites, waste disposal or bombs; second, ozone depletion; third, the waste products of the chemical industry. In other words, the first three priorities are carcinogenic or mutagenic to humans. As an independent scientist I see things very differently. To me the vast, urgent and certain danger comes from the clearance of tropical forests.

The tropical rainforests are both a habitat for humans and a physiologically significant ecosystem. That habitat is being destroyed at a ruthless pace. Yet, in the 'first world' we try to justify the preservation of tropical forests on the feeble grounds that they are the home of species of plants and animals—even of plants containing drugs that could cure cancer. They may be. They may even be slightly useful in removing carbon dioxide from the air. But they do much more. Through their capacity to evaporate vast volumes of water vapour and of gases and particles that assist the formation of clouds, the forests serve to keep their region cool and moist by wearing a sunshade of white reflecting clouds and by bringing rain that sustains them. Every year we burn away an area of forest equal to that of Britain, and often we replace it with crude cattle farms.

Unlike farms in the temperate regions, such farms rapidly become desert, more trees are felled and the awful process of burning away the skin of the Earth goes on.We do not seem to realize that once more than 70 or 80% of a tropical forest is destroyed, the remainder can no longer sustain the climate and the whole ecosystem collapses. By the year 2000, given the present rate of clearance, we shall have removed 65% of the tropical rainforests. After that it will not be long before they vanish, leaving the billion poor of those regions without support in a vast global desert. In some ways this is a threat greater in scale than a nuclear war. Imagine the human suffering, the refugees, the guilt and the political consequences of such an event. And it will happen at a time when we in the first world are battling with the surprises and disasters of the greenhouse effect, intensified by the extra heating from the forest clearance.

A different civilization

Common sense now tells us that in the absence of a clear understanding of the consequences of what we are doing to the Earth we should cut back our pollution and land abuse to the point where at least there is no annual increase. But, like all acts of self-denial, it is only too easy to put it off until something happens. I can't arrange, or predict, anything exciting enough to cause us to give up polluting, but what I can do is to tell you a fable about an environmental problem that afflicted an imaginary industrial civilization 15 000 years ago.

Just about the time that our immediate ancestors appeared on the Earth, 2.5 million years ago, the planet itself was changing from a state where the climate was comparatively constant to one where the climate cycled periodically between glacial and interglacial phases. The ice ages were long; they lasted about 90 000 years. In the intensely cold winters, ice extended to within 45° of the equator. The warm periods, the interglacials, were brief, lasting only about 12 000 years, and the climate was like the one we enjoy, or at least did until quite recently.

I would like you to imagine that civilization became industrial 15 000 years earlier than it did. This requires an increase of only 0.5% in the rate of evolution of human society. I would ask you to envisage a civilization very like ours now, but existing 15 000 years ago. Just as developed and just as polluted. The main difference would be that the Earth was then in the cold stage of an ice age. The climate in the position of the UK would be like the present climate of Iceland and there would be few inhabitants. The oceans would be more than 400 feet lower than now. A vast area of land, mostly near the equator, that is now under the ocean, would be dry and populated.

Let us imagine that the civilization developed and became industrial somewhere in the region of Japan and China. The cold winters, with the need for housing and heating, stimulated invention. The region was also rich in coal, oil and mineral deposits. Soon these were exploited and there followed a rapid progression through water and wind power to steam electricity and nuclear power, just as we have seen take place in a mere two hundred years.

Greenhouse gases, carbon dioxide and methane, from extensive agriculture began to rise and before long the climate became perceptibly warmer. A large part of the civilized world was in the tropical zones and these were becoming uncomfortably warm for their inhabitants. The nations of the north were efficient at producing consumer goods. They were like the Victorian British, or the present day Japanese. Needs drive invention, and soon refrigerators using CFCs were pouring from the production lines and were shipped to customers worldwide.

It was not long before scientists began to realize that the global environment was changing. A few of them stumbled on the fact that CFC gases leaking from refrigerators were accumulating in the air without any apparent means for their removal. Soon it was discovered that the CFCs were a threat to the ozone layer and that if their growth in abundance in the air continued, ozone in the stratosphere would be so depleted that many, especially the fair-skinned, would be in grave danger from the ultraviolet component of sunlight and would develop skin cancers. There was an explosion of hype in the media over this threat and funds flowed for science as never before. Governments were reluctant to act because they knew the CFCs to be harmless in the home and were the most efficient refrigerant gases that could be used. And they were the basis of a large and profitable industry. They were reluctant also because there was no evidence of any increase in solar ultraviolet at ground level; indeed, there was a decrease. So nothing was done to stop CFCs rising in abundance at 10% each year.

A few scientists felt frustrated because they knew that the real threat from the CFCs was not ozone depletion but their property of blocking the escape of outgoing heat radiation for the planet. The CFCs are more than 10 000 times as potent as greenhouse gases than carbon dioxide. The fear of cancer always seems to transcend other dangers and as a consequence ozone depletion was the issue that received the most attention. Greenhouse warmth was known about, but regarded as a good thing, as the world was cold anyway.

Nobody then knew that in 2000 years the planet was destined to make one of its characteristic jumps in temperature to an interglacial. The polar regions in the ice age were so inhospitable that there was none of the clear, strong data from ice cores that we now have to help us understand the past. The jump in temperature due 2000 years ahead would come because the position of the Earth with respect to the Sun was changing in a way that increased the heat received from the Sun. These were small increases in solar heating and by themselves insufficient to precipitate an interglacial, but at the end of a glacial period the planet was in a state highly sensitive to small perturbations.

A minority opinion among the scientists held that the increasing warmth from greenhouse gas pollution would start to melt the ice caps and that the flooding of low-lying tropical forest land would then take place. This in turn would release vast volumes of methane gas as the vegetation rotted beneath a few feet of sea water. The methane would cause more greenhouse warming and soon, by a runaway positive feedback, the planet would heat and melt the vast polar ice caps. They warned that the rise in sea level would ultimately be 450 feet, enough to drown most of the large towns and cities of the civilized world. Then, as now, most centers of civilization were close to sea level.

This pronouncement was treated with derision and contumely. Ozone depletion, and the dangers from nuclear power, were the main interest to government and environmentalists alike. Soon the CFCs reached five parts per billion in the air and ozone holes appeared over the poles. By themselves the ozone holes were of no consequence as nothing lived at the ice age polar regions, but their presence was enough to tip the balance in favor of legislation to ban the use of CFCs. Unfortunately, it was too late, for the greenhouse balance had also tipped and the planet was now like a boat passing over the edge of a waterfall, moving ever faster towards the heat of the interglacial. The polar ice was already melting, and within a few hundred years all of this Atlantean civilization was deep under the ocean. The legend of a flood and of a great empire beneath the ocean persisted. The stories about it were reiterated over the camp fires of the wandering tribes of hunters.

If there is any moral to be drawn from this tale it is that we are very lucky to have chosen to pollute the air now when the planet is least sensitive to perturbation by greenhouse gases. But if you look at the Earth, as I do, as a superorganism, then we need to make sure that some other surprise may not be waiting to do us some other unexpected damage. A surprise as great as that which confronted those imaginary Atlanteans.

So let me conclude with some further thoughts about the dangerous illusion that we could be stewards of the spaceship Earth.

Everyone these days is or aims to be a manager, and this may be why we talk of managing the whole planet. Could we, by some act of common will, change our natures and become proper managers, gentle gardeners, stewards, taking care of all of the natural life of our planet?

I think that we are too full of hubris even to ask such a question, or to think of our job description as stewards of the Earth. Originally, a steward was the keeper of the sty where the pigs lived; this was too lowly for most humans and gentility raised the styward so that he became a bureaucrat, in charge of men as well as pigs. Do we really want to be the bureaucrats of the Earth? Do we want the full responsibility for its care and health? I would sooner expect a goat to succeed as a gardener as expect humans to become stewards of the Earth, and there can be no worse fate for people than to be conscripted for such a hopeless task; to be made accountable for the smooth running of the climate, the composition of the oceans, the air and the soil. Something that, until we began to dismantle creation, was the free gift of Gaia.

I would suggest that our real role as stewards on the Earth is more like that of the proud trades union functionary, the shop steward. We are not managers or masters of the Earth, we are just shop stewards, workers chosen because of our intelligence, as representatives for the others, the rest of life on our planet. Our union represents the bacteria, the fungi, the slime molds and invertebrates, as well as the nouveau riche fish, birds, reptiles and mammals and the landed establishment of noble trees and their lesser plants. Indeed, all living are members of our union and they are angry at the diabolical liberties taken with their planet and their lives by people. People should be living in union with the other members, not exploiting them and their habitats. When I see the misery we inflict upon them and upon ourselves, I have to speak out as a shop steward. I have to warn my fellow humans that they must learn to live with the Earth in partnership, otherwise the rest of creation will, as part of Gaia, unconsciously move the Earth itself to a new state, one where humans may no longer be welcome.

Annotated List of Further Reading

Gaia: The Growth of an Idea, Lawrence E. Joseph, London: Penguin, 1990.

Venus and Mars are utterly dead lumps of rock, against which the living planet Earth shines like a dappled sapphire. Was it the impersonal laws of geology that made her habitable? Or did the different forms of life on Earth *create* (or decisively modify) the environment they needed for survival? Despite the excesses of 'New Age' Gaia enthusiasts, Joseph makes clear that the theory remains both convincing and intensely stimulating.

Microcosmos, Lynn Margulis and Dorion Sagan, London: Allen & Unwin, 1987.

Much has been written about the big scene, the cosmos, but what of inner space? Lynn Margulis and Dorion Sagan's enthralling and elegant book takes us on a journey to a gentler world, the microcosmos. It is a wonderfully interdisciplinary voyage; no academic passports are needed, yet specialists in all fields will enjoy and learn from it.

Scientists on Gaia, Stephen Schneider and Penelope Boston, Boston: MIT Press, 1991.

The proceedings of the first wholly scientific conference on the Gaia hypothesis, held by the American Geophysical Union in 1989. Rather technical in parts, but wide ranging and readable.

From Gaia to Selfish Genes: Selected Writings in the Life Sciences, Connie Barlow (Ed.), Boston: MIT Press, 1991.

Spanning scales from the biosphere to the cell to DNA, Connie Barlow weaves together writings from more than 30 scientists and science writers who explore links between biology and philosophy, encompassing disciplines from global ecology to behavior and genetics.

Claude Alvares

Author biography

Claude Alvares is an editor with the Other India Press, a small independent publishing house located in Goa, the major source of alternative publishing in India. Earlier, Alvares worked as an investigative journalist whose work led the then Prime Minister, Indira Gandhi, to order an investigation into Europe's Operation Flood milk scheme in India. Educated in Bombay, Alvares completed his PhD at the Technische Hogeschool in Eindhoven in the Netherlands. He has written extensively, including *De-Colonizing History: Technology and Culture in India, China and the West: 1500 to the Present Day*, and *Science, Development and Violence*. Alvares is also secretary of the Goa Foundation, which has taken legal and other measures for the protection of Goan ecology in the wake of the depredations inaugurated by luxury resorts. This chapter is reproduced by permission of Zed Books.

Chapter 4

Claude Alvares

Does the Real World Need 'Modern' Science?

I WAS born into a culture that continues to exercise greater influence and power over behavior than modern science does, or will ever do. If *that* were properly understood, then this obituary would not appear either scandalous or scurrilous. Every culture enjoins on its members respect for certain entities. Modern science does not find a place in *our* pantheon.

Far from it. From this side of Suez, in fact, modern science appears akin to an imported brand of toothpaste. It contains elaborate promises and much sweetness and glamour. It can be used, is often used (many times pointlessly), yet can be dispensed with at any time precisely because it is still largely irrelevant to *life*.

Toothpaste has become a significant universal commodity: for some, it has even evolved into a category of mind. For decades now, it has remained (with the toothbrush) an essential adjunct of modern civilization, available from Managua to Manila. Those who have ingratiated themselves with modernity are prone to find any absence of toothpaste (either for themselves or for others) a source of acute anxiety.

In *our* society, however, the moment we find toothpaste unavailable, we return to neem sticks, or cashew or mango leaves, or mixtures composed of ginger, charcoal and salt. All excellent, locally available and dependable materials for keeping the mouth fresh and disinfected and the teeth clean.

Now modern science is a universal commodity too, also distinctly recognizable from Managua to Manila, also approved by many whose devotion to its tenets and its propagation is more often than not related to its ability to provide a high living wage and, often, in addition, power, prestige and a chauffeur-driven car. Like the early morning toothbrush, science is considered a precondition for a freshly minted worldview uncontaminated by unlearned or unemancipated perceptions. For its part, it offers to flush out the many disabling superstitions from all those hidden crevices of a society's soul, to eliminate any and every offending bacterium to produce a clean and ordered world. Most importantly, it promises a materialist paradise for the world's unprivileged through its awesome, magical powers. But not for any reason difficult to understand, it also continues to require as big an advertising budget as toothpaste. There is something about modernity's leading prestige product that is actually so bland it has to be rendered spectacular by sensational copy and a fertile imagination.

Such an irreverent view of modern science will not be comfortable for those who have chosen to remain imprisoned within the dominant present day perceptions of the age. But for us, it always was *another* culture's product, a recognizably foreign entity. We eventually came to see it as an epoch-specific, ethnic (Western) and culture-specific (culturally *entombed*) project, one that is a politically directed, artificially induced stream of consciousness invading and distorting, and often attempting to take over, the larger, more stable canvas of human perceptions and experience. In a world consisting of dominating and dominated societies, some cultures are bound to be considered more equal than others. This heritage of inequality, inaugurated and cemented during colonialism, has remained still largely intact today. So the culture products of the West, including its science, are able to claim compelling primacy and universal validity only because of their (as we shall see later) congenital relationship with the political throne of global power.

Colonialism, we know, subjects, undermines, subordinates and then replaces what it eliminates with its own exemplar. It is natural to expect that Western science, an associate of colonial power, would function not any less brazenly and effectively: extending its hegemony by intimidation, propaganda, catechism and political force. In fact, being a culture product, it was only to be expected that it would be associated with the various (mostly aggressive) thrusts of that culture. It would attempt to extend its hegemony to other cultures through an elite class, which social commentators today call 'modernizers', whose distinguishing characteristic, following a period of schooling at Oxbridge, was a thorough-going alienation from the life and culture of their own people. And true to its origins, this science has remained in the service of Western culture to this day, a crucial component in the hysterically active hegemony of the West.

However, due to stupendous and unrecognized inner strengths, the cultures on which modern science was sought to be imposed were able to prevent themselves from being fully incorporated. Its inability to deliver the goods and its general incompetence to deal with specific problems have also led to its decline. A global overview today of its actual hegemony would, in fact, be quite distressing to its devotees. In many areas of the non-Western world, it has been reduced to the status of a commodity (like toothpaste) or a gadget (to be purchased with money). Its promise to transform the world into a materialist paradise and thereby put an end to poverty and oppression has lost all credibility. There is evidence indeed to show that it has accomplished just the contrary. As for its offer of a new metaphysical worldview to provide us with ethical guidance, this has also been largely rejected. *Dharma*, conversation, community, interaction with sacred entities and their associated symbols, still remain prime movers within our societies. One even encounters significant desertions from the imperium of science in the very citadels of Western culture.

Thus, the geographical area of its influence has turned out to be far less than was originally desired or attempted. In comparison, other ideas have dominated (and sometimes unsettled) human societies for far longer periods of time. Buddhism, for example, which like Western science had its own theory of causation, was born on Indian soil, from where it was exported to entire civilizations. In societies like Japan, it exercised influence for centuries. It unsettled most South and South-East Asian societies with its radically new notions of what a society should be like and of the relationship between the sangha and the state. In comparison with Buddhism, the sway of modern science is impressive, but less pervasive. We should also remember that Buddhism, in contrast with science, was not propagated and imposed by violence.

The actual self-perception of modern science as a recognizably distinct human activity does not go back more than 200 years in Western society. The very term 'scientist' (used as an analogy to the word 'artist') was first suggested by William Whewell as late as 1833 at a meeting of the British Association for the Advancement of Science. It was only used without distaste by its practitioners towards the end of the first quarter of this century.

This is not to deny that the world's citizenry did suffer greatly from the temptations of modern science. It did. Just as it did until recently from the promises of development. But just as one now routinely encounters the 'stink of development', one is also compelled to concede that three centuries of science have raised their own trail of disturbing odors. Not surprisingly, therefore, one discovers that whatever is being said in obituaries about development can equally be said about modern science.

Science and Development: A Congenital Relationship

What has been responsible for the gross influence of science over the imagination of men in our times? One major factor has been the intimate relationship between science and development. They cannot be understood in isolation from each other, as India's policy-makers made clear 30 years ago

The key to national prosperity, apart from the spirit of the people, lies, in the modern age, in the effective combination of three factors, technology, raw materials and capital, of which the first is perhaps the most important, since the creation and adoption of new scientific techniques can in fact make up for a deficiency in national resources and reduce the demands on capital.

Generally speaking, development was merely modern science's latest associate in the exercise of its political hegemony. Earlier, science had linked itself with enlightenment and millennial claims, before going on to associate itself with racism, sexism, imperialism and colonialism, and then settling down with development, an idea in which most of these earlier inheritances are encoded.

If one, in fact, reflects on the events of recent decades, one is indeed reminded that development and science have run through the period, tied together as intimately as a horse and carriage. Development was desired by us non-Western societies precisely because it was associated with science. What existed prior to development, either in the form of pure nature or non-Western subsistence, did not have, we were told, the rationality, slickness and efficiency of modern science. People, societies, nature itself were backward because of its absence. Planners labeled entire zones 'backward' simply because they lacked factories. (The factory has remained until today a concrete symbol of the new processes developed by science.) Backwardness was to be substituted by development, an allegedly better way of organizing man and nature based on the rich insights of up to date science.

Science, in turn, was desired because it made development *possible*. If one developed its associated skills, one could have unlimited development and riches. Science and development both reinforced the need for each other; each legitimized the other in a circular fashion popularly rendered: 'I scratch your back, you scratch mine.'

If development had had no special relationship with science, there would have been no need to displace subsistence and the new standard of living that development proposed.

However, the relationship between modern science and development was much more than merely intimate: it was congenital. This congenital relationship can be traced back to the industrial revolution when a relationship was first established between science and *industry*. This should not unduly surprise the reader. Some of the principal laws of science arose originally out of industrial experience. For instance, the second law of thermodynamics resulted from efforts to improve the working of the steam engine with a view to advancing industry.

India produces different forms of sugar. The most important of these are white sugar and *gur*. According to official opinion, the processes used for the extraction and production of white sugar are superior to those that lead to *gur*. Not only is the extractive efficiency of large mills higher, the produce (white sugar) stores well. It can be transported and hoarded, and otherwise abused for reasons of state. The attendant pollution wreaked by sugar mills is acknowledged, but is considered a small price to pay for the benefits of progress.

Gur, on the other hand, is mostly manufactured in open furnaces, using agricultural waste, timber or bagasse. The extraction of sugar cane juice is not as high as in the big industry process. The final product also does not keep well beyond a certain period. However, no pollution results from the production process: neither the Earth nor its atmosphere is damaged. And, of course, hoarding and speculation in *gur* is less easy.

From a bare accounting of the two processes, it would seem to be in the public interest for the state to support the replacement of *gur* production with modern sugar mills. *Development is white sugar.* And this is what has occurred in countries like ours in the post-independence period. Credit policy towards farmers in the vicinity of large sugar mills stipulates that if farmers take loans for growing sugar cane from government financial institutions, they are duty-bound to sell all their sugar cane only to the large refineries. They may not make *gur* out of it. Special officers of government, designated Sugar Commissioners, actually oversee such development. Indeed, this authoritarianism of

71

development has been upheld by the Supreme Court of India. A farmer was ordered by a Sugar Commissioner to deposit all his sugar cane with a large sugar mill. He refused because he wanted to process it into *gur* instead. The matter went up to the Supreme Court. The Court upheld the orders of the Sugar Commissioner.

A different picture emerges, however, when a closer investigation is made of the *qualities* of the two processes and their end-products. We then discover how modern science highlights certain qualities to the exclusion of others and how the blind adoption of its procedures can lead us to emphasize the wrong values. White sugar is dangerous to health for a number of reasons long tested and proved. The bodily processes involved in the metabolism of white sugar end up destabilizing the health of the consumer. In addition, the human body has no physiological requirement for white sugar as such. It is recognized that white sugar is, after all, nothing but empty calories. *Gur*, on the other hand, is a food. It contains not merely sugar, but iron and important vitamins and minerals.

Thus, if the two sugars are compared in the round, *gur* would make a positive contribution to human welfare, whereas white sugar would not. This, however, is not apparent in any comparison of the mere production processes that produce white sugar and *gur*, and in any case the criterion of this comparison resides only in the particular, and biased, terrain of modern science's view of efficient energy conversion. The technology for white sugar production is simply assumed to be more efficient than the technology used in the production of *gur*. Besides, whether it is worth producing a commodity that is harmful to human health and also damages the environment (waste heat and effluents) is not part of the efficiency debate.

Symbolic, nevertheless, of the new status sought for modern science by third world ruling elites was an international conference on the Role of Science in the Advancement of New States held in August 1960 in Israel. At that conference, S.E. Imoke, Minister of Finance for Eastern Nigeria, told his audience

> *We do not ask for the moon nor are we anxious for a trip there with you just yet. All we seek is your guidance, assistance and co-operation in our efforts to gather the treasures of our lands, so that we may rise above the subsistence level to a life more abundant.*

Revamping Society

The drive to advance big industry in the West was paralleled by an equally powerful project to reorganize society along scientific (i.e. efficient) lines. Auguste Comte set out the general design. His vision of applying the principles of rationality, empiricism and enlightenment to human society in every detail has already had a pervasive influence on the so-called advanced societies.

A roughly similar Comtean vision received a fresh lease of life with the political independence of the less developed nations. Here science (the archetypical instrument) was entrusted with the turn-key role of promising undreamed of standards of material wellbeing to the so-called poor of the planet.

The most well-known specimen of this innocent worldview was Jawaharlal Nehru, the first Prime Minister of free India. No leader of a less developed country was as enamored of the glamour and promise associated with modern science as Nehru. For him, development and science were synonymous. The original Comtean vision is starkly revealed in Nehru's insistence on scientific temper as a *sine qua non* of material advancement. According to him (in his *Discovery of India*), it was science and science alone that 'could solve the problems of hunger and poverty, of insanitation and illiteracy, of superstition and deadening custom and tradition, of vast resources running to waste, of a rich country inhabited by starving people.'

This alarming naivety was passed on by him to the country's leading bureaucrats. India adopted a science policy resolution in March 1958, which read, in part

The dominating feature of the contemporary world is the intense cultivation of science on a large scale, and its application to meet a country's requirements. It is this which, for the first time in man's history, has given to the common man in countries advanced in science, a standard of living and social and cultural amenities, which were once confined to a very small privileged minority of the population. Science has led to the growth and diffusion of culture to an extent never possible before. It has not only radically altered man's material environment, but, what is of still deeper significance, it has provided new tools of thought and has extended man's mental horizon. It has thus even influenced the basic values of life, and given to civilization a new vitality and a new dynamism.

Science and technology can make up for deficiencies in raw materials by providing substitutes or, indeed, by providing skills which can be exported in return for raw materials. In industrializing a country, a heavy price has to be paid in importing science and technology in the form of plant and machinery, highly paid personnel and technical consultants. An early and large development of science and technology in the country could therefore greatly reduce the drain in capital during the early and critical state of industrialization.

Science has developed at an ever-increasing pace since the beginning of the century so that the gap between the advanced and backward countries has widened more and more. It is only by adopting the most vigorous measures

and by putting forward our utmost effort into the develop-
ment of science that we can bridge the gap. It is an inherent
obligation of a good country like India, with its tradition
for scholarship and original thinking and its great cultural
heritage, to participate fully in the march of science, which
is probably mankind's greatest enterprise today.

Likewise, the authors of the country's First Five Year Plan noted: 'In the planned economy of a country, science must necessarily play a specially important role . . . Planning is science in action, and the scientific method means planning.'

These great 'self-evident truths', however, did not seem so obvious to many ordinary people in the less developed nations, particularly tribals, peasants and others not yet converted to the Western paradigm. In fact, if the benefits of modern science were not immediately obvious to them, neither did development seem to symbolize a better way of doing routine tasks. On the contrary, development seemed more of a con-game to ordinary folk. To these perceptive observers, it actually demanded greater sacrifices, more work, and more boring work, in return for a less secure livelihood. It required the surrender of subsistence (and its related autonomy) in exchange for the dependence and insecurity of wage slavery.

Left to its own, development would have made little headway across the globe. That it did eventually get moving was due purely to the coercive power of the new nation-states which now assumed, in addition to their earlier controlling function, a conducting function as well. Every nation-state stepped in voluntarily to force development, often with the assistance of police and magistrates. If their citizens were so ignorant that they were unable on their own to recognize the 'benefits of development', the new states would have no option but to 'force them to be free'.

Development became coercion: forced relocations to *ujamaa* villages, compulsory cooperatives, and tying people up in new forms of organization 'for their own good'. Said Abel Alier, Sudan's Southern Regional President, during an Assembly discussion of the controversial Jonglei Canal: 'If we have to drive our people to paradise with sticks, we will do so for their good and the good of those who come after us.' The modern state does not understand, much less accept, the right of people not to be developed.

We must recognize that the state's commitment to development stemmed from its equal commitment to modern science. Science was an ideal choice because it claimed to be able to *remake* reality. It redefined and invented concepts and laws, and thereby remade reality as well. It manufactured new theories about how nature worked, or more importantly, should work.

Therefore, when the state in the non-Western world assumed the role of developer, desirous of creating a new society and economy, with an entirely new set of temples and all, science naturally became the most attractive and crucial instrument for the purpose. It was Nehru, after all, who called mammoth development projects the 'temples of today'.

Neither people nor nature have been spared as victims of a science-fuelled developmentalism driven on by the state. Today, the remaking of nature has become a major preoccupation of officialized ecology. A classic illustration comes from the approach of scientists to what is called forest development. Foresters are unable to recreate natural forests. But that does not bother them. Instead they redefine forests as plantations, and carry out monocultures under the label of scientific forestry. Nature is thus replaced with a substandard substitute. In reality, the afforestation engineered by modern science becomes the deforestation of nature.

The state claims its right to 'develop' people and nature on the basis of a vision of progress set out in blueprints supplied by modern science, itself a cultural product of the West. The people have no role other than as spectators or cogs in this 'great adventure'. In exchange, they, or some of them at least, are privileged to consume the technological wonders that result from the heady union of development and science. In the eyes of a patronizing state, this is adequate compensation for a surrender of their natural rights. As for those who cannot or will not participate, they must lose their rights. They can be displaced from the resource arena, their resources being transferred instead to big industry.

A Totalitarian Edge

The democratic idea remains the one potential element available to counter these twin oppressions of modernity. For democracies are based on the principle of fundamental human rights. Let us turn to how this potential for checking the totalitarianism of modernity was, however, effectively undermined.

We have probed the congenital links between modern science and development, and the implied bias in science against both nature and handicraft production. We have also discussed how the new nation-states, heavily committed to development, found in this science an attractive instrument for their project of remaking their people in the image of what they believed was an advanced form of man.

Both these features of the modern science/modern state relationship indirectly undermined the natural rights of humans. In the first instance, science dismissed all existing processes in nature and traditional technics as inferior or of marginal value, thus enabling big industry (capitalist or statist) to substitute the blueprints supplied by science. Yet in human history, at least up until the scientific and industrial revolutions, the technical knowledge necessary for survival had mostly remained noncentralized and radically dispersed. Literally millions of arts and technologies existed—all using a vast variety of accumulated knowledge and productive of a huge quantum of goods, cultural ideas and symbols stemming from the rich diversity of human experience, and based principally on exploiting processes at ambient temperatures. In many ways, this technical diversity of the human species more or less paralleled the genetic diversity of nature itself.

In the second instance, the very conception of what constituted human normality was itself redefined. People lost the right to claim that they could function as competent human beings unless they underwent the indoctrination required by modernity. It was *a priori* assumed that they were deficient as human beings and had to be remade. As the scientific policy resolution quoted earlier noted: 'India's enormous resources of manpower can only become an asset in the modern world when trained or educated.' If in the process they emerged as pale caricatures of human beings in more powerful cultures, this was nothing to worry about. Science and its experts would decide how human beings would be brought up, trained and entertained, and what they should consume.

This is not too difficult for modern science to achieve primarily because it claims to be associated not only with greater efficiency, but also to have greater explanatory power. What is more, it claims its explanatory power to be superior to anything ever achieved before in the human past, because it alone is impartial and therefore objective. Objectivity was also easy to associate with equality and democracy, as neutrality was beneficial to all. (The biases of monarchical forms of administration, for instance, were notorious.) Modern science therefore seemed ideally suited for modern democracies.

By implication, everything 'nonscientific' was devalued as subjective and arbitrary, of marginal value and could hardly be made the foundation of public policy.

The so-called scientific revolution of the 17th century constituted a watershed in thinking about thinking. The revolution was successful in insinuating a general consensus that, for the first time in human history, human beings had succeeded in unraveling a method of gaining knowledge as certain as the knowledge that earlier had only been available via revealed scripture. This technique of knowledge acquisition was so reliable that the knowledge acquired thereby was for all practical purposes non-negotiable. It was this claim which would soon conflict with the natural rights of humans.

The indisputable knowledge that science presumed to offer was kept outside the arena of politics: in no way was it the consequence of bargaining or choice. In fact, one was no longer at liberty to choose scientific knowledge as an option from among other systems of knowledge. Scientific knowledge was a given. No-one was any longer free to reject its statements, as one was free (and often encouraged) to reject the statements of religion or art. The individual who refused to accept the basic scientific worldview risked being labeled not merely ignorant, but obscurantist, deviant or irrational.

Two important points here. Firstly, fallible beings, equipped with an equally fallible instrumentality, reason, were now staking a claim to an infallible method of generating and certifying knowledge. Secondly, rationality itself was being reduced to nothing more than a narrow and biased scientific rationality which has precious little to do with how the human mind actually thinks, although much to do with how some people think the mind ought to think.

We have to acknowledge that, in its drive for power, modern Western science could hardly afford to be diffident about the nature of its claims. It was compelled by its own premises to concentrate and arbitrate all epistemes, and to pretend to do so impersonally. As the need for certification increased, so did modern science become less democratic and access to knowledge itself turned into a matter of privilege and special training. The layman was now seen as an empty receptacle to be filled up with the contents of science. He was to forgo his own knowledge and knowledge-rights.

Another curious paradox here. Scientific reason operated with a logic that was allegedly independent of personal factors or whims. It aimed at the formulation of laws existing independently of persons. Yet its certifiers were persons, often persons who had a vested interest in the power of science, and who were dependent on it for their livelihood. Fallible individuals thus exploited the prestige associated with their discipline to gain a share of political power. The ballot was surreptitiously replaced, increasingly by the new scientific priesthood indoctrinated by its shared assumptions.

This, of course, was diametrically opposed to democratic functioning where rights are unique and universal and belong to individuals primarily because they are members of the species. Such rights include the right to claim true knowledge and the right to reject impersonal knowledge. A right which, in other words, includes the power to certify knowledge. Under the new tyranny of modern science, such rights were first assaulted, then extinguished, and ordinary people were no longer considered as being capable by the fruit of their own activity of providing or obtaining true and certain knowledge of the world. This political right was taken away from all people falling within the ambit of science's dictatorship. In fact, for the ruling classes which felt that human rights had been too early democratized, or unnecessarily so, science now provided the means by which they could take back with the one hand what they had earlier been compelled to give away with the other.

Thus planning, science and technology—the technocracy—now became the principal means for usurping the people's rights to the domains of knowledge and production, for dismissing the people's right to create knowledge, and diminishing their right to intervene in matters of public interest or affecting their own subsistence and survival.

The non-negotiability of modern science, the much vaunted objectivity of scientific knowledge, the seeming neutrality of its information, all these seemed positive features to most reasonable and educated men of different religions, values and nations. Rationality, the scientific temper and modern education seemed indisputable and necessary assets to human life.

However, although science itself advanced its knowledge by dissent, by the clash of hypotheses, it summarily dismissed dissent from outside the scientific imperium regarding either its content or its methods and mode of rationality. The non-negotiability of scientific assumptions, methods and knowledge became a powerful myth elaborately constructed over several centuries, fed by a feigned ignorance among its propagandists concerning how it had actually negotiated its rise and apparently unassailable position.

Scientific knowledge—seen as above emotion, caste, community, language, religion, and transnational—became the preferred and primary instrument for transformation not only above the interest of all, but more importantly, enforceable on all. Never, in fact, was there so much agreement among the intellectuals of so many nations, whether liberals, communists, reactionaries, Gandhians, conservatives or even revolutionaries: all succumbed to the totalitarian temptation of science.

What we have said concerning the power relationship of modern science with other epistemologies is also true of what came to pertain between it and technics. Development based on it came to constitute a dynamic (actively colonizing) power, committed to compromising the survival possibilities and niches of larger and larger masses of people. By and large, it found the people's knowledge competitive and therefore offensive. And as it maintained a contemptuous attitude towards folk science, it also treated people's rights to use resources in their own way with scant respect.

Most important of all, the modern state's interest in such development itself owed much to the latter's constant search for ways and means to compromise, erode and often severely diminish personal autonomy and the creativity and political freedom that went with it. In a democracy, people can govern themselves, but they can hardly do so if their governments are seriously attempting at the same time to see whether they can be successfully managed and changed.

Once the ordinary people's epistemologic rights were devalued, the state could proceed to use allegedly scientific criteria to supplant such rights with officially sponsored and defined perceptions and needs.

Science's propaganda, that it alone provided a valid description of nature, was turned into a stick with which to beat trans-scientific, or folk-scientific, descriptions of nature. The various 'people's science movements' in India took this job quite seriously, by functioning as an unofficial establishment, gallantly attempting to replace the science of the village sorcerer or *tantrik* with the barbarism of modern science's electric shock treatment or frontal lobotomies.

This expansion of the domain of scientific epistemology involved the most sustained deprivation of others' epistemologic rights. State policy, being committed to this one epistemology exclusively, abused or ignored others. In medicine, to take just one example, the bias exercised against Indian systems of healing in favor of imported allopathy needs little documentation.

All imperia are intolerant and breed violence. The arrogance of science concerning its epistemology led it actively to replace alternatives with its own, superimposing on nature new and artificial processes. Naturally, the exercise provoked endless and endemic violence and suffering as the perceptions of modern science sat clumsily and inappropriately on natural systems. Thus, just as the Europeans eliminated millions of indigenous Indians from North and South America and other indigenous populations elsewhere to make place for their own kind, and just as their medicine uprooted other medicine, and their seeds displaced other seed, so their knowledge project called modern science attempted to ridicule and wipe out all other ways of seeing, doing and having.

Knowledge is power, but power is also knowledge. Power decides what is knowledge and what is not knowledge. Thus modern science actually attempted to suppress even noncompetitive, but different ways of interacting with humans, nature and the cosmos. It wanted to empty the planet of all divergent streams of episteme to assert the unrivaled hegemony of its own batch of rules and set of perceptions, the latter being clearly linked with the aggressive thrusts of Western culture.

It is an illusion to think that modern science expanded possibilities for real knowledge. In actual fact, it made knowledge scarce. It over-extended certain frontiers, eliminated or blocked others. Thus it actually narrowed down the possibilities for enriching knowledge available to human experience. It did *appear* to generate a phenomenal information explosion. But information is information, not knowledge. The most that can be said of information is that it is knowledge in a degraded, distorted form. Science should have been critically understood not as an instrument for expanding knowledge, but for colonizing and controlling the direction of knowledge, and consequently human behavior, within a straight and narrow path conducive to the design of the project.

Is, then, the defeat total? No. The planet has not succumbed to appropriation by modern science everywhere. Indeed, the outward symbols of science—agribusiness food, nuclear reactors, gigantic dams—are facing rebellion across the globe. And if those who have tasted the empty fruits of modern science are disillusioned with them, others have refused to taste them at all. Millions of farmers, for instance, reject the modern rice strains manufactured by cereal research centers controlled by agribusiness. Citizens across the planet are rejecting modern allopathic medicine to varying degrees. Millions of ordinary people reject the idea of living by the distorting (and distorted) values associated with modern science.

In a country like India, 40 years of state sponsorship of science and all its works have been unable to bolster its failing reputation. In 1976, the late Prime Minister Mrs Indira Gandhi made the propagation of the scientific temper one of the fundamental duties of Indian citizens, and amended the Constitution accordingly. Despite this, there is an even greater sense of crisis among the Indian scientific community, which finds itself every decade more and more out of tune with Indian society's principal preoccupations.

This sense of failure has irreversibly crippled much of the thrust to push India into the straitjacket prepared for it by the project of modern science. The people in non-Western societies do not merely not cooperate with its principal designs, they indicate they do not care a fig for the West and its creations.

In many areas, the noncooperation has become aggressive. People, groups and villages have openly rejected modernizing development and stubbornly insisted on maintaining their ways of life, their ambient interactions with nature and the arts of subsistence. The revolt against development is bound to be at another level a revolt against modern science and the violence it symbolizes. This was Mahatma Gandhi's view. It will eventually become the view of those interested in protecting the natural rights of humans and nature everywhere.

Annotated List of Further Reading

Hind Swarj, Mahatma K. Gandhi, pp. 81–208 in *Collected Works of Mahatma Gandhi*, Delhi: Government of India, Vol. 4.

An early radical and vigorous critique of science and its claims to truth. This work is basically an assault on all bourgeois civil institutions, including modern science.

Science, Hegemony and Violence: A Requiem for Modernity, A. Nandy (Ed.), New Delhi: Oxford University Press, 1988; *Science, Development and Violence*, Claude Alvares, New Delhi: Oxford University Press, 1992.

These two books bring together a comprehensive critique of development and modern science, the twin oppressions of our age, and their intimate relationship with violence.

My Works and Days, Lewis Mumford, New York: Harcourt B. Jovanovitch, 1979.

Underwrites Gandhi's themes with extraordinary scholarship, as does his classic, *The Myth of the Machine*.

Development and Thermodynamics, C. V. Seshadri in *Equity is Good Science: The Equity Papers*, Madras, 1993.

This was a crucial influence on my critique of modern science and its ethnocentric origins.

The One-Straw Revolution, Masanobu Fukuoka, Goa: Other India Press; *Living, Dying*, Manu Kothari and Lopa Mehta, Goa: Other India Press; *The Other Face of Cancer*, Manu Kothari and Lopa Mehta, Goa: Other India Press.

These books take apart the rationality of modern agriculture and modern medicine, respectively. All three writers deeply repudiate modern science and restore the primacy of nature. J.P.S. Uberoi does a europology in his classic little book, *Science and Culture*, New Delhi: Oxford University Press, 1978.

The Development Dictionary, Wolfgang Sachs (Ed.), London: Zed Books, 1992.

The last 40 years can be called the 'age of development'. In the *Dictionary*, I join some of the world's most eminent critics of development to write its obituary. This takes the form of a direct intellectual assault on key everyday concepts like 'environment', 'resources' and 'science' (a longer version of this chapter). The authors expose the political origins of these concepts, their historical obsolescence and intellectual sterility.

However, no work of academia can be as compelling as human experience. Enmeshed in day to day village cosmology, it was not long before the scales fell quickly from my eyes. If one attempts to live close to the peasants or within the bosom of nature, modern science is perceived differently: as vicious, arrogant, politically powerful, wasteful, unmindful of other ways. Life in Thane, a village northeast of the State of Goa, on India's West Coast, and for the past six years in Parra, a more accessible coastal village, provided me with enough education to see through the emperor's new clothes.

Part II

DIFFERENT TERRAINS

George Monbiot
Credit: Adrian Arbib

Adrian Arbib

Author biographies

George Monbiot is an investigative journalist concentrating on environmental politics, land tenure and indigenous peoples. He is author of the books *Poisoned Arrows, Amazon Watershed*, which won the Sir Peter Kent Award for Conservation Writing, and *No Man's Land*. His broadcast work has won a Sony Award and the Lloyds National Screenwriting Prize. He is a Visiting Fellow of the Green College Centre for Environmental Policy and Understanding, University of Oxford and co-founder of the land-rights campaign *The Land is Ours*.

Adrian Arbib currently works in development and documentary photography. Having studied at the London College of Printing, he now works freelance for aid agencies in the UK. Working with Survival International, he has concentrated on minority groups around the world, with a large body of work being carried out in Irian Jaya (West Papua New Guinea) and most recently in East Africa with the Turkana, Maasai and Dinka, backed by the UK charity, Oxfam.

Chapter 5

George Monbiot

The Tragedy of Enclosure: The Science of Disposition and Destruction, with a Photographic Essay by Adrian Arbib

DURING the long, dry seasons in the far northwest of Kenya, the people of the Turkwel River keep themselves alive by feeding their goats on the pods of the acacia trees growing on its banks. Every clump of trees is controlled by a committee of elders, who decide who should be allowed to use them and for how long.

Anyone coming into the area who wants to feed their goats on the pods has to negotiate with the elders. Depending on the size of the pod crop, the elders will allow them in or tell them to move on. If anyone overexploits the pods, or tries to browse their animals without negotiating with the elders first, he will be driven off with sticks. If they do it repeatedly they may even be killed. The acacia woods are a common: a resource owned by many families. Like all the commons of the Turkana people, they are controlled with fierce determination.

In the 1960s and 1970s the Turkana were battered by a combination of drought and raiding by enemy tribes armed with automatic weapons. Many people came close to starvation, and the Kenyan government, the United Nations (UN) Development Programme and the UN's Food and Agriculture Organization decided that something had to be done to help them.

The authorities knew nothing of how the Turkana regulated access to their commons. What they saw, in the acacia forests and the grass and scrublands of the savannahs, was a succession of unrelated people moving in, taking as much as they wanted, then moving out again. If the Turkana tried to explain how it worked, their concepts were lost in translation. It looked like a free for all, and the experts blamed the lack of regulation for the disappearance of the vegetation. This was, in fact, caused not by people, but by drought.

They decided that the only way to stop the people from overusing their resources was to settle them down, get rid of most of their animals and encourage them to farm. On the banks of the Turkwel River they started a series of irrigation schemes, where ex-nomads could own a patch of land and grow grain. They spent US$60 000 per hectare in setting it up.

People flocked in, not, on the whole, to farm, but to trade, to find paid labor or to seek protection from their enemies. With the first drought, the irrigation scheme collapsed. The immigrants reverted to the only certain means of keeping themselves alive in the savannahs— herding animals. They spread along the banks, into the acacia woods.

Overwhelmed by their numbers, the elders could do nothing to keep them away from their trees. If they threatened to kill anyone for taking pods without permission, they were reported to the police. The pods and the surrounding grazing were swiftly exhausted and people started to starve. The commons had become a free for all. The authorities had achieved exactly what they set out to prevent.

The overriding of commoners' rights has been taking place, often with similarly disastrous consequences, for centuries, all around the world. But in the last two decades it has greatly accelerated. The impetus for much of this change came from a paper published 25 years ago, whose title has become a catchphrase among developers.

In *The Tragedy of the Commons*, Garrett Hardin, an American biologist, argued that common property will always be destroyed, because the gain that individuals make by overexploiting it will outweigh the loss they suffer as a result of its overexploitation. He used the example of a herdsman, keeping his cattle on a common pasture. With every cow the man added to his herds he would gain more than he lost: he would be one cow richer, while the community as a whole would bear the cost of the extra cow. He suggested that the way to prevent this tragedy from unfolding was to privatize or nationalize common land.

The paper, published in *Science* magazine, had an enormous impact. It neatly encapsulated a prevailing trend of thought, and appeared to provide some of the answers to the growing problem of how to prevent starvation. For authorities such as the World Bank and Western governments it provided a rational basis for the widespread privatization of land. In Africa, among newly independent governments looking for dramatic change, it encouraged the massive transfer of land from tribal peoples to the state or to individuals.

In Africa, Asia, Europe and the Americas, developers hurried to remove land from commoners and give it to people they felt could manage it better. The commoners were encouraged to work for those people as waged labor or to move to the towns, where, in the developing world, they could become the workforce for the impending industrial revolutions.

But Hardin's paper had one critical flaw. He had assumed that individuals can be as selfish as they like in a commons because there is no-one to stop them. In reality, traditional commons are closely regulated by the people who live there. There are two elements to common property: common and property. A common is the property of a particular community which, like the Turkana of the Turkwel River, decides who is allowed to use it and to what extent they are allowed to exploit it.

Hardin's thesis works only where there is no ownership. The oceans, for example, possessed by no-one and poorly regulated, are overfished and polluted, as every user tries to get as much out of them as possible, and the costs of their exploitation are borne by the world as a whole. These are not commons, but free for alls. In a true commons, everyone watches everyone else, for they know that anyone overexploiting a resource is exploiting them.

The effects of dismantling the commons to prevent Hardin's presumed tragedy of overexploitation from running its course can scarcely be overstated. In Brazil, for example, peasant communities are being pushed off their land to make way for agro-industry. Land that supported thousands of people becomes the exclusive property of one family. Mechanization means that hardly any permanent labor is needed.

Some of the dispossessed go the the cities where, instead of an industrial revolution, they find unemployment and destitution. Others go to the forests, where they may try to move into the commons belonging to the Indians, defying their regulations by cutting and burning the forests.

No group has suffered more than the people singled out by Hardin's paper: the traditional herders of animals, or pastoralists. In Kenya the Maasai have been cajoled into privatizing their commons: in some parts every family now owns a small ranch. Not only is this destroying Maasai society, as tight communities are artificially divided into nuclear families, but it has undercut the very basis of their survival.

In the varied and changeable savannahs, the only way a herder can survive is by moving. Traditionally, the Maasai followed the rain across their lands, leaving an area before its resources were exhausted and returning only when it had recovered. Now, confined to a single plot, they have no alternative but to graze it until drought or overuse brings the vegetation to an end. When their herds die, entrepreneurs move in, buy up their lands for a song and either plough them for wheat and barley, exhausting the soil within a few years, or use them as collateral for securing business loans.

In Somalia, Siad Barre's government nationalized the commons, nullifying the laws devised by Somali communities to protect their grazing lands from people of other clans. When charcoal burners moved in to cut their trees, the local people found that there was nothing they could do to stop them. The free for all with which the commons regime was replaced was one of the reasons for the murderous chaos that later governed the country.

The enclosure of the commons, of which these are examples, has always been ruinous for the commoners. In Britain, we choose to remember what we consider the positive effects of enclosure: the creation of a workforce to drive the Industrial Revolution. But the expropriation of common land by private landlords in many cases took place centuries before industrialization.

The dispossessed commoners became vagrants, hounded from county to county, without licenses permitting them to work, begging and stealing to get by, sometimes expressing their fury by rioting or burning the new owners' hayricks. It was only after hundreds of years of proscription, destitution and starvation that jobs for the dispossessed became widely available in the cities.

These changes in the ownership of land lie at the heart of our environmental crisis. Traditional rural communities use their commons to supply most of their needs: food, fuel, fabrics, medicine and housing. To keep themselves alive they have to maintain a diversity of habitats: woods, grazing lands, fields, ponds, marshes and scrub. Within these habitats they need to protect a wide range of species, different types of grazing, a mixture of crops, trees for fruit, fibers, medicine or building. The land is all they possess, so they have to look after it well.

However, when the commons are privatized, they pass into the hands of people whose priority is to make money. The most efficient means of making it is to select the most profitable product and concentrate on producing that. So, in Kenya, the Maasai's savannahs—a mixture of woods and scrub, grasslands and flowering swards—are replaced with uniform fields of wheat. The crofts of Scotland, whose forests, marshes, fields and pastures answered all the commoners' needs, gave way to sheep and conifer plantations. As the land is no longer the sole means of survival, but an investment that can be exchanged, the new owners can, if necessary, overexploit it and reinvest elsewhere.

As land changes hands, so does power. When communities own the land they make the laws and develop them to suit their own needs. Everyone is responsible for ensuring that everyone else obeys them. As landlords take over, it is their law that prevails, whether or not it leads to the protection of local resources.

The language in which the old laws were expressed gives way to the language of the outsiders. With it go many of the concepts and cautionary tales encouraging people to protect their environment. Translated into the dominant language they appear irrational and archaic. As they disappear, so does much that makes our contact with the countryside meaningful: it becomes a series of unrelated resources, rather than an ecosystem of which we, economically, culturally and spiritually, are a part. For human beings, as for the biosphere, the tragedy of the commons is not the tragedy of their existence, but the tragedy of their disappearance.

Tragedies of enclosure are not confined to other lands or other periods. In Britain, the commoners' battle for the land has largely been lost: 75% of the land surface is in the hands of less than 1% of the population. Most of the changes in land tenure occurred so long ago that we are no longer aware of their significance. It is not considered strange that 92% of our population lives in towns; that even access and recreation should be forbidden in most of the countryside; that the landscape should consist of open and relatively uniform fields, rather than a complex of different habitats. All these are direct results of enclosure.

Most of the remaining 'commons' in Britain are, paradoxically, privately owned. Norman barons forcibly dissolved the communal owner-ship of common land, but upheld communal rights to its use. Both the commons themselves and these rights of usufruct have diminished since then: today only 4.5% of the land is registered as commons, and across much of this all commoners' rights have been extinguished. But even the commoners' few residual rights are, in many places, still being eroded. As they diminish, so does the diversity of the land they have protected.

Weaver's Down, near Liphook in Hampshire, is a 200 acre common of heathland, grass meadow, scrub and copse on the Hampshire/West Sussex border. The commoners, few of whom are officially registered as such, use it for walking and occasional grazing. The farmer who owns it replaced some of the rough pastures with enhanced grazing for his animals but, after protests from local people, started to allow the heath on those parts of the common to regenerate. Enough of the original vegetation survives on the untouched areas for Weaver's Down to remain one of the few sites in Britain where sand lizards, smooth snakes, slow worms, nightjars and Dartford warblers remain.

A Japanese corporation recently bought the land and applied for planning permission to turn it into a golf course. For a number of reasons, including the fact that there was no vehicular access to the area, permission could not be granted. While Chichester City Council and Hampshire District Council considered the application, the corporation applied pesticides to part of the heathland and drove a motor mower over the common to make a rudimentary road. Commoners discovered that several protected reptiles were killed in the blades: as a result the corporation is currently subject to court action.

If the golf course is approved, the heath and remaining rough pasture will probably be replaced by fairways seeded with one species of grass and maintained by the use of pesticides and piped water. Inconveniently placed trees will be removed. Those that are planted are likely to be fast-growing exotics, rather than native species, although the company promises otherwise.

The commoners complain that these plans will deprive them of the landscape they valued. They successfully petitioned the District Council to reject the planning application, but the corporation has now appealed to the Department of the Environment.

The point here is that biological diversity does not depend so much on the use of the land, but on who has control or influence over this use. The two parties to the dispute both want to use the land for recreation. The local people, who use Weaver's Down for most of their outdoor recreational needs (children's play, walking dogs, birdwatching, botany, sitting and taking in the view), demand habitat diversity. Outsiders, whose need for recreational diversity may be answered by a number of different places (such as marinas and running tracks as well as golf courses), demand uniformity in each one.

Annotated List of Further Reading

The Tragedy of the Commons, Garrett Hardin, *Science*, Vol. 162, pp. 1243–1248, 1968.

This paper has had an enormous impact on development policy over the last 25 years. It applies game theory, originally developed for military strategists, to the ownership of resources, arguing that common property will inevitably be destroyed by overexploitation and, in the case of land, must be privatized or regulated by external institutions to be protected.

Failing to Cope With Drought: the Plight of Africa's Ex-pastoralists, J. Moris, *Development Policy Review*, Vol. 6, pp. 269–294, 1988.

Pastoralists, whose activities have been restricted by land loss and externally imposed regulation, have reduced ability to recover from drought. Those forced to settle by the privatization or nationalization of land also impose a greater burden on the environment.

Whose Common Future? The Ecologist, Vol. 22, No. 4, 1992.

Documents, in a Special Issue, the worldwide alienation of common property and shows how enclosure changes social and environmental relationships, concentrating power and resources in the hands of a small number of people and institutions—changing the ways in which land is used.

Intention of Implication: The Effects of Turkana Social Organization on Ecological Balances, F. Storas in P. T. Baxter and R. S. Hogg (Eds), *Property, Poverty and People: Changing Rights in Property and Problems of Pastoral Development*, Manchester: University of Manchester Press, 1987.

Describes traditional Turkana property relations, and how restrictions on access vary with the abundance of natural resources. Shows how settlement schemes in the Turkana district have failed to take traditional systems into account, leading to the overuse of resources.

On Common Ground, Francis Reed, London: Working Press, 1991.

Historical analysis of common property ownership in Britain and prescriptions for improvements in the built environment arising from studies of the relationship between people and space.

The Reality of the Commons: Answering Hardin from Somalia, Gillian Shepherd, pp. 73–86 in *Forest Policies, Forest Politics, Overseas Development Institute Occasional Paper 13*, 1992.

Common lands in the Bay Region of Somalia were nationalized, with the result that outsiders were permitted by the government to enter them and cut the trees for charcoal. Local people were not allowed to stop them, yet the weak state institutions were insufficiently motivated or empowered to intervene to prevent overexploitation.

Settlement, Pastoralism and the Commons: The Ideology and Practice of Irrigation Development in Northern Kenya, Richard S. Hogg in D. Anderson and A. T. Grove (Eds), *Conservation in Africa: Policies and Practice*, Cambridge: Cambridge University Press, 1986.

Shows how irrigation schemes in northern Kenya, designed to conserve the rangelands and alleviate poverty, were premised on a misunderstanding of pastoralist land management. They exacerbated famine and pauperization and led to an increase in grazing pressure.

A Turkana child drinks straight from the cow. The Turkana are totally dependent on their livestock. Without them, they and their culture perish

Every day the young boys take the herd from the village to grazing land, usually near the communal acacia forest, to feed on the fallen pods

Turkana elders spend much of their time discussing the movements of the community as well as social issues

Young Turkana boys have left their pastoralist communities due to famine, raiding and drought to seek a life on the streets of Kitale

Turkana pastoralists in the Kibera shanty town, Nairobi—hundreds of miles from home, stuck in an alien lifestyle

Maasai herding cattle in the hills of Loita, one of the last places left in Kenya where the Maasai maintain a relatively traditional lifestyle

Maasai herders graze their cattle along the edge of the Maasai Mara game reserve. Laws no longer allow them to enter where they have herded for years

The Maasai have been excluded from good grazing lands and are now reduced to taking their cattle to graze alongside roads

Maasai herd their livestock in the background on the wheat stubble as a combine harvester works the land where they once herded them

A Maasai mother tends her crops, a concept alien to her. Traditionally, the Maasai are nomadic herders, but land pressure has denied them grazing areas

Once the rangelands of the Maasai and their cattle herds, most of the land south of Nairobi has been ploughed into prairie and wheat fields

A Maasai herder has sold his cattle. Once a mark of status, large herds are now often sold because of the increasing land pressure and the need for money

Maasai men in a bar in Kajiaido. Many Maasai men, having sold their cattle and land, spend their time drinking in the local bars

John Whitelegg
Credit: John Wakeford

Author biography

John Whitelegg uses the way human society transports itself as a barometer for its sustainability. Formerly Head of the Department of Geography at the University of Lancaster, he now acts as an independent researcher and consultant to governments, academia and business. His latest book is called *Transport for a Sustainable Future*. He is Chairman of Transport 2000 International, a global organization that campaigns for sustainable transport policies and environmental responsibility in the transport field. The work of Transport 2000 International has involved research and support for the tram system in Melbourne and Calcutta, arguments against the bridge between Sweden and Denmark, and activity within the European Community on the trans-European road network.

Chapter 6

John Whitelegg

The Pollution of Time

IN THE enormously wide-ranging and important discussion about the world's finite resources and the rate at which we are consuming them, there is a deafening silence about time. In some ways this is not surprising. Our cultural evolution has led us to believe that we can 'save time' or increase our efficiency by using time more effectively. Indeed, time-saving has become synonymous with a technological arrogance that assumes our destructive activities will somehow be transformed into nurturing and sustainable activities. Language is suffused with references to time-saving devices or derogatory remarks about time-wasting, and there is an all-embracing assumption that our technologies and management sciences make us better and better at getting more out of the irreducible 24 hour day.

Sustainability itself, the rallying point for global and national environmental policies, has at its core a time transformation. If it does not mean reducing consumption so as to extend the life of our finite resources, then it does not mean anything. If it cannot embrace a more measured and time-wasting approach to the organization of human activities, then it is a fraud. Independent of our consumption of finite resources is the rate at which we consume them and the extent to which this rate leads or lags is the rate at which the planet can cope, repair and manage the damage. Time is the crucial element in this equation. If we cannot slow down processes that pollute the atmosphere, reduce biodiversity, precipitate climatic change, destroy communities and destroy bonds between people and places, then our historic battle against time will ensure that we run out of it. Wasting time, in the sense of having long-time horizons, not seeking returns on investments in three years or five years, and taking time to enjoy our local environments and the experience of place, might well turn out to be the most important environmental strategy we could adopt.

Time and space (in the terrestrial sense) define human activities, set boundaries around what is possible and determine levels of energy consumption, social interaction, pollution and quality of life. Time and space mean very different things to different groups in society. This is certainly true at a global level, where some groups can operate in an environment almost completely free of time–space constraints and others are deeply rooted in places and temporal rhythms that effectively define their culture and language. The dealer on the financial markets in the City of London operates globally and in a 'non-place' virtual reality that permits and encourages actions that are destructive to environment and culture. Instant pay-back, instant gratification, profit-taking and a global stage without a global commitment are a powerful inducement to environmental destruction and rejection of long-term thinking.

A liberation from time–space constraints has both a physical and a psychological impact. Most of the problems we now categorize as environmental problems can be described as the result of reallocating time which has been liberated by some technological means and assigned to other activities, which in their turn consume time and resources at a faster rate. If we 'save' time by driving to work rather than walking to work we will consume that gain by living further away. If we 'save' time by the adoption of labor-saving devices of some kind, then we might well feel the need to purchase consumer goods or travel by car to some leisure destination to use up the time saved. Time-savings are unlikely to be resource-neutral in their implications. Benefits arising from time-saving are likely to be consumed by some other activity, which in its turn requires energy, produces pollution and intensifies resource consumption.

Caesare Marchetti has commented on the relationships over time between the expenditure of time, money and effort on transport. He notes that the expenditure of time on transport in developed countries is approximately one hour per day per person and accounts for 15% of our disposable income. Interestingly, in the context of this discussion on time-savings and the consumption of that saving as more distance, increasing energy and resource consumption (time pollution), Marchetti argues that the allocation of time and money over the available transportation modes is made to maximize distance. His conclusion, therefore, is very clear indeed and is central to the notion of time pollution. The twin goals of transport systems are 'as fast as possible, as cheap as possible'. Technological gains that allow us to travel further within a fixed time budget will generate changes that increase the distances over which we travel and over which we move goods.

The psychological dimension of these physical changes is just as important. If we are 'freed' of living, working and socializing within a narrowly defined geographical area, we experience a transformation of experience from locality-specific to no-locality. Our experiences are now characterized not by meeting people informally as we go about our daily business on the streets of a city between home and work, play group, school, café and pub, but by the daily commute, the experience of sitting inside a metal box insulated from reality, rushing past pedestrians, cyclists, children and the elderly, and always intent on origins and destinations and not the bit in the middle. The journey by car or plane or high-speed train imposes enormous social and environmental costs on those who experience the impact on their neighborhood. The individuals passing through have no interest in the corridors they are devastating; they want to save time, get there, finish their journey. Their time has been valued by society but *the time that has been polluted* along the corridors is devalued. It is not important.

New roads or railway lines can be built to save five minutes of the traveler's time. Each time one traveler saves that five minutes, he or she imposes noise, dirt, danger and pollution on thousands of local residents who, by virtue of their residential address, must suffer the consequences. Their conversation will be disrupted, the time it takes to cross streets, to get to school, to go shopping in a neighborhood will be lengthened because the new road or increased traffic on adjacent roads generated by the new road has divided their community. Thousands of hours of local time will be sacrificed so that those in transit can save traveling time.

The deterioration of local environmental conditions caused by the growth in traffic will persuade parents to stop their children crossing roads, walking and cycling. Parents and other adults will then spend thousands of hours sitting in cars ferrying children to and from schools, swimming pools, friends and organized activities. They do this because they are frightened for the safety of their children on the roads. The time-savings built into the planning of new roads and their elaborate cost–benefit calculations have imposed huge time burdens on other parts of the system. For many groups, particularly the elderly, the time redistribution which the new road has precipitated is disastrous. It means that they can no longer cross roads at all and so are deprived of activities such as spending time with friends and relatives (unless they are driven or drive themselves, thereby adding to the problems for those without access to a car). It means that they must spend more time in their own home and not on the street, where their presence is a vital part of community life and can encourage others to become involved in a rich street life.

The theft of public space from ordinary residents by traffic has been accomplished by the valuation of drivers'/passengers' time in a computer model of cost–benefit analysis (CBA) that simply delivers the result intended. If a value is put on the time of car occupants and inserted into a rigged mathematical procedure, it will produce the answer that we need new roads. Everything else to do with the quality of life of pedestrians, cyclists, children, the elderly and community is ignored. Time has been usurped to justify a crude political choice in favor of new roads.

One of the most impressive characteristics of cars is that no matter how powerful, laden with sexual imagery and supportive of flagging ego and status, they are no use if everyone has one. This might suggest the interesting conclusion that time-saving must be carefully rationed by social class so that the wealthy can continue to enjoy 'it' whilst the masses are deprived of 'it'. This is very similar to concepts of slavery and working below stairs, which essentially involved a view of whose time was important and whose time was to be devoted to the service of others. In the case of cars it is not working out very well. A motorized trip of only a few miles length across London will result in serious loss of time for rich and poor alike in the ubiquitous congestion. It is very obvious indeed that the freedom and liberation promised to the car owner cannot now be delivered. Time spent in a car in gridlock or near-gridlock conditions consumes significant parts of people's lives in Los Angeles, Bangkok and London. Time 'lost' in this way adds to pollution and adds to the cost of industry. The UK Confederation of British Industry claims that the losses can be converted into cash, and work out at about £15 billion per year in Britain.

This loss of time on roads is one measure of 'real' time to be compared with the fantasy time of CBA calculations. Roads continue to be justified and built by procedures enshrined in CBA and based on a view of time that has little resemblance to reality. Another measure of 'real' time might be some concept of useful time. Time spent on public transport as long as the public transport vehicle is reasonably clean and comfortable is all usable time for reading, writing and sleeping. This is not normally the case with car driving. We do not have a mechanism with which we can compare real time with useful time, though we can compare the prediction of journey times made in support of new roads with the result some years later. What is clear is that current concepts and measures of time in transport planning and associated investment appraisal all work to produce unsustainable transport policies, pollution and community destruction.

The pursuit of time-savings represents a social transfer of environmental destruction. Globally, we are witnessing environmental degradation in large parts of the world (normally called the less developed) because of the desire to support non-sustainable lifestyles in the 'developed' world. In Manchester, Berlin and Los Angeles, those who are free of time–space constraints (i.e. the wealthy) can travel long distances by car through poorer neighborhoods, exposing local children to increased chances of road traffic accidents. They can travel by air to remote parts of the world and wreak havoc on traditional lifestyles, cultures and ecology. Tourism is basically a frantic search for time-compressed experiences in the virtual reality of an exotic location. The expenditure of so much effort to consume so much in such a short burst of time is a major contributor to global pollution, particularly around airports, at tourist destinations and at 10–12 km above the Earth's surface, where aircraft emissions inject greenhouse gases into the atmosphere.

The growth in the demand for air travel, which is closely locked into the growth in demand for tourist trips, is possibly even more unsustainable than car and lorry use, creating as it does significant atmospheric problems and an insatiable demand for termini, car parks, runways and other paraphernalia on the ground. Although even under difficult circumstances it is possible to plan for a shift from cars to public transport, foot or bicycle, it is not possible to envisage a shift from air transport to alternative modes. Air transport, which is the essence of distance-intensive and time-saving lifestyles, is not easily switched to other modes and requires a reduction in demand. This will be difficult.

Our transport system and its massive state funding represents a systematic transfer of time from weaker groups (economically and socially) to stronger groups. That is exactly what CBA on road construction proposals actually means. The process is cumulative and opportunistic. The more we destroy the urban environment or the countryside around urban areas with bypasses justified on 'environmental grounds', the more we exclude people from public space and from time-demanding ('time wasting') social interaction. More travel must then be accomplished by car because no responsible parent would let their child walk to school. More travel by car feeds the demand for more road space and deprives collective transport and, more importantly, walking and cycling, of its credibility.

The result is a £23 billion road-building program in the UK over the next 10 years to increase the supply of road space by 5% when forecasts indicate an increase in miles driven by car of 83–142%, or double that in rural areas.

The road-building program, the extraction of aggregates, the production of cement, the 60% of all journeys by car that are less than five miles in length and the resource consumption associated with car manufacture and use, account for significant amounts of noise, pollution, land take and greenhouse gas emissions.

Time-saving or time-wasting: the car's balance sheet

It is evident that the car can save large amounts of time spent on journeys and can also make available a large number of opportunities within a constrained time budget. Multiple journey purposes are made possible by a car and would be impossible by public transport or on bicycle or foot. These are real benefits and can be quantified. There are, however, two caveats: (1) the car cannot be obtained and serviced without an expenditure of time and effort, and this time and effort imposes a significant time penalty on the car user; and (2) the car feeds a number of changes in land use allocations and spatial organization that respond to the new movement opportunities by spreading society out over longer distances. Time-savings are therefore quickly absorbed in the necessity to travel longer distances to do exactly the same kind of things that we could have done over shorter distances 20 years ago.

The time demanded by cars, and indeed by travel itself, is a basic measure of society's progression towards increasing levels of consumption, and, as in transport this is largely fed by fossil fuels, increasing levels of pollution, global warming and health damage.

One calculation of time demands imposed by cars in Germany was made by the Institute of Applied Environmental Research and is summarized in Table 6.1. These calculations can be compared with those in Figure 6.1 showing the 'average social speed' of large cars compared with smaller cars and with bicycles. Clearly, the environmentally sounder vehicle (the bicycle) delivers a much better return on time expended than does the car. The concept of 'average social speed' is far more revealing about the relationships between resource expenditure, time

Table 6.1. How much time is required for a car?

Yearly outgoings on vehicle (DM)	5424.20
Average hourly wage (DM)	19.99
Time spent working to pay for the vehicle in hours per annum	262.24
Travel time for 15 000 km per year, assuming 35 km/hr to include jams and parking place searches, repairs, tank-filling, washing, etc.	528.57
Total time devoted to the car in hours per year	790.81
Average speed assuming 15 000 km per year and 790.81 hours time expenditure	18.97

Source: Institut für angewandte Umweltforschung (1987).

Calculated speeds taking into account the total amount of time spent in transport

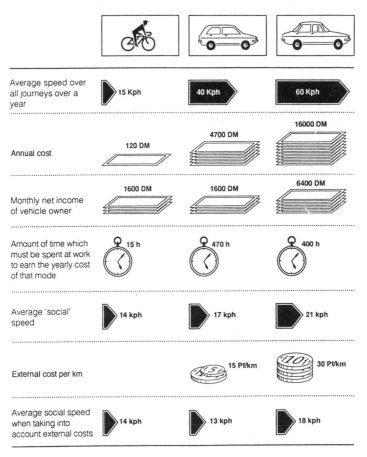

Average speed over all journeys over a year	15 Kph	40 Kph	60 Kph
Annual cost	120 DM	4700 DM	16000 DM
Monthly net income of vehicle owner	1600 DM	1600 DM	6400 DM
Amount of time which must be spent at work to earn the yearly cost of that mode	15 h	470 h	400 h
Average 'social' speed	14 kph	17 kph	21 kph
External cost per km		15 Pf/km	30 Pf/km
Average social speed when taking into account external costs	14 kph	13 kph	18 kph

Figure 6.1. Bicycles can overtake cars?

expenditure and environmental destruction than the naive assumptions about speed as measured on the speedometer. To achieve the high speeds that can be reached on motorways, and in illegal bursts in residential areas, considerable amounts of energy have to be consumed and paid for by the expenditure of work time to earn the cash. Even more revealing would be an extension of average social speed to cover the amount of time that would have to be worked to earn the cash to carry out the remedial work to clean up the air and noise pollution, repair the injured in road traffic accidents and pick up the health costs of those whose respiratory systems have been damaged by exposure to vehicle exhaust emissions. The search for time savings is not only illusory, it is usually counter-productive and sometimes deadly. A road traffic accident fatality deprives someone of all their time forever.

At a more basic level, German data summarized in Table 6.2 show an increase over time in the amount of time spent traveling and very low and stable average speeds.

Similar UK data (Table 6.3) show an increase over time in the amount of time we spend on the move. These increased time allocations are corroborated by increases in the distances that have to be covered in journeys to work and recreational activities and in making connections with increasingly remote shops, schools and health care facilities. The processes that are responsible for concentrating these activities on a smaller number of sites and the increasing average distances that separate origins from destinations are the basic processes that generate demand for transport, vehicle ownership and use and impose time penalties. One

Table 6.2. Development of mobility in Germany

	1976	1982	1989
Journeys per person per day	2.84	2.93	3.01
Motorized journeys	1.63	1.80	1.89
Time budget (minutes per person per day)	71	78	80
Average length of journeys (km)	15.5	16.5	17.7
Average speed (km/hr)	13.1	12.7	13.3

Table 6.3. Time spent traveling according to mode of travel in 1975-1976 compared with 1985-1986 (minutes per person per week)

Mode	1975–1976	1985–1986
Walk	80	111
Bicycle	9	6
Car/van/lorry	158	192
Local bus	61	46
Rail	15	21
Other	17	20
Total	340	396

of the ironies implicit in these processes is that the imposition of time penalties is generally described as an increase in freedom and choice, and the marketing of vehicles and the support of road construction by organizations such as the UK Automobile Association (AA) and Royal Automobile Club (RAC) is couched in terms of liberty, freedom of choice and increase in quality of life. The reality is somewhat different, with larger and larger amounts of time spent traveling, usually in unpleasant conditions, to satisfy needs and wants that only 10 years ago could have been satisfied nearer to each other and nearer to residential locations.

The manipulation of concepts of choice and freedom, linked to speed and status, is a major source of the increased demand for transport, with all its associated environmental damage and self-reinforcing demand for more road space to try and keep up with the illusion of choice and freedom and utilization of time. Because time has been hijacked by the illusion of speed and choice, more time is wasted riding around on infrastructure justified on the grounds that it saves time. Meanwhile, modes of transport that take more time (walking and cycling) suffer because the corruption of time by vehicular transport has put facilities out of reach of the time budget of non-car users. The desire to save time on the part of motorists, and the desire to service large numbers of consumers in new shopping centers or large hospitals, has robbed the non-car user of local facilities and basic opportunities within range of non-car time budgets.

If we could imagine a situation where all travel was car-based so that there were no social and spatial inequalities borne out of lack of access to cars and remoteness of facilities, then we would have genuinely equitable mass pollution, gridlock and immobility. The advantages of the privileged are once again purchased at the expense of the relative immobility of the less wealthy. The wealthy have the resources to buy time through their vehicles, but this is only possible as long as vehicle ownership and use is not a mass phenomenon. This is the reason why road pricing or its equivalent will be necessary to ensure that time (like wealth) can be made unequally available.

Time pollution is a shorthand description for the processes which feed the delusion of time-savings whilst increasing time allocations spent on traveling to increasingly distant locations. The pursuit of time-savings generates significant increases in vehicle ownership and use, especially as it is so successful at exterminating the conditions conducive to 'time wasting' activities. This feeds increases in pollution, global warming, health damage and community destruction. It also feeds social inequities with its damage to walking, cycling and local facilities, and stimulates totally inappropriate responses such as more road-building and road-pricing strategies, all of which heighten social inequalities by ensuring time benefits can be kept only within reach of the wealthy.

Death on the streets

Road traffic accidents exact an enormous price in the deaths and injuries they produce. Over half a million citizens of the European Union have been killed in the last 10 years and 10 million injured. Victims are often slow and vulnerable whereas the vehicles that kill them are fast and kitted out with technology to protect their occupants, such as emergency 'air-bags'. Between 1980 and 1990 in England and Wales an average of 239 children were killed each year on the roads as pedestrians. For every death, 10 children were admitted to hospital with injuries. All that fashionable air-bags would have achieved would have been a reduction in bruising of the offending car drivers. The pursuit of speed in the service of time-saving is a major component in the causation of serious and fatal accidents. The apparent fall in deaths and injuries in the UK in recent years has been purchased at the expense of use of public space. Children in particular have been severely restricted in their use of streets to make room for more and faster cars.

The relationship between speed and accident severity is well known. Injury and fatality risks at 50 km/hr are more than double those at 30 km/hr. The empirical relationship between speed and the severity of the injury resulting from a road traffic accident is very clear indeed and is summarized in Figure 6.2.

In a remarkable example of societal trade-offs, we routinely accept child fatalities so that we can get to work five minutes quicker or drive to a social event and 'save' 10 minutes. Higher speeds are more polluting in terms of emissions than lower speeds (Figure 6.3), though even these negative consequences of time pollution pale into insignificance when compared with the consequences for human life of speeds in excess of 20 km/hr.

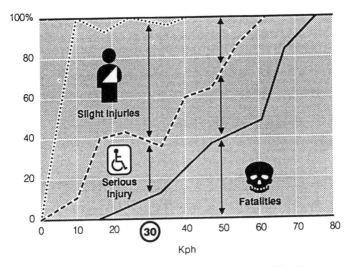

Figure 6.2. Injury and fatality risks at various speeds. Risks at 50 km/hr are more than double those at 30 km/hr

Significant savings in accident numbers, fatalities and injuries can be achieved very easily simply by reducing speed. Reducing speed in the context of traffic calming in a German city (maximum speed 30 km/hr) or imposing 100 km/hr limits on sections of German motorways means reversing our normal image of time and convenience, but shows very clearly that actually making cars take longer to complete a journey brings about substantial savings in life, resource costs and pollution. It is paradoxical that the whole UK road building program is built on the concept of saving time when the opposite has so much to offer.

German traffic calming projects show reductions of 100% in fatalities and over 75% in injuries as well as large cost savings. Figures 6.4 and 6.5 show the results of traffic calming and speed limitation in the city of Cologne. The imposition of a 100 km/hr limit on the autobahn around Cologne produced a reduction of 23.8% in fatalities.

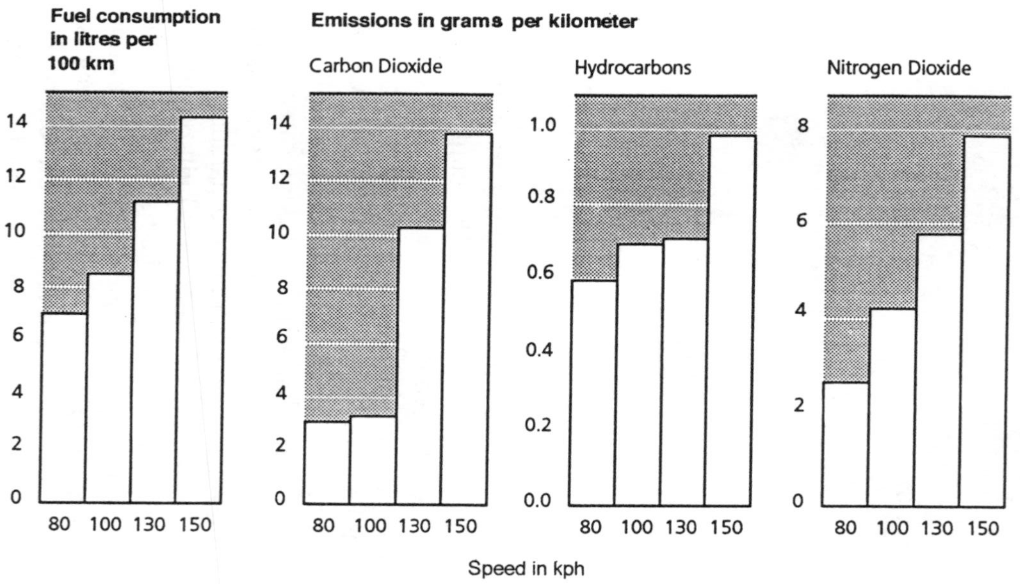

Emissions in grams per kilometer

Figure 6.3. Fuel consumption and emissions from petrol engine cars at constant speeds (average value for 30 vehicles)

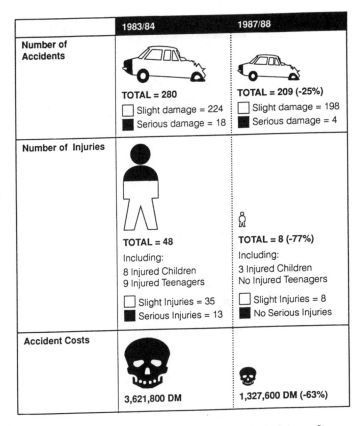

	1983/84	1987/88
Number of Accidents	TOTAL = 280 ☐ Slight damage = 224 ■ Serious damage = 18	TOTAL = 209 (-25%) ☐ Slight damage = 198 ■ Serious damage = 4
Number of Injuries	TOTAL = 48 Including: 8 Injured Children 9 Injured Teenagers ☐ Slight Injuries = 35 ■ Serious Injuries = 13	TOTAL = 8 (-77%) Including: 3 Injured Children No Injured Teenagers ☐ Slight Injuries = 8 ■ No Serious Injuries
Accident Costs	3,621,800 DM	1,327,600 DM (-63%)

Figure 6.4. Results of traffic calming and speed limitation in Cologne, Germany: program area Nippes um Baudri- und Schillplatz

Reduced speeds (i.e. deliberately imposing a time penalty on motorists) reduces the amount of space needed for traffic (Figure 6.6). At higher speeds it is necessary to leave longer gaps between cars and lorries to take stopping time and reaction time into account.

In a lifecycle analysis of the car, the Institute for Environmental Prediction demonstrated the serious time penalties exacted by auto-dependence. Lifecycle analysis

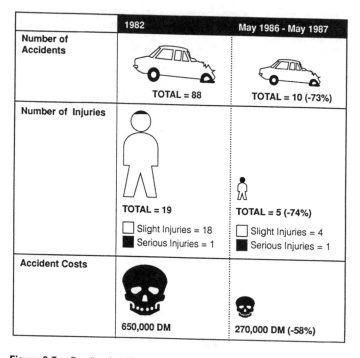

	1982	May 1986 - May 1987
Number of Accidents	TOTAL = 88	TOTAL = 10 (-73%)
Number of Injuries	TOTAL = 19 ☐ Slight Injuries = 18 ■ Serious Injuries = 1	TOTAL = 5 (-74%) ☐ Slight Injuries = 4 ■ Serious Injuries = 1
Accident Costs	650,000 DM	270,000 DM (-58%)

Figure 6.5. Results of traffic calming and speed limitation in Cologne, Germany: program area Agnes-Viertel/Teilbereich östl. Neusser Strasse

is particularly important in the environmental debate because of its detailed tracking of environmental and social impacts at every stage in the life of a product. Simply looking at the environmental impact of a car whilst in use is to focus on a very small bandwidth of time. If we start the clock when those raw materials that will eventually make up a car are extracted from the ground and keep the clock running until the waste products of tyres, exhaust systems, batteries and cars themselves have 'finished' polluting water supplies and aquifers and have released all their pollutants back into the biosphere, then the total damage is enormous.

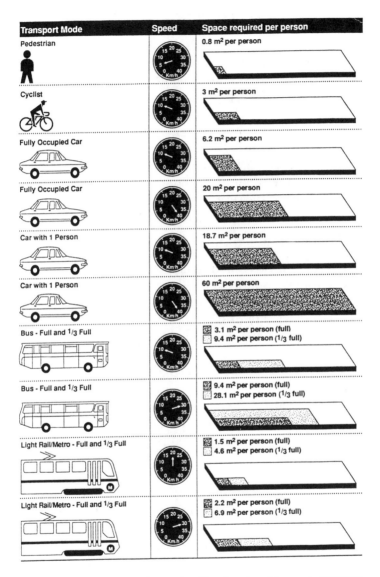

Figure 6.6. Consumption of space by different modes of transport: occupancy and speed

The Heidelberg researchers have quantified all these elements effectively, demonstrating the literal meaning of time pollution. Resource consumption on the scale displayed by our levels of car and lorry dependence casts a deep shadow over future generations and pollutes future environments. It also affects the health of those who, as children in the 1990s, are routinely exposed to air pollution, which beyond any doubt damages their respiratory systems.

There can be very few indicators of non-sustainability that are clearer than the respiratory damage to children from current traffic levels. These levels will certainly double over the next 15–20 years across the European Union and possibly more than double as a result of the release of a mountain of suppressed demand in Eastern Europe and the former Soviet Union. Our commitment in Britain to destroying the railway system and to moving 92% of our freight by road makes the pollution of the future inevitable and the possibility of meeting international conventions on reductions/stabilization of NO_x and CO_2 non-existent.

The lifecycle analysis of the car shows that over the lifetime of a car in Germany it will be responsible for the loss of 820 hours of human life and incalculable damage to the rest of the biosphere. Each car in its lifetime is responsible for 2800 hours of a life damaged by a road traffic accident injury resulting in some kind of handicap. Looking at an individual over his or her lifetime, one in every hundred will be killed in a road traffic accident and two out of every three injured.

Converted into production data, every 50 minutes a new car is produced that will kill someone and every 50 seconds a new car is produced that will injure someone.

The conquest of distance by the destruction of time: the case of high-speed trains

The global surge of interest in high-speed trains has sharpened the debate about time-saving and the importance of time in the struggle for market share in transport. High speed in the context of new rail investment is normally taken as a speed in excess of 200 km/hr. High-speed trains in Europe can produce time savings of 25–50% when new services such as those operated in France or Germany are compared with the conventional rail services they replace. Savings in time of 50% on most journeys are claimed by the railway operators.

The long-term plan for Europe comprises 23 000 km of high-speed lines including 12 000 km of new lines at a cost of 180 billion ECUs.

The European Commission is a very important agent in the process of designing and funding new networks to increase speed, mobility and economic growth. Its commitment to 12 500 km of new motorways in Europe as part of its drive to secure economic gains from completing the single market is a major blow to the environment of over 20 of Europe's most important ecologically sensitive regions. Motorways are proposed through the Snowdonia and Pembrokeshire National Parks in the UK, the Pyrenees, the west of Ireland and undeveloped areas of Spain, Portugal and Greece. These plans for new networks are at odds with commitments to sustainability and the objectives of the 5th Environmental Action Programme. The new road program, like the new rail program, is aimed at increasing mobility and increasing resource consumption through time-savings.

High-speed trains have rapidly gained acceptance and have won large-scale governmental support in a way that local transport provision, particularly urban rail and integrated urban public transport, has not. The success of high-speed rail is another consequence of the time fetishism that afflicts transport planning. Only a small proportion (less than 5%) of trips in Europe are over 500 km in length and hence suited to high-speed rail travel. In Australia the government has supported the Very Fast Train (VFT) concept between Melbourne and Sydney, whilst mounting a savage campaign in 1989 against Melbourne's urban rail system and against country rail services throughout the state of Victoria. Although support for high-speed rail in Britain is less comprehensive than in France or Germany, it nevertheless attracts more support than the mundane business of running buses and trains in cities.

High-speed rail is usually justified on the grounds that it will substitute for air trips, certainly over distances of 500–800 km, and will therefore be a net contributor to the environment. Here we have a very good example of time-savings being used as a basis for investment that will result in environmental gains. The air substitution argument is seductive. Paris–London comparisons show a total journey time (including check-in, security, trips to airport/station) of 4 hours 15 minutes by high-speed rail and 4 hours 35 minutes by air. Such comparisons are helped by making assumptions favorable to rail and unfavorable to air, but the point is still relevant. The experience on the Paris–Lyons TGV, which has been running for more than 10 years, is very revealing.

Between 1980 and 1984 the annual number of passengers between Paris and Lyons (in both directions) increased from 1.5 to 3.7 million and has continued to grow steadily at a rate of 6% each year since then. This is very impressive indeed and is frequently quoted in the justification of investment proposals for high-speed rail. The TGV has captured half the air travelers between Paris and Lyons, mainly because the rail ticket is half the cost of the air ticket for a similar journey time. More importantly, it has stimulated a great deal of extra travel. The passengers who formerly traveled by air represent only one-third of the TGV passengers. Another third have transferred from existing rail and the final third are accounted for by entirely newly-generated journeys. The impact of time-savings therefore has been to increase the demand for transport, just as it does with new road construction. Arguments about environmental gains arising from transfers from air are specious as airlines take advantage of the reduction in congestion to reallocate air traffic control slots to accommodate longer distance journeys and the massive demand of air travel for tourist purposes (currently increasing at over 10% each year).

The time-savings have not only generated more travel on the Paris–Lyons corridor, they have made room for an increase in air travel overall. Both types of passenger travel demand are damaging to the environment.

Plassard has provided some details about the impact of TGV services on travel behavior. He notes a 'mobility effect', pointing out that the availability of high-speed trains has increased the number of journeys made by each traveler by 30%. This is a very important dimension of time pollution. Saving time through the application of technology and cash produces more demand and more environmental damage. The extra travel by rail will be associated with car journeys to stations, with changes in residential location to take advantage of more rural locations because the high-speed trains permit journeys to be made in similar amounts of time even though changes in domestic address, business address or other activities now necessitate travel over much longer distances. The time gain has simply been consumed by increasing distances traveled.

Instead of making a single trip to Paris for several appointments, travelers now make one trip for each appointment. Their time-savings have emerged as an increase in time spent traveling on a per appointment basis. He also notes that the experience of high-speed trains in Japan has been to reduce employment and economic vitality at intermediate points such as Nagoya. The economic gains frequently claimed by road and rail builders are far from clear, and such evidence as is available indicates a redistribution effect, with job losses at intermediate centers.

'Just-in-Time', but not for the environment

The growth in road freight in Europe over the last 20 years has been one of the strongest areas of increase in the demand for transport. Road and rail are compared in Table 6.4. This growth, and the associated decline of rail, has serious environmental implications. The environmental impact of road freight in comparison with rail freight is summarized in Figure 6.7.

Lorries are five times more damaging in terms of carbon dioxide emissions than are trains, and 25 times more damaging in terms of road traffic accidents. Given these

Table 6.4. Average annual growth rates in freight transport in the European Union (percentages)

Time period	Rail	Road
1970–1975	− 3.1	+ 4.0
1975–1980	+ 1.8	+ 4.8
1980–1985	− 1.2	+ 1.1
1985–1989	− 0.1	+ 6.7
1989–1990	− 2.7	+ 1.7

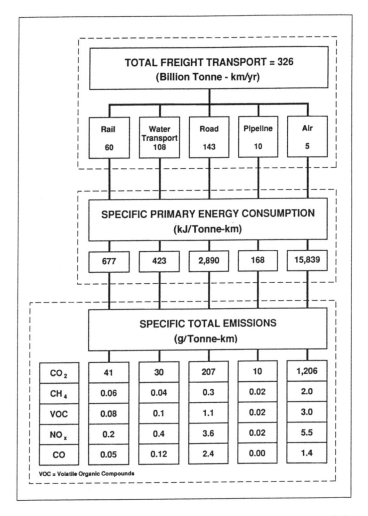

Figure 6.7. Different modes of freight transport in terms of energy use and pollution

enormous disparities in environmental performance, it is all the more remarkable that European industry, distribution and related activities are moving inexorably into road freight and abandoning the alternatives.

This process is particularly well advanced in Britain, with major transfers of freight from rail to road. Cement traffic from Lancashire to Scotland, oil movements from Ellesmere Port to Mid-Wales and Aberystwyth and quarry traffic in the Yorkshire Dales have been transferred to road. The economics of rail and road freight have accelerated this shift. The road sector receives massive investment, whilst rail facilities decline in number and increase in prices in the UK as the government imposes unreasonable and discriminatory financial rates of return on rail investment.

More important than the economics are the wide-ranging changes in the organization of production and consumption. These have reduced the need to store materials at points in the production chain and have substituted the highly efficient transport of materials so that they arrive 'just in time'. The transport function then becomes a highly integrated component of the total manufacturing and distribution system. This shift to higher levels of dependence on road haulage and to more movement of goods is referred to as logistics or 'just in time transport'.

The spatial concentration of production over time and the increased length of haul in road freight have all been made possible by the time-saving possibilities afforded by motorways. Firms are externalizing their internal costs by incorporating the motorway system into their production process. This is only possible because of time-savings and because of the low cost of transport in Europe, which makes massive increases in transport costs a much more profitable route to take than manufacturing and storing goods in a large number of smaller operations, with more local distribution arrangements. The more local distribution arrangements would produce a reduction in kilometers driven by lorries and a lowered environmental impact, but would be more expensive to industry. Time-savings in road transport have completely reorganized corporate behavior, location and distribution, to produce a major increase in environmental damage.

Spatial concentration to reduce the number of depots and increase kilometers traveled by lorries continues. The number of depots operated by a sample of firms fell by 68% between 1969 and 1978. Another sample compiled in 1990 had reduced their number of depots by 44% over the period 1978–1990.

These spatial concentration processes and application of logistic concepts will all be intensified by the single market and the changes in transport market regulation associated with that development. The deregulation of international haulage to permit lorries from any European Union country to operate on domestic journeys in another country will add to the downward price for road haulage as well as to levels of pollution, road traffic accidents and congestion. In the meantime, the railways and combined transport modes (rail and road working together with appropriate infrastructural support) will decline as logistics emphasizes the advantages of road-based operation.

Time-savings and the restructuring of accessibility surfaces have generated considerable amounts of extra transport activity and given the road-based modes, with their flexibility to respond quickly to changes in locational preferences, a major boost. Future levels of road freight, at both inter-urban and intra-urban scales, will constitute one of the most intractable environmental problems within the European Union and eastern Europe in the next few years.

Time and sustainability

It is very unlikely that those parts of the globe exhibiting high rates of consumption can achieve sustainability without reconceptualizing time and time-savings. Michael Ende, in his children's novel *Momo*, described the differences between a society geared to achieving time-savings and one operating in a way where human activities were conducted over shorter distances, with greater levels of social interaction. It is not necessary, however, to fantasize about a new utopia to alter course and to value time in a way that does not accelerate the pace of resource consumption nor generate higher and higher demands for infrastructure to support longer and longer distances for both people and freight transport.

A reconceptualization of time would put more emphasis on resource conservation, local production and consumption, nonmotorized transport for short trips, and socially rich neighborhoods. If time were valued in a way that did not assume time-savings translated into monetary benefits, then the road bias in national transport policy would be eliminated and transport policies would shift dramatically in the direction of sustainable transport, accessibility rather than mobility, and a hierarchy of modes, with walking and cycling the most important, followed by public transport and, much further down the list, cars.

An acceptance of the very real benefits which stem from valuing time spent in social interaction, utilizing local shops, local facilities and local green space, puts considerable emphasis on land-use planning changes and changes in the organization of facilities so that a large proportion of our daily activities can be satisfied by local travel rather than travel over distances of up to 100 km. Writing 30 years ago, Jane Jacobs showed how much cities can benefit from strong local communities, especially when compared with the 'spaced-out' alternatives encouraged by motorways, air transport and high-speed rail.

Because of our fascination with time-savings, spatial concentration and increasing mobility, we have very little idea about the environmental, social, community and economic benefits of regional production and consumption systems. A regional structure would provide the highest quality infrastructure for local trips (up to 5 km in length) and for groups of urban areas and their rural hinterland. Essentially, regional structures and rich networks of local facilities provide one of the few ways out of the rising spiral of transport demand and infrastructure provision. The environmental impacts associated with this demand for transport—e.g. greenhouse gases, acid rain, stratospheric ozone depletion, loss of habitat and threats to biodiversity— cannot be reduced by technical means (e.g. catalytic converters) or by regulation (e.g. the sulfur content of fuels). Taxation might produce some results, but debates within the European Union and lack of conclusion about carbon/ energy taxes show the difficulties of moving in this direction.

Changes in land-use planning, locations nearer to each other and to homes of those facilities for which people travel, investment in modes of transport which support local travel and a commitment to multimodal freight transport are capable of delivering reduced demand and a quality of life better than that delivered by hypermobility and growth. All these policies would be discriminated against by analysis and investment appraisal, processes which regard time-saving as valuable, and time as a commodity which can be converted into monetary units and used as a very large 'benefit' to set against limited 'costs' in a crude cost–benefit calculation. This distortion and usurpation of time is time pollution at its simplest.

Annotated List of Further Reading

Momo, Michael Ende, London: Puffin Books, 1985.
  First published in German in 1973. Also published in English as *The Little Grey Gentlemen*, this is a fairy-tale introduction to the theme of this chapter. For adults as well as children.

The Death and Life of Great American Cities, J. Jacobs, London: Random House, 1961. Republished London: Penguin Books, 1984.

   The best thing written on the condition of urban life and its links with transport and excessive mobility. Its 1961 analysis is as relevant in the late 1990s as it was then, and in many ways industrial society has made very little progress towards solving these problems.

Technocratic Dreaming: Of Very Fast Trains and Japanese Designer Cities, P. James, Melbourne: Left Book Club, 1990.

   Identifies the links between large-scale global capitalism, highly environmentally damaging transport and urban development projects and the collusion between national governments and representatives of large corporations in environmental destruction. The analysis of high-speed trains and their wider ramifications is highly recommended for understanding the full context of transport investments.

Death on the Streets: Cars and the Mythology of Road Safety, Robert Davies, Hawes: Leading Edge, 1993.

   Throws down a series of challenges to the road safety lobby and points out that in the vast majority of cases, road 'safety' policies work in favor of drivers and cars while being to the disadvantage of cyclists and pedestrians. It also describes ways in which a road safety policy would evolve if it took as its priority the protection of the latter group, and their use of the urban environment.

Sir Crispin Tickell

Author biography

As an international diplomat, Sir Crispin Tickell has long taken a special interest in environmental issues. In 1974–1975 he took a sabbatical year at Harvard University, leading to the publication of his book *Climate Change and World Affairs*. He was later Ambassador to Mexico, Permanent Secretary of the Overseas Development Administration and British Permanent Representative to the United Nations. He has often been credited with the 'greening' of Margaret Thatcher when Prime Minister and has played a key role in putting climate change on the world's agenda. He is now Warden of Green College, Oxford, Chairman of the British Government's Advisory Committee on the Darwin Initiative for the Survival of Species and Convenor of the British Government Panel on Sustainable Development.

Chapter 7

Sir Crispin Tickell

Cities and Climate Change

PEOPLE have been coming together in villages, towns and cities over the last few thousand years. Until the last century, cities were dangerous places. Death rates exceeded birth rates, and cities could only maintain themselves by sucking in people and resources from outside. We have become such urban creatures that we forget the vulnerability of cities. There are three main contributory factors: dependence on external resources; hazards to health through concentration of numbers; and liability to environmental change.

Such resources as food, water, timber, building materials and fuel must be brought in from surrounding areas, while rubbish, sewage and waste of all kinds must be disposed of. Cities, and their support systems, create an environment of their own. There are almost imperceptible effects over time, both within the city and without. Depletion of the external resource base with deforestation, soil erosion, overuse of groundwater, salting up of irrigation works and consumption of fuel, in particular wood, from ever further afield, can create what would look from space like devastated areas. Such devastation can eventually drain away the life of the urban organism.

Historical examples include the fate of the Harappa culture in the Indus valley about 3500 to 4500 years ago. The destruction of forest cover and removal of topsoil probably led to the creation of dust clouds, up to 30 000 feet, which maintained a downward flow of cool air and prevented the rise of moisture, even in summer. With sharply diminishing rainfall and declining fertility of soils, Harappa society lost its means of support and eventually collapsed. Similar changes in the sustaining environment could well have happened in the valleys of the Tigris and Euphrates; around Petra in the Wadi Araba; and in parts of the Sahel belt across Africa today. Disposal of the output of cities in the form of waste, toxic and otherwise, is an acute and growing problem everywhere, particularly in industrial countries.

The second factor of vulnerability relates to health and numbers. Air and water pollution reduce resistance to disease, and crowded conditions enhance its communication. The spread of such diseases as the Black Death, typhus, cholera and now AIDS is far more rapid in cities, especially the poorer parts, than elsewhere. Yet cities are increasing their drawing power. Life expectancy today is longer in the city than in the country. Figures for overall human population growth (10 million 12 000 years ago, 2 billion in 1930, 5.4 billion in 1990, around 8.5 billion in 2025) tend to conceal still steeper growth in urban populations. In the 1990s, 83% of population growth is likely to be in cities. This is the equivalent of 10 cities the size of London every year. In 1950, 29% of the world's population was urban; in 1965 it was 36%; in 1990 50%;

and by 2025 it is expected to be at least 60%. The world annual growth rate of urban population between 1965 and 1980 was 2.6%; but between 1980 and 1990 it was 4.5%. Nearly all the current increase is in poor countries, by definition those with the least resources and the lowest capacity to manage and dispose of waste. In extreme cases, such as Djakarta, the increase in population is 6% a year.

Obviously, the more precarious an urban society, the more vulnerable it is to change in external circumstances. Apart from the changes cities bring upon themselves— the search ever further for food, water and fuel, leading to political, economic and even military consequences— there are the longer term environmental changes over which humans have limited control. The most crucial of these is climate.

The variability of climate is a prime factor in the process of evolution. Usually change takes place so slowly that we do not notice it. Animals, plants and other forms of life have time to adapt or migrate. The Thames Valley provides a good example. About 130 000 years ago it was the habitat of swamp-loving hippos; 18 000 years ago reindeer and mammoth roamed the tundra not far from the ice sheet which weighed heavily on the land to the north; and only 900 years ago the French were trying to close down vineyards in southern England which were too competitive.

We are living in one of the brief warm periods in the recent history of the Earth. For the last two and a half million years there has been a broad 100 000 year rhythm, with over 20 glacial periods, interspersed with 10 000 to 15 000 year interglacials. These cycles are the product of a combination of the Milankovic cycles (in which the proximity of the Earth and its angle of rotation with respect to the Sun vary); tectonic plate movement and the rise and fall of mountains (which affect the relationship of land and sea); changes brought about by volcanic emissions;

149

and the influence of living creatures, for example algal blooms, which can provide seeding for clouds. There is variation between the warm periods. During a warm period, about 6000 years ago, the average temperature was about 1.5 °C more than it is today and sea levels were a little higher. Cooler conditions then set in and did not reverse until around 2000 years ago. The early Middle Ages were the warmest in recorded memory. But in the 'Little Ice Age', between the 14th and 18th centuries, temperatures were between 1 and 2 °C below those of today.

Within this broad picture there is clear evidence of human-induced change. Even before the Industrial Revolution, and as far back as the Bronze Age, there were variations in microclimate due to changes in land use, in particular deforestation. There is a close relationship between trees and rainfall. Without a quantum of trees there is less than a quantum of rainfall. Examples can be seen in the eastern Mediterranean, along the coast of North Africa and in Arizona. In modern times the changes wrought by desertification and urbanization are evident on every continent except Antarctica.

Macro-changes—alterations in whole weather systems—may already be happening. There is an acceleration of previous factors: further changes in land use and the expansion of cement, stone and brick accompanying the growth of cities. In Britain, urban areas already cover around 10% of the total. Since the Industrial Revolution we have been using the sky as a waste unit by enhancing the natural greenhouse effect with emissions of carbon dioxide, methane, nitrous oxide, chlorofluorocarbons and related molecules into the atmosphere. Without some greenhouse effect the Earth's temperature would be around 33 °C cooler, and life as we know it would be impossible. Carbon dioxide accounts for the largest proportion of greenhouse gases. We know from the analysis of ice cores that during the last glaciation the concentration in the atmosphere was 190 parts per million (ppm). It had risen to 280 ppm before the beginning of the Industrial Revolution. It is now 355 ppm and rising by 0.5% annually. The main source is the combustion of fossil fuels and biomass, in particular forest burning.

Public anxiety about the possible effects of environmental changes has greatly increased over the last 20 years. First there was the UN Conference on the Environment in Stockholm in 1972, followed by the creation of the UN Environment Programme, the first World Climate Conference in 1979, the production of many papers, including *Global 2000*, the Brundtland Commission report on Environment and Development and declarations on the environment by industrial and non-industrial countries alike. Then came the Second World Climate Conference in 1990 and the Earth Summit at Rio in June 1992.

Scientific consensus on the key factor of climate was obviously essential. Hence the creation of the Intergovernmental Panel on Climate Change (IPCC) in 1987. The IPCC published its first assessment in 1990. On what it termed a business as usual scenario, the Panel predicted, on the basis of modeling, an average rise of 1.0 °C by 2025 and 3.0 °C by the end of the next century. This would not be steady because of the interplay of many other factors. Such an average rise might well seem small, but it can be compared with a drop of only 5.0 °C in the last big glaciation.

The IPCC also predicted an average rate of global mean sea-level rise of about 6 cm per decade over the next century (with an uncertainty range of between 3 and 10 cm per decade). This would be caused by thermal expansion of the oceans and the melting of some land ice. The rise could thus be about 20 cm by 2030 and 65 cm by the end of the next century. Not all models confirm this prediction.

In the past, warmer climates have brought more precipitation, including more snow at the poles, and thus thicker ice. But even if sea levels fell as a result, the effect could be temporary as warming continued, and most models show a substantial increase as in previous warm periods in the Earth's history.

There would be markedly different results in different places with, for example, relatively little change at the equator, but big changes in the temperate and polar regions. Temperature change is always more pronounced over land. In the north the most marked increases have so far been in minimum night-time temperatures rather than maximum daytime temperatures. Southern Europe and North America would have less summer precipitation and lower soil moisture. In general, there would be more precipitation and more extreme and irregular rainfall. Snow cover and ice would generally be reduced. Modeling capacity cannot yet, if ever, predict precise geographical results.

In 1992 the Scientific Working Group of the IPCC met in China to check the 1990 conclusions. Some interesting new evidence was produced about the short-term cooling effect of sulfates and other human-made pollution in the lower atmosphere (especially in the north). Airborne particles, such as those from volcanic eruptions (in the upper atmosphere) or sulfur emissions (in the lower atmosphere), can affect the radiation scattered and absorbed by the atmosphere and also affect the micro-physics of clouds, increasing cloud cover and therefore increasing reflectivity. Both these have a cooling effect, but overall warming remained clear (1990 was the warmest year on record).

There are many uncertainties, but none, singly or together, affects the main predictions. Among the uncertainties are variations in solar radiation; clouds and the hydrological cycle; the role of the oceans as a thermostat and exchanges with the atmosphere; the nature of the carbon cycle; and the behavior of polar ice sheets and sea ice. It is the speed of change which is important. According to the IPCC, this is likely to be greater now than at any time in the last 10 000 years, and the rise in sea level will be three to six times faster than in the last 100 years. We are already embarked on an unstoppable course of global warming. Even if all human-made emissions of greenhouse gases were to be halted, about half the increase in carbon dioxide concentration caused by human activities would still be evident at the end of the next century.

So what will be the future effect on cities? Again, we look at their resource base, health and numbers, and external factors. In an increasingly urban world, cities will be more vulnerable to degradation of their sources of supply of food, water and fuel, with accompanying problems of land, water and air pollution. More land is given over to brick, stone, concrete and urban sprawl. But the most significant change in land use is the acceleration of the destruction of forests worldwide and the declining fertility of soils. According to a report by the World Resources Institute published in 1992, about 10% of the vegetation-bearing surface of the Earth is suffering from moderate to extreme degradation, an area the size of China and India combined. Although forest cover is slightly increasing in industrial countries, its destruction elsewhere, with accompanying loss of species, is on a scale to change the global ecosystem. Poor countries continue to depend on wood for fuel.

Waste disposal may soon become a bigger problem than the consumption of resources. No part of the world is now exempt from the wastes produced by industrial activity. Pollution and recent accidents have demonstrated the international character of industrial hazards. Within the vast land mass of the former Soviet Union, about 16% (or 1 382 000 square miles) was recently judged an ecological disaster area by the Academy of Sciences. Chemical accidents may be limited in their effects, but disposal of chemical wastes is a worldwide problem.

Demand for freshwater doubled between 1940 and 1980, and will double again by 2000. More people need more water. Many countries already suffer severe shortages and droughts. Competition for water was a prime source of conflict in the past, and will be in the future. Problems of meeting this demand are exacerbated by increasing contamination, including problems arising from drainage and sewage disposal, algal blooms from nitrate pollution, salinization and aluminum toxicity. There is a dangerous dependence on irrigation.

By the middle of the next century pressure on food supplies for a still-growing population will come from many quarters: shifts in climatic zones, changes in methods of crop, livestock and fish-farming, less good water for irrigation and loss of arable land through desertification or rise in sea-level. Semiarid areas are particularly vulnerable to droughts or floods.

Cities are especially vulnerable to climatic change because they already have an artificial climate. Less greenery means less rainfall and transpiration of plants, more absorption of radiation and higher temperatures. Buildings absorb heat and do not retain moisture, so there is less evaporation. All this leads to what have been called urban heat islands: higher temperatures, less wind, lower humidity, more cloudiness, fogs and smogs.

Human health is obviously at risk. Temperature rise and precipitation change affect the ability of viruses, bacteria and insects to multiply and prosper. The proliferation of fast-adapting organisms leads to an increase in vector-borne diseases. A subsequent increase in pesticides could itself be damaging to health, and deteriorating water quality benefits water-borne pathogens such as cholera.

Poor quality air leads to inflammatory and respiratory diseases. Over 4.2 million children die each year in poor countries from respiratory diseases. Cities such as Athens, Budapest, London, Los Angeles, Mexico City, Prague, Santiago and São Paulo have high levels of ozone, carbon monoxide, sulfur dioxide and other pollutants. Exposure to air pollution is worse than was hitherto believed. Autopsies carried out on young accident victims in Los Angeles showed 80% to have significant lung abnormalities and 27% severe lung lesions. Children, who breathe about four times more air (due to smaller lungs and greater activity) are especially vulnerable to air pollution. Mexico City closed its schools for six weeks due to high ozone levels in 1990. The crisis there continues. Increases in harmful ultraviolet radiation, due to depletion of the ozone layer by such human-made molecules as chlorofluorocarbons, lead to immune suppression, skin cancer and cataracts.

All problems of health are several orders of magnitude worse in poor countries, when urban increase is greatest. But a particular problem arises from swelling numbers of refugees. On a strict political definition there was a rise from fewer than six million in 1978 to 18.5 million in 1992. There is an unquantified number of environmental refugees or economic migrants, but it is increasing fast, and there are certainly more than 10 million.

Obviously cities will contribute to and be affected by a multiplicity of external factors, ranging from political and economic instability to worldwide competition for resources. Cities are capable of reacting to short-term crises, but are not easily adaptable to long-term change. Thus, freshwater can be brought from long distances, but the cost of doing so can eventually become intolerable. Sea-level rise is a more direct danger. Almost half the world's population lives alongside coasts, rivers and estuaries. Eighty percent of cities are at risk: among them are Alexandria, Bangkok, Dhaka, New Orleans, Amsterdam, St Petersburg, Sydney and London. A rise of half a meter by 2100 would have widespread effects. The Netherlands is particularly vulnerable, with 27% below sea level and 60% lying less than 1 m above it. Even a small rise would lead to the disruption of sewers and drainage, undermining of structures, increased susceptibility to storms and other hazards, habitat modification, raised water-tables, salt water intrusion and contamination of freshwater supplies.

In the past, urban planners have tried to avoid the issues, or go for short-term expedients. People travel further and further for resources. They take waste somewhere else. Higher chimneys are built to disperse pollution. Barrages and coastal defense systems are constructed against rising sea levels. Suburbia spreads. Greenery is brought back into the urban landscape.

Clearly something more radical is required in the longer term. This is not the place to look into the future of the city itself at a time when, with the current revolution in information technology, more and more people, at least in industrial countries, will be able to work from home. It is too late to prevent—if we ever could have prevented— environmental change. But there is much we can do to mitigate its effects and to adapt ourselves, our institutions and our cities.

In conclusion, let us recall that we are not dealing with one factor—climate—but with a vast combination of factors: population increase, environmental degradation, pollution and loss of biodiversity. Science, like life itself, is full of surprises, some good, some bad. The problem is not change, but the rate of change. Human society is fragile in or out of cities. All previous civilizations have collapsed. Ultimately, we are as subject to biological restraints as any other animal species. But unlike them we can consciously shape our future. If we fail to do so, there will be no-one to blame but ourselves.

Annotated List of Further Reading

The Gaia Atlas of Planet Management, Norman Myers, London: Gaia Books, 1994.
  Inspired by Jim Lovelock's Gaia hypothesis, this is the first in a series of books which takes an overview of global ecological, social and economic forces. Beautifully and professionally illustrated, Myers has produced a useful introduction to environmental issues, especially for those new to the subject.

The Gaia Atlas of Future Cities, Herbert Girardet, London: Gaia Books, 1992.
  An excellent book which continues the theme of this chapter, and expands on its author's case study of London, the TV documentary *Metropolis*.

Tony Cooper and Aubrey Meyer

Author biography

Tony Cooper and Aubrey Meyer are founding members of the Global Commons Institute (GCI), an independent research and advocacy group working on economic and political issues relating to global change and the protection of the global commons. It was founded in 1990 and is based in the UK. The GCI receives no statutory or institutional funding. Its operations have thus far been maintained through occasional small grants from sympathetic parties, mostly individuals. The Global Commons Trust was recently formed to support the work of the GCI. Charitable status has been agreed with the UK Charity Commissioners.

Chapter 8

Tony Cooper and Aubrey Meyer

'Green' Economics: Still a Dismal Science?

ECONOMICS has been disparagingly labeled the 'dismal science' ever since the phrase was first coined by the 19th century Scottish writer Thomas Carlyle, who attacked an economic and political climate where 'Cash payment' had, he suggested, become 'the sole nexus between man and man'. A century and a half since Carlyle's writing heralded a new generation of novels with a social conscience, the ability to produce 'cash payment' is too often the only means by which a human life is valued, even by many 'green' economists. Universal human rights appear not to fit into their computer models, which carry the implicit assumption that such rights are subsidiary to monetary values. As Hazel Henderson put it

Economics has enthroned some of our most unattractive pre-dispositions: material acquisitiveness, competition, gluttony, pride, selfishness, short-sightedness and just plain greed.

In this chapter, however, we see South Africa as a microcosm of the world's economic and political dilemmas, and view events there during the past few years as a cause for hope. Its rich ruling minority ceded political power to a new democratic government because it was ultimately in its own self-interest to do so. We see the same process as able to bring long-term solutions to many of humanity's current environmental dilemmas.

We argue in this chapter that the prevention of catastrophic changes to the human life support system, the biosphere, is also in everyone's interest—even billionaires, economists and politicians. Focusing on the negotiations surrounding global climate change, we suggest that proposed solutions which are not based on equity have little chance of long-term success. We see signs that an increasing number of individuals who shape world economic policy believe that the current environmental crisis can only be overcome if the solutions proposed are based on the equal worth of every human life on Earth.

Economics seeks the honorific status of being a science, yet its divorce from ecological processes, upon which every economic process ultimately depends, is among the factors which limit its utility in the real world. As Lynn Margulis has suggested in Chapter 2, the only truly productive beings on Earth are those which carry out the remarkable biological process of photosynthesis by which CO_2 and water are transformed into oxygen and carbohydrates. Such organisms include plants and many bacteria, whereas humans just convert such productivity, consume, excrete and (hopefully) recycle. A nation's gross national product can ultimately only be a biological and, to a lesser extent, a geological one, not the meaningless economic statistic that is currently calculated. To be sustainable such a total cannot increase indefinitely, but will eventually stabilize. Any society that does not undertake to democratically agree where such an increase in human throughput should stop will either end up in internal conflict, or in conflict with its neighbors.

Most economists have been unable to take on this broader perspective because they straddle the worlds of both academic ideas and political power, as described by Harmke Kamminga in Chapter 15, and because both politicians and economists are oblivious to, maybe even wilfully ignorant of, fundamental ecological truths such as the finite nature of many of the Earth's resources. Their solutions are often an uncomfortable mix of 'objective' mathematical models with political pragmatism. Although microeconomics, occurring within specific small-scale political frameworks where, for example, individuals share a common interest in survival and are constrained within clear ecological limits, has seen some success, the intellectual basis of macroeconomics is fatally undermined by being forced to factor out such uncomfortable truths because of the subject's intimate relationship with political pragmatism and compromise. Economists who share in power often share in its arrogance and its ignorance of the unutterably awful living conditions they impose on millions of people, even if such people exist on their own doorstep.

The biggest obstacle for economists in modifying their models to fit reality was the notion, prophesized by Carlyle, that everything—pure air, football matches, even people—has a monetary value. Once money became more than a convenient local substitute for swapping resources such as food, livestock and building materials, then the lunacy of people-less money in the stock market controlling money-less people became inevitable. The rules by which most economists operate only allow for the creation of more money, without any reference to the people or resources required, apart from the assumption of their inexhaustible ability to allow increased production of colored pieces of paper. When built upon these foundations, 'green economics' is an oxymoron.

The Intergovernmental Panel on Climate Change (IPCC) was set up by the United Nations (UN) Environment Programme and the World Meteorological Organization to find out whether human activities might be disturbing the world's climate and, if so, what can be done. Over the past 130 years the global mean temperature has risen by at least 0.6 °C. Sea levels have risen. Weather-induced insurance claims are, in real terms, an order of magnitude higher than 20 years ago. Beyond this, a rapid and irreversible rise in temperature could develop within 50 years.

In 1990, the IPCC confirmed that there was a risk of catastrophic climate change unless greenhouse gas levels were stabilized. This, they said, would require humans to reduce their greenhouse emissions by 60–80%. Greenpeace conducted a survey of all international climate scientists involved in the IPCC study, and others who have published on issues relevant to climate change in the journals *Science* or *Nature* during 1991. Of 113 responses, 13% agreed that if greenhouse gas emissions continue at their present rate, a runaway greenhouse effect would be 'probable'; 32% said a runaway greenhouse effect was 'possible'; while 47% said it would 'probably not' happen. The OECD (Organization for Economic Co-operation and Development) suggest that there is going to be a rate of death in hundreds of thousands due to global climate changes.

As a result, many environmentalists hoped that economics might be forced to reacquaint itself with some ecological realities. In 1992, certain economists were invited to join the climate change negotiation process and have subsequently explicitly or implicitly attempted to capture that process for their profession. They applied a standard procedure, cost–benefit analysis or CBA, which balances one person's costs against another's benefits. As we will show, when applied to environmental problems, CBA has serious drawbacks in addition to the fundamental questions, 'whose costs?' and 'who benefits?' These difficulties are addressed by the United Kingdom's Centre for the Social and Economic Research of the Global Environment (CSERGE), who developed a concept called global cost–benefit analysis. Global warming and the costs and benefits of climate change are now assessed by them in these monetary terms. This assessment is being aggressively pushed by the economists in the UN's IPCC. Part of this exercise, they assert, entails giving cash values to human lives. They accept that there are going to be hundreds of thousands of deaths worldwide as a result of global climate changes.

The logical conclusion of global-CBA is reached in a recent CSERGE publication. In the document, an impeccable chain of reasoning, albeit from a questionable set of premises, leads to a conclusion that in global climate negotiations countries with different gross national products have different values attached to their citizens. Therefore the 'statistical life' of a citizen of the European Union (EU) or the USA is worth $1.5 million, whereas in China it is only $150 000. Thus these influential economists believe that one real Chinese life is 10 times more easily discarded than a real life in the EU and the USA. Ironically, these lives are now at risk as a result of damage to the global environment for which citizens in the EU and the USA have been and are at least 10 times more responsible per head than citizens in China. An average citizen in the EU or the USA uses between 10 and 100 times the resources of an average citizen in the less developed world.

There may be some potential local professional benefit to economists in industrialized nations by their domination of the sustainable development agenda, but it is outweighed by the obvious global political cost. People in the EU and the USA are outnumbered by everyone else by ten to one. Thus the need to value human rights as equal would seem extremely prudent.

In fact, global-CBA is a misnomer in that it is trying to compare subglobal costs with global benefits. Clearly everyone on the planet stands to benefit from avoiding the damages resulting from emissions-driven global climate changes, and this benefit is therefore global. But the 'costs' of cutting back these emissions pertain only to that minority of industrial countries who are disproportionately responsible for creating them, and are therefore subglobal by definition.

Despite this anomaly, World Bank economists suggest that the right to emit CO_2 should be proportional to the size of a country's gross domestic product (GDP). In other words, rights should be vested in those countries which already have substantial GDPs, virtually all generated by fossil fuels. They suggest that, because of the 'costs' of reducing emissions, stabilization should be achieved by a combination of small fossil-GDP states (developing countries) not using fossil fuels, and major users not expanding their use (rather than cutting back). Although this proposal could lead to an eventual stabilization of *emissions*, it provides no basis for the universally accepted goal of the stabilization of atmospheric CO_2 *levels*, which would require a long-term reduction in total emissions.

Furthermore, whilst these arguments are being made, 'policy instruments' are being designed by the economists and prepared for promotion through the IPCC. Prominent amongst these is the instrument called, 'tradable CO_2 emissions quotas'. It is intended that these quotas will be introduced into international trading arrangements and that the basic allocation of quotas (or the right to pollute) will not only be matched to the maldistribution of global economic development of a particular country, but also that the maldistribution will be structurally consolidated through trading operations in the existing exchange rate regime. Because currencies are traded, exchange rates bear little relation to purchasing power. An allocation by GDP, apart from its fundamental immorality, has the effect of systematically under-allocating to less developed countries by a factor of two to four.

The International Monetary Fund (IMF) intends that global macroeconomic policy development will sustain the purchasing power advantage of the G7 countries at the expense of currencies elsewhere. The 'tradable CO_2 emissions quotas' represent a thrust to set up a market in the international trade of what are, in reality, global common property resources. In effect, the quotas represent bits of the global ecological services provided by the global climate system. We believe that the allocation of quotas per capita rather than by GDP is the only fair and sustainable method, and the only one with any chance of obtaining widespread international recognition.

Overall, global-CBA designed mechanisms for the management of global climate change are the rearticulation of a two-tier global economy. They are the culmination of centuries of colonialist and current neocolonialist distortions of the economies and ecologies of less developed countries to suit the needs of the industrialized world. In contrast with this analysis, Figure 8.1 summarizes the actual divide: 'debitors' can achieve high incomes by ecologically inefficient overconsumption with a high environmental impact, but are ultimately unsustainable. 'Creditors' have long lived sustainably by underconsuming their resources with low environmental impact, but are threatened—first by colonialism and more recently by the neocolonialist implications of global-CBA. The ability of

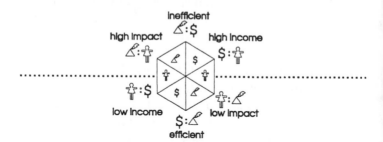

DEBITORS

over-consuming and living unsustainably

inefficient

high impact   high income

low income   low impact

efficient

underconsuming but living sustainably

CREDITORS

People

$ Production = Income $

Pollution = Impact

low - per capita income - high

low - per capita impact - high

efficient - inefficient

Figure 8.1. Who are the real creditors and debitors of the global commons?

economists to make their work appear 'objective', when in fact their modeling ignores the basic right of every human to be judged of equal worth whatever their nationality, creed or color, is described in Figure 8.2.

To progress we need far-reaching reforms of international institutions. The UN must be democratized. More radical and much harder to achieve would be the

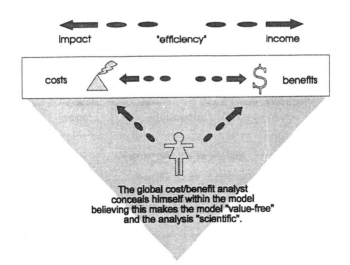

Figure 8.2. A global commons critique of cost-benefit analysis

establishment of Structural Adjustment Programmes (SAPs) for the industrialized countries. Current SAPs are imposed on less developed countries to drive them towards export-led growth in accordance with conventional 'wisdom'. The SAPs lead to the replacing of subsistence crops by cash crops, encouraging deforestation, reducing welfare spending, lowering standards of living and forcing dependence on a market where the terms of trade remorselessly deteriorate as the countries concerned are forced to compete with each other on rich men's terms. Such SAPs are a result of the power of people-less money. So we suggest an OECD that is 'structurally adjusted' to include money-less people. This would guide the OECD countries towards the greening of their economies and exact very modest reparations from them for past damage to the biosphere.

Outbreaks of common sense and sanity keep occurring all over the world. If you need cheering up, read Guy

Dauncey's *After the Crash*, a superb compendium of mostly small-scale ecological–economic success stories such as credit unions, local currencies and cooperatives. Democracy, most spectacularly demonstrated by recent events in South Africa, is breaking out in many places in the world. Full democracy, the siting of real power with people rather than with money, is a prerequisite for sanity. The fissioning, if peaceful, of large- and medium-sized countries into smaller units is encouraging too: small places are much easier to democratize.

Another sign of hope is the vibrant new economics movement, which is much too large and diverse to do justice to here. The New Economics Foundation in the UK is one leading light. So internationally is TOES (The Other Economic Summit), the series of parallel conferences to the annual jamborees of the G7 heads of state. There is increasing interest in these organizations from the media and from sections of political and economic orthodoxy.

Here at the Global Commons Institute we are concentrating on the democratization of the climate change negotiations, steering them away from people-less money and empowering money-less people. The *global commons* is a term which has entered the sustainable development debate, particularly in the context of global climate change. It signifies that there are, by definition, subglobal limits to the creation of private property arrangements. We also take the term to signify that a free market in these subglobal private property arrangements cannot sustainably exceed subglobal limits. The phrase *global commons* also acknowledges the basic collateral, or equity, of human existence in the totality of the biosphere's life supporting systems and recognizes the interdependence of all the stake-holders in this global equity and addresses their fundamental rights of existence. It recognizes therefore that the stake-holders' global rights precede subglobal rights derived from private property arrangements.

Economics need not be dismal, it merely needs to be conducted on a more democratic, human scale, together with a recognition that humanity together constitutes a global common.

Annotated List of Further Reading

The Growth Illusion, Richard Douthwaite, London: Green Books, 1992.
Subtitled 'How Economic Growth Has Enriched the Few, Impoverished the Many and Endangered the Planet.' A passionate presentation of the case against economic growth, with in-depth case studies of Holland, India and Ireland.

Global Warming Damage Costs: Some Monetary Estimates, Samuel Frankhauser, CSERGE Working Paper GEC 92-29, 1994.
An attempt to calculate money values for all aspects of the damage expected to be caused by a doubling of atmospheric CO_2. Destined for notoriety due to its valuing an OECD life at $1.5 million and a Chinese life at $150 000.

The New Protectionism, Tim Lang and Colin Hines, London: Earthscan, 1993.
Details the case against so-called 'free' trade. Argues for a new progressive variant on protectionism which favors local production, local and minimal consumption of resources and high quality of life.

A Green History of the World, Clive Ponting, London: Penguin, 1993.
Presents an ecological perspective on world history, starting with the development of agriculture. A telling vignette portrays the history of Easter Island as a stark role model for today's anti-ecological world society.

Alternative Economic Indicators, Victor Anderson, London: Routledge, 1991.
Describes national accounting, summarizes the case against economic growth, and presents a strong case for the replacement of GDP by

a basket of 16 social, demographic, financial and environmental factors.

After the Crash, Guy Dauncey, London: Green Print, 1988.
A vision of pieces of a different future that are starting to happen; with many examples of inspiring practice from all over the world.

New Economics, quarterly magazine published by New Economics Foundation, 88/94 Wentworth St, London E1 7SA, UK.
Lively articles on subjects including fair trade, green taxes and local initiatives.

Benefits and Taxes: A Radical Strategy, James Robertson, London: New Economics Foundation, 1994.
Proposes a comprehensive reform of UK institutions to reconcile economic efficiency with social justice and ecological sustainability.

Small is Beautiful, E. F. Schumacher, London: Blond & Briggs, 1973.
The subtitle, 'A Study of Economics as if People Mattered'. A classic.

Nigel Woodcock

Author biography

Nigel Woodcock is an award-winning geologist in the Department of Earth Sciences at the University of Cambridge. He has completely revised relevant geological parts of the science degree course at Cambridge to reflect the finite nature of most geological resources and the geological components of many environmental impacts. He has led efforts to make geological scientists more aware of the global warming implications of fossil fuels that they find. His latest book *Geology and Environment in Britain and Ireland* marks an important change of direction for the teaching of applied geology. He also researches the early Paleozoic rocks of Britain.

Chapter 9

Nigel Woodcock

Earth's History as a Guide to the Earth's Future

ASK the average person to name a site of geological interest and they'll probably say Stonehenge. Ask them how the fuel for their car was found and they'll describe drilling wildcat wells to strike oil. These are just two examples of the public ignorance of geology as a science of the Earth—a science of investigating subsurface composition, architecture and processes of deciphering the Earth's history from its rock record and of applying that knowledge to find or manage underground resources.

But this communication gap between geology and society is two-way. If the public awareness of geology is low, so too is the level of concern amongst geologists for the social context in which their science is done. Ask most geologists whether eroding coastlines should be defended or allowed to retreat and they'll say let planners decide. Ask them about the global warming risk from burning the fossil fuels that most geologists are employed to find. They'll say that they only discover the stuff—it's up to society how to use it. Getting involved in political issues is 'non-scientific' and will threaten the objectivity of their geological research.

The mutual misunderstanding between geology and society is being brought into sharper focus by the growing environmental awareness of the past two decades. Take, for example, the underground disposal of toxic wastes. Many cases of rapid leakage into water-supply aquifers or agricultural soils have shown the risks of a poor under-standing of the local subsurface geological environment. Take the threat of impending global change. Decision-makers ask 'has it happened in the past?—this climatic warming, sea-level rise, or melting of ice sheets?' The geologists who answer yes are the same scientific body who find the fuels mostly responsible for posing these same threats.

Something is wrong here—both in a society that aspires to being scientifically aware and in a profession that claims to be the science of the Earth. This chapter explores the worrying and increasingly serious gap between geology and society as a whole. How did it arise? What is its nature? How can it be narrowed?

The scientific context of geology

One place to start is with the definition of geology as a scientific discipline. Does it differ from 'geoscience', or 'Earth science' or even 'Earth system science'? The public at large have reason to be confused when a science changes its name every decade or so.

The essence of geology

Geology is a science of the Earth—but then many sciences are. However, physics, chemistry, biology and their related

174

disciplines deal with components of the working Earth. What distinguishes geology is firstly its concern for all natural processes that leave a record in the rocks, and secondly, its aim to piece together the local and global interplay of these processes over the four and a half billion years of Earth history. Geology is essentially holistic science done in the four dimensions of space and time.

Watch geologists investigating a unit of limestone rock. The physical size, shape and arrangement of the mineral grains will tell them the strength and variability of the tidal or wave currents that deposited the original sediment. The types of fossils embedded in the rock will reveal its geological age. The fossils and the burrows or tracks left by fossilized organisms allow the geologists to reconstruct the ancient biological community. Then they can estimate environmental conditions—water depth, salinity, temperature, oxygen content. Under the microscope the mineral cement that binds the rock grains may record the changing composition of water passing through the rock as it was buried. The physical state of any plant fragments in the rock records the maximum depth of this burial. Laboratory analysis of the different isotopes of strontium in the fossil shells will indicate the chemistry of the old seawater. Indirectly, this can show the rate that sediment was eroding from the continent and the amount of volcanism beneath the past oceans. Oxygen isotope analysis gives the seawater temperature. And so on—no aspect of the limestone is irrelevant to the problem of its origin. The best hypothesis is the one that fits all the diverse evidence.

The limestone study is a small-scale example from one part of geological time. But such local evidence can be integrated in space up to a global scale, and in time through successive geological periods. Always, it is the holistic approach which marks out geological science. Good paleobiology can be done on the fossils, sedimentology on the grain shapes, or paleo-oceanography with the chemical isotopes. Geology provides the systematic links between these subjects.

The shift towards Earth science

Charles Lyell's dictum that 'the present is the key to the past' has acted both as a unifying scientific strategy for geologists and, over the past 40 years, as a force to disperse them into specialized subdisciplines.

The processes of the ancient Earth cannot be studied directly. Only the material consequences remain in the rock record. These signs must be read with reference to presently active processes—the growth of a coral reef, the ebb and flow of the tides, the flooding of a river. This relevance of present day processes forged links between geologists and other scientists of today's Earth, such as marine biologists, oceanographers and hydrologists. But the broadening influence of this collaboration was counteracted by a fragmentation of geology into specialist groups. Each group focused on a particular subset of Earth processes, dissecting it into its component mechanisms. This reductionist approach to science has made rapid detailed advances in understanding, but at the expense of the holistic view that characterized the old geology.

This fragmentation of geology even affected the study of deep Earth processes. The convection in the Earth's core, the melting rocks in the mantle or crust, the production of earthquakes—these geological processes cannot be observed directly like those at the Earth's surface. A suite of chemical and physical techniques was devised to decipher the deep Earth. The specialized nature of this geochemistry and geophysics also began to divide these disciplines from mainstream geology. Geophysicists, in particular, came to feel uneasy about being included as geologists at all.

The labels 'geological science' and 'Earth science' were born of attempts to regroup the disciplines that geology had spawned. But the labels are less powerful than ideas. Ironically, about 25 years ago, it was geophysicists who provided the unifying concept to turn the scientific tide. Plate tectonics offered a coherent working model of the outer part of the 'solid' Earth. Most importantly, this model could be tested against data from almost every other discipline in 'Earth science'. Paleontologists started talking again to volcanologists, sedimentologists to geochemists, and petrologists to geophysicists. The specialization within each discipline continues, but now within a framework of plate tectonics which all 'Earth scientists' can understand. Holistic 'Earth science' is at least possible, if not always practiced.

A new Earth systems science?

Now a larger framework is needed to study the workings of the whole Earth, and most immediately to address the problems of the global environment. 'Earth science' is not enough. This term has unfortunately come to mean the study of the 'solid' Earth—the Earth stripped of its presently active atmosphere, hydrosphere and biosphere. There has been some attempt in North America to broaden 'Earth science' to include these other components, but also a recognition that a new concept is needed.

This concept is Earth systems science (Figure 9.1). It embraces all Earth processes and, most crucially, stresses the interactions between them. But in the same way that Earth sciences would not have achieved a coherence without the unifying concept of plate tectonics, so Earth systems

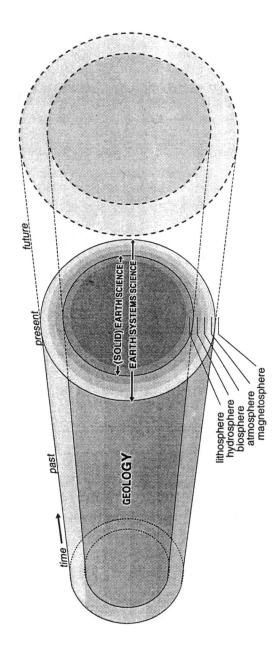

Figure 9.1. Conceptual relationship between geology, Earth science and Earth systems science

science needs to be more than just terminology. The unifying concepts are the biogeochemical cycles that continually move material through the atmosphere, biosphere, hydrosphere and the solid Earth. One well known example is the hydrological cycle (Figure 9.2). Within a framework like this, a meteorologist concerned with atmospheric weather patterns can talk meaningfully to a river hydrologist, or a plant scientist can understand a hydrogeologist studying groundwater. All cycles ultimately operate on a global scale, but the methodology is equally useful on a local scale if the transfers with the global system can be quantified.

Earth systems science has been conceived in terms of interactions on the present Earth and specifically includes cycles which human activity itself is perturbing in a major way. However, some of its cycles operate so slowly that they can only be understood by looking back over millions of years, back through geological time. In this way the science of geology can be viewed as the fourth dimension to Earth systems science (Figure 9.1). It provides the perspective into the Earth's past that makes sense of its long-period processes. Moreover, it provides the scientific basis for looking the other way through the telescope of time and predicting future global change—particularly now human activity threatens to induce it. Geology is a science of the once and future Earth.

Geology and the environment

The public face of geology

Watch a popular television program on threats to the local environment. You see an ancient wood being razed in

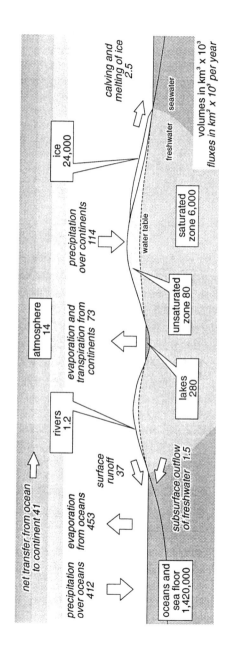

Figure 9.2. Hydrological cycle, with global values for the main (water) reservoirs and the fluxes between them

the path of a motorway, a river being poisoned by industrial effluent, or air quality in a city being affected by exhaust gases from motor vehicles. Much less often you see the groundwater polluted by seepage from an old municipal land infill site, or the subsidence above old mine workings. For many people 'the environment' ends at the Earth's surface. Below ground is out of sight and out of mind. This 'geological environment' is presumed to be at once infinite, inactive and irrelevant.

The same television program will probably also portray the environment as a permanent fixture. The 'ancient' woodland is 'hundreds of years old'—no mention that ten thousand years ago this land was Arctic tundra. The eroding coast must be defended at its present line—no matter that a thousand years ago it was a kilometer seaward and that in another thousand it will be a kilometer further inland. The television producer is merely reflecting the public ignorance of geological history. The environment is here, now, and to be preserved, preferably without much changing our lifestyle. There is little feel for the constantly shifting mosaic of subenvironments which marks out geological time, both past and future.

At best, then, the popular view of the environment is distinctly two dimensional, restricted to the spherical surface of the Earth. The third dimension, upwards into the atmosphere, is poorly understood, and downwards into the lithosphere is unknown. The fourth dimension of geological time is popularly ignored. But no one-sided blame should be inferred from this public misunderstanding of geology. If society has been slow to learn, so too have geologists been reluctant to teach. We shall return later to this communication gap and its consequences.

The environmental relevance of geology

Despite our television parody of public awareness, geology pervades the workings of society (Figure 9.3). At one end of the engine of civilization, geologists provide the many material inputs from under the ground. Oil, gas and coal supply most of the world's energy needs. Rocks and minerals provide raw materials for the built environment and many of its industrial products. Metallic minerals yielding iron or aluminum, industrial minerals such as china clay, sand, gravel, limestone for cement—the list is long and varied. Most necessary of all is subsurface water, which supplements or substitutes for surface water supplies in many areas of the world.

Next comes the involvement of geology with the workings of society itself. Geologists help to assess the appropriate use for land. They assist in engineering the foundations of buildings, bridges and other large structures. They advise on surface excavations or tunnels, particularly their stability and effect of groundwater flow.

At the output end of society, geologists are concerned with the safe storage or dispersal of fluid and solid wastes on or under the ground surface. They are also called on for remedial action where unplanned toxic releases have polluted land and groundwater.

The fourth concern of environmental geology is in predicting or minimizing the impacts of 'geological hazards'—earthquakes, volcanic eruptions, landslides, ground subsidence, coastal erosion or the seepage of radon gas.

Depicted in this way (Figure 9.3) the interaction of geology with society is a cycle, one of the human-involved components of Earth system science. But this cycle is poorly understood. Firstly, as we have seen, its existence is little known to the general public. Secondly, and more seriously,

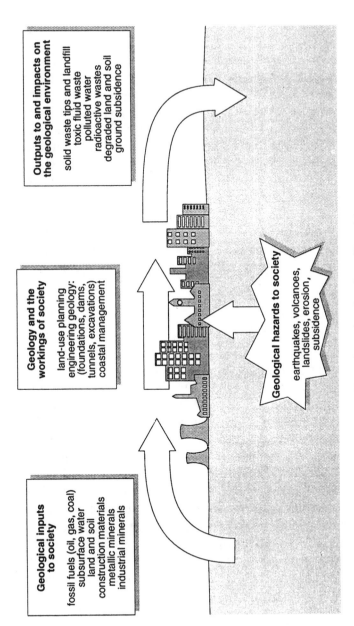

Geological inputs to society

fossil fuels (oil, gas, coal)
subsurface water
land and soil
construction materials
metallic minerals
industrial minerals

Geology and the workings of society

land-use planning
engineering geology:
(foundations, dams,
tunnels, excavations)
coastal management

Outputs to and impacts on the geological environment

solid waste tips and landfill
toxic fluid waste
polluted water
radioactive wastes
degraded land and soil
ground subsidence

Geological hazards to society

earthquakes, volcanoes,
landslides, erosion,
subsidence

Figure 9.3. Interaction of geology with society

183

one feature of this cycle is widely ignored by the geological profession itself—that the cycle is open, not closed. Apart from groundwater, the resources that are being removed from the Earth as inputs to society are not renewable by natural processes at anything like their removal rate. Their exploitation is not sustainable. Similarly, many of the outputs from society cannot be recycled back into the system. They remain as toxic concentrations or incomplete dispersions, above as well as below the ground surface. Some of these pollutants may even degrade otherwise renewable resources such as groundwater or the atmosphere. The geological profession therefore operates within a linear system for exploiting resources, more often than not unconcerned for the incompatibility of this system with a more holistic Earth view that the profession itself likes to teach.

The tarnish of petroleum

To generalize about blinkered environmental attitudes within geological science is to overlook many areas of informed concern and action. But the geological profession is overshadowed by one conspicuous example of flawed thinking which tarnishes the image of geology as holistic science. This example is the exploitation of fossil fuels.

Over half of the professional geologists in countries such as the UK and the USA are employed directly to find oil and gas. Others work for government energy agencies. Some academic geologists run research programs funded by petroleum companies. Add to these the numbers involved in finding and producing coal, and probably between 65 and 75% of the profession is dependent on the fossil fuel business. The mission of this business is to supply inputs of fuel to society in as great a volume and with as large a profit margin for its shareholders as the economic market will bear.

Exploration geologists are the first human link in the chain of oil supply and use (Figure 9.4). Using their knowledge of Earth history they can identify periods when sediments formed with a high content of organic material—the source rocks for oil and gas. They can identify the regions where these sediments may have accumulated and been heated and compressed to the right amounts to mature the hydrocarbons. Using geophysical sounding techniques they can explore the subsurface structure in the target region to identify specific areas where the upward migrating petroleum fluids may have been trapped in a porous reservoir rock. They can explore more accurately by drilling test wells and measuring the thickness, sequence and properties of the rock units. If their predictions are correct, and some of these wells strike oil or gas, the exploration geologists hand over to the production geologists who design a strategy for pumping the maximum volume of petroleum from that oil field.

Exploration for petroleum is now far removed from the still prevalent public image of wildcat drilling and lucky strikes. Drilling wells is too costly, particularly offshore, to do without good reason. Rather, exploration is the scientific hypothesis testing of a most sophisticated and expensive kind. The exploration geologist is operating within an established paradigm for petroleum formation based on the best scientific research into relevant Earth processes, and on a large database of past successes and failures in explored areas. Oil exploration is mainstream geological science.

Unfortunately, exploration and production are merely the upstream end of a cycle of petroleum use whose logic runs against the conclusions of more holistic Earth systems science. In fact, the petroleum cycle hardly merits the name

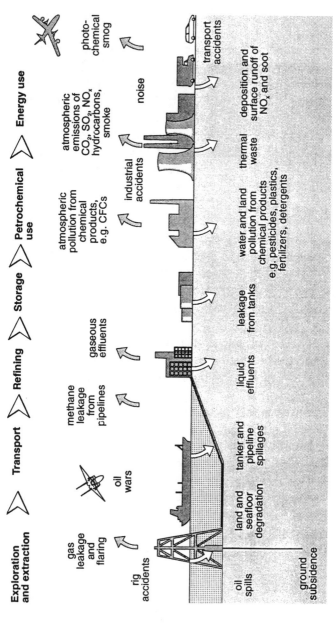

Figure 9.4. Some of the impacts on society from the cycle of petroleum use

(Figure 9.4). It is at best an open cycle in which energy resources are introduced at one end and their waste products are allowed to escape unplanned into the environment at the other end, often to pollute other life support systems. Of course, thermodynamic theory dictates that the input matter–energy is not destroyed. It is converted from a low entropy state—ordered and concentrated—into a high entropy state—disorganized, dissipated and less available for productive use. Pollution and wastes are high entropy states almost by definition.

The effluents from petroleum exploitation affect all parts of the environment (Figure 9.4). Near the upstream end of the cycle, attempts are made to limit the escape of toxic wastes. Society has seen fit to hold oil companies responsible for tanker spillages or pipeline leaks. But this responsibility is not extended to downstream pollution from petroleum use. Oil companies are not charged for the environmental cost of the greenhouse gases emitted to the atmosphere when oil and gas are burned, or the pesticide and fertilizer residues that accumulate in groundwater when these petroleum byproducts are overused.

The current ethic allows oil companies to show on their balance sheets the revenue from extracting and selling a natural resource, but to omit the cost of the damage to natural systems caused by use of this resource. This same ethic is the defense for the geological profession that 'only finds the oil and gas' for a resource-hungry society who must be responsible for its use. But this ethic is being questioned. Ironically, some of the questions can be best posed by that same geological profession. With their aspirations to holistic science they are well placed to see the dangers of the incomplete petroleum 'cycle'.

Human and natural economies

One danger, probably the main danger, from petroleum use is starkly revealed by completing just one of the many natural cycles perturbed by this use: the carbon cycle. A simplified version of this (Figure 9.5) shows how carbon is stored in major reservoirs and transferred between them by biological, chemical and physical processes. The largest fluxes involve the transfer of carbon dioxide (CO_2) to and from the atmosphere. Carbon dioxide is pumped down by photosynthesizing organisms and converted into the biomass of the oceans and continents. Carbon dioxide is emitted again by respiring animals. Inorganic solution and release of CO_2 from seawater add to fluxes.

The amount of CO_2 in the atmosphere is crucial in controlling the amount of heat trapped by the greenhouse effect—letting solar radiation in, but preventing heat radiation getting out. Without human intervention, the levels of atmospheric CO_2 vary slowly and regularly in response to changes in the orbit of the Earth and the Sun. But since the Industrial Revolution CO_2 levels have been rising exponentially, fed by the extra carbon released when coal, oil, gas and forests are burned (Figure 9.5). Serious enhancement of the greenhouse effect is threatened by this human-derived CO_2, and by the gases such as methane, nitrous oxides and chlorofluorocarbons. The consequent risks are global warming and its destabilizing effect on established climatic patterns.

The fossil fuel carbon which is being released so rapidly by human activity was safely locked away in coal swamps or marine shales tens or hundreds of millions of years ago. Indeed, the rapid photosynthesis that pumped down CO_2 from the atmosphere in these past times may itself have been a response to threateningly high atmospheric levels of CO_2. Maybe the same natural response of increased

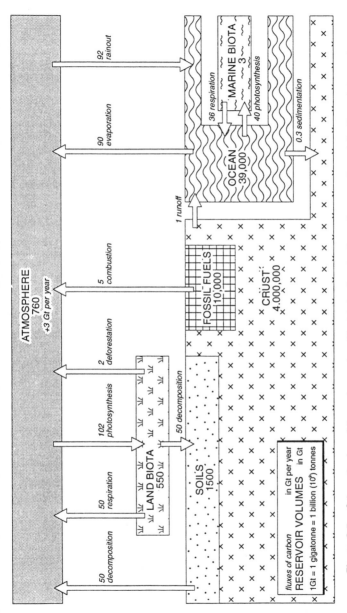

Figure 9.5. Schematic view of the carbon cycle, with global values for the main reservoirs and the fluxes between them

189

plant activity has kicked in now and will prevent an unsafe rise in CO_2? But if photosynthetic activity has increased, it is only absorbing about half the extra carbon load from fossil fuel burning. Five billion tonnes go up and three of these stay there in the atmosphere.

The other main way in which carbon is stored in rocks is as the calcium carbonate hard parts of animals. Dissolved CO_2 in seawater is extracted by the organisms, to be replaced by further solution of atmospheric CO_2. But, as with photosynthesized carbon, this transfer of carbon into safe rock storage happens extremely slowly compared with mutual fluxes between the atmosphere, hydrosphere and biosphere. More pertinent to the petroleum business is that the total flux of carbon into the rock reservoir is much slower than the reverse flux due to extraction of fossil fuels. This part of the cycle is not sustainable in the long term.

The carbon cycle is one example of a 'natural economy'—one of the Earth's life support systems where budgets always balance (Figure 9.5). Set against it, the 'human economy' of the fossil fuel business looks naive (Figure 9.4). The economic model is essentially linear. Carbon is pumped out from one reservoir and mostly ejected into another on the assumption that both reservoirs are infinitely large. In fact, at presently increasing rates of extraction, the fossil fuel reserve will last a very short time, even in the perspective of human history, let alone geological time—hundreds of years for coal and decades for oil and gas. Even more importantly, the 'infinite' carrying capacity of the atmosphere is already being exceeded. The narrow linear thinking of conventional economics records 'healthy' rises in gross national products and large profits on the bottom line of oil company accounts. The balance sheet of natural economics shows that this growth and profit is illusory and achieved by overdrawing on both the resource-supply account and the waste-processing accounts. Unless human economists realize soon the full constraints imposed by the natural economy, there is a danger that our credit facility may be withdrawn and that the human being business may be forced to downsize rapidly.

The silent voice of geology

The geological profession has taken to claiming that the impacts of using fossil fuels and other geological resources are beyond its control and therefore outside its concern. This ethic, which allows scientists to absolve themselves from the downstream effects of their research, is itself of debatable validity. It is the same ethic which would distance chemists from the side-effects of their pesticides or drugs, and has excused physicists for the effects of nuclear weapons. But the general detachment of geologists from debates about the overuse of resources rests on even more shaky foundations. It assumes that industrialists, economists and politicians are best placed to gauge the effects of resource use. In fact, the holistic scientific training of geologists makes them better able than most professionals to see the impending risks to the Earth's life support systems.

Why the reluctance to get involved in these wider debates from geologists, and indeed scientists in general? The impasse is, of course, the well-identified and much-discussed rift between the two cultures of science and the humanities. 'Good science is pure and objective and should not be polluted by concern about its social and political context.' This attitude has been even easier to sustain in the Earth sciences than, for instance, in medical or agricultural science. It is in urgent need of revision.

Looking back and looking forward

We have seen how society's low awareness of geological science permits misunderstandings of large proportions. Society's decision-makers can allow depletion of subsurface resources at unsustainable rates, and the leakage or disposal of wastes into the underground environment as though it was infinite, homogeneous and inert. This low awareness is balanced by that of geologists for the social context of their science. They can be experts both in finding petroleum and in budgeting the carbon cycle without ever questioning the socioeconomic precepts which link them. A recent review by the US National Research Council has as two objectives of Earth science 'to sustain sufficient supplies of natural resources' and 'to minimize and adjust to the effects of global and environmental change' without commenting on the mutual incompatibility of these goals.

The route forward is clearly through better two-way communication between geologists and the society within which they operate. Specific policies must depend on national circumstances, but some general strategies should be:

1. better geological training in schools, both of students and of their teachers, within a framework of a holistic science of the Earth;
2. in particular, a teaching that the environment does not end at the Earth's surface, but continues underground;
3. more cross-disciplinary opportunities in higher education, allowing interaction between students of sciences and the humanities;
4. a shift to more holistic systems science teaching in geology and other natural sciences at all levels;

5. a greater willingness by scientists to criticize and shape policy, not just on 'scientific' issues but in all areas, such as modern economics, whose logic runs counter to the natural economy of the Earth;
6. an appreciation by scientists that the advances in their subject are incomplete, and maybe even dangerous, without wider public discussion of how they might be applied.

A greater mutual awareness between geologists and society can speed the necessary shift away from the demand-led exploitation of the Earth's resources which has characterized the 20th century. Understanding of the Earth's natural economy can guide the development of a human economy that is sustainable, at least on a human time-scale. Comparison of geological rates of global change with the changes driven by human activity can highlight the urgency of the situation. Society is fast running out of that most abundant of geological resources—time.

Annotated List of Further Reading

The Ages of Gaia: A Biography of our Living Earth, James E. Lovelock, Oxford: Oxford University Press, 1988.
   The most geologically oriented of books on the Gaia hypothesis. A stimulating view of how Earth history is relevant to predicting future global change.

The End of Nature, Bill McKibbin, London: Viking Penguin, 1990.
   A stimulating view of human attempts to manage the Earth.

An Introduction to Global Environmental Issues, Kevin T. Pickering and Lewis A. Owen, London: Routledge, 1994.
   Written by two geologists, this up to date, yet inevitably selective, text deals with the world's major environmental concerns.

Environmental Geology, Donald R. Coates, Chichester: Wiley, 1981.
Chapters 1 to 3 contain a helpful discussion of the ethical and philosophical problems involved in applying geology to finding natural resources and to investigate environmental impacts.

Solid-Earth Sciences and Society, National Research Council, Washington DC: National Academy Press, 1993.
A manifesto for the systems science approach to geology. Includes valuable descriptions and illustrations of the main Earth systems.

Richard Lindsay

Author biography

RICHARD Lindsay has worked professionally in nature conservation for nearly 20 years. Having begun work in 1976 with the Nature Conservancy Council, the then UK government watchdog on nature conservation, he was later appointed Senior Peatland Specialist. He was closely involved in a number of high-profile peatland conservation issues, including the large-scale afforestation of the Flow Country peatlands of northern Scotland and, more recently, the debate about the use of peat in gardening and horticulture. He has taken part in a number of Public Inquiries and encountered a wide range of environmental impact assessments of proposed developments. He is Chairman of the International Mire Conservation Group, and now works for Scottish Natural Heritage, the NCC's successor body in Scotland (this chapter does not represent official SNH policy), and is an adviser on environmental issues to HRH the Prince of Wales.

Chapter 10

Richard Lindsay

Galloping Gertie and the Precautionary Principle: How is Environmental Impact Assessed?

THERE should be a law which states that every scientist intending to carry out an environmental impact assessment (EIA) must first be presented with a statue of a dog. Not just any animal, of course; the statue, or, more properly, a memorial, would be of a dog which once belonged to the daughter of Leonard Coatsworth from Washington State, in the USA. The dog's name was Tubby and, alas, poor Tubby was killed by Galloping Gertie on a November morning in 1940. The death of Tubby, and indeed that of Galloping Gertie, who died at the same time, was a direct result of something which has always been a feature of scientific investigation, but whose effects are now increasingly becoming the focus of many environmental issues. The problem can be summed up thus:

Q: What's the difference between a 'correct' and an 'incorrect' theory?

A: About ten years.

This dictum, for which I am indebted to Dr Hans Joosten of Utrecht, neatly expresses the fact that any existing scientific model is almost certain to be modified or even completely overturned by subsequent discoveries. Predictions for much more than 10–20 years hence, based on present day models, have a significant probability of ultimately proving to be, if not wrong, then at least not quite right. The greater the complexity of the system being modelled, the greater the probability that this will prove to be so. It is a fact which environmental consultants would do well to consider before making unduly optimistic predictions about the likely impact of a particular development. They should also reflect on the fate of poor Tubby.

Bridge building, oscillations and vortices

The Tacoma Narrows Bridge (Figure 10.1a and b) was designed by one of the leading bridge designers of his day, Leon Moitseief. At the time, it was considered to be a daring, innovative example of engineering, but ultimately its intended purpose was simply to bridge the Narrows. It was expected to do this within the limitations of known engineering safety tolerances because no-one was going to pay for a bridge which was unsafe to use; but that was exactly what Moitseief eventually provided for the people of Washington State.

Within weeks of opening, it was observed that, in any sort of wind, the bridge would oscillate up and down, very slowly. The Tacoma Narrows Bridge, rapidly renamed

Figure 10.1a. The last moments of Galloping Gertie

'Galloping Gertie', was proving to possess aeroelastic properties which had never before been encountered or even dreamed of within bridge-building circles. While sightseers came simply to gaze in amazement, engineers came to measure the process. They considered the various stresses on the fabric of the bridge and declared that, although the motion was unusual, the bridge was nevertheless quite safe and could remain open even when 'galloping'.

This view prevailed until one November morning in 1940. On that day, a 40 mile/hr wind blew steadily down the Narrows and people began observing a new phenomenon. Whereas, on all previous occasions, Gertie had simply oscillated up and down, now she was going up and down and beginning to twist from side to side. By the time Leonard Coatsworth and Tubby reached the bridge in

Figure 10.1b. Gertie after her last gallop

Leonard's car, the combined oscillations were just getting into their stride. Once on the bridge, further progress was clearly impossible. Mr Coatsworth, Tubby and several other motorists found themselves stranded on a bucking leviathan. Police closed the bridge and managed to persuade all of the occupants in stranded vehicles to run to safety—all, that is, except Tubby, who absolutely refused to leave the vehicle. Newsreels of the time show Mr Coatsworth, minus Tubby, staggering from the bridge like a drunken man as steel and concrete heave and roll around him in the manner of a confused sea.

A short while later the newsreels also show the entire structure finally tearing apart and collapsing into the Narrows, carrying poor Tubby and Gertie to a watery grave. When asked later about the cause of the phenomenon, Moitseief simply said 'I have no idea.' He died not long after the disaster, a mystified and broken man.

With the Tacoma Narrows Bridge, Moitseief had employed engineering techniques which were well tested and thoroughly researched. He had taken the design just a little way into new territory by making the ratio of width to length slightly greater than had been attempted before, but, because there was no existing evidence to suggest otherwise, no problems were anticipated with this. It was only 52 years later, in 1992, that scientists finally caught up with Nature and were able to show that Gertie's self-destructive change from vertical to lateral oscillations was a result of von Karmen vortices. The effects of such vortices on a structure such as Gertie were an entirely unknown phenomenon in the 1930s.

The Ferrybridge disaster

Despite the name, Ferrybridge is not another bridge disaster, nor was it a project intended to push back the frontiers of engineering. The construction of cooling towers for power stations was, by the early 1960s, a well-established and somewhat prosaic engineering process. The several towers of the Ferrybridge Power Station in Yorkshire were all constructed using standard techniques. Nothing novel here.

Except that, on the afternoon of a windy November day in the early 1960s (perhaps the patron saint of engineers takes a break every November), one of the concrete and steel towers in the complex began to behave in a distinctly novel way. It started to oscillate, wobbling like a badly made pot on a potter's wheel. The wobbles became increasingly violent, until, as anyone who has attempted pottery will recognize, the instability moved rapidly and inexorably towards an unavoidable and catastrophic climax. Millions of fascinated TV viewers watched the evening news to see the violent wobbles cause the flailing upper parts of the tower finally to shear off. The whole 375 ft construction then collapsed in a heap of rubble and twisted steel.

What happened next was almost as incredible. Even before the dust had settled on the TV screens, an expert was wheeled on to explain how the disaster had happened. With the day's gale gusting at up to 85 miles/hr, huge vortices caused by adjoining cooling towers had created such powerful forces of suction that the fabric of one particular tower had been quite unable to cope with the resultant stresses and had simply disintegrated. I well remember the sense of wonder which this revelation provoked. 'Good Heavens!', we exclaimed as we listened to this expert, 'then why were the towers not designed either to avoid, or to cope with, such vortices? After all, gales of 85 miles/hr are not so unusual in Britain.' The answer, of course, lay in the undisclosed fact that the possible development of these vortices, and their subsequent impact, had been unsuspected by engineers *until* they were observed to occur in the real world, at Ferrybridge.

Engineering and the real world

In effect, to carry out an experiment and then develop a model which can provide useful predictions, a scientist will try as far as possible to provide an environment which is entirely controlled or measured. Even bridge-builders, however, in their relatively rigidly defined world of concrete and steel, recognize the limitations of their craft when faced with the unpredictable real world. Rod Rhys Jones, an engineering consultant, observes

> How much can engineers possibly know about the future? Bridges are there a long time. Engineers have to know the unknowable, predict the unpredictable. They have to be able to account for Acts of God[1].

Bridges are certainly there a long time, some even predate the origins of some valued wildlife habitats, but although the common objective of both bridge-building and conservation is to maintain the working fabric of a bridge or habitat as far into the foreseeable future as possible, the bridge-builder always knows that, should the need arise, another bridge can be built to replace the existing structure. For the majority of valued wildlife habitats, such artificial reconstruction is simply not possible—existing attempts at habitat recreation or regeneration have yet to show any significant level of success. They currently represent no more than the first stumbling steps of ecological engineers into a vast and largely uncharted territory. Over-confidence at such an early stage in the exploration of this relatively new field could all too easily lead entire species groups into blind alleys from which there is no return—unlike bridge design, the luxury of two bites at the cherry is not one of the characteristic features of extinction.

Klaus Ostenfield, Bridge Director of COWI engineering consultants, recognizes that, in relation to projects where the bridge-builder is also going into uncharted territory

> [The designer] runs the risk of having overseen something, so every time you make a long extrapolation in technology, you have to watch out and be very careful in order to make sure you see what you cannot see[1].

Such cautionary thoughts come from engineers who deal for the most part quite literally in concrete facts. The majority of bridge design is utterly predictable. The designer's biggest worry is that the real world will intrude on this ordered, measured and precisely defined exercise with some previously unrecognized mischief. For a bridge-designer the majority of facts are solid, and only a few elements of unpredictability are expected to seep into the final process.

The one major change in circumstances, when the engineer finally takes a design or a model from the laboratory out into the real world and begins construction, is that the design is then subject to the much more complex environment of the real world, and this may throw up a few surprises. Indeed, the common causative factor in the collapse of both Galloping Gertie and Ferrybridge was nothing to do with engineering *per se*. Both resulted from a series of atmospheric tricks which were, until that point, completely unknown to the engineer, and which only became apparent when the design was subjected to the unpredictability of the real world.

It is important to understand that 'unpredictability' does not mean some Luddite view of a world which is beyond any possibility of measurement and thus whose future behavior is subject only to, in footballer Diego Maradona's famous phrase, 'the Hand of God'. The word is used here very deliberately to contrast conditions in the outside world with the 'controlled conditions' of a laboratory environment. The very idea of experiments carried out in 'controlled conditions' logically indicates that everything outside these conditions must be 'uncontrolled'—i.e. unpredictable, or at least *not measured*.

The furore over 'cold fusion' centers, in part, over accusations that physicists Pons and Fleischmann failed to control their experimental conditions sufficiently closely, and that perhaps some of the products they observed were therefore derived from entirely unrelated and unrecorded external processes. This accusation may or may not be true, but it does illustrate the very rigorous application by the general scientific community of the concept of 'controlled conditions'. It also highlights the common problem which faces scientists when carrying out any experiment—namely the ease with which unpredictable factors can slip into what is a supposedly controlled environment. One of the biggest problems in maintaining this set of conditions is ensuring that the real world is not inadvertently allowed to intrude on the experiment. All scientists know the problem, even within the closed world of the laboratory—low readings from a dirty electrode, a fault in the deionized water supply, stray *Penicillium* mold on an agar plate . . .

In an engineering project, the actual process of design and construction rests largely on the use of materials and techniques which have already undergone exhaustive tests and trials under laboratory conditions. Othmar H Ammann, chief designer of the Brooklyn Bridge, produced 'a design so precise that engineers considered the job half-finished when workmen appeared on the site, in 1959'. He knew that the 693 ft twin towers would need to support 150 000 tons of roadway and cable, and that the towers themselves would weigh 48 000 tons. He calculated, and was subsequently proved right, that the weight of the completed road deck would cause the suspension cables to sag by exactly 28 ft below their unladen arc. He was able, because of laboratory tests which showed the behavior of metals under differing conditions, to allow for summer expansions and winter contractions which would alter the height of the span by as much as 6 ft, and when the wind blew, enable the whole span to distort up to 14 ft sideways. Ammann was able to do this because the vast majority of steps in the design process were already robustly proved techniques, some of which went back to Roman times or even earlier. The construction process was almost entirely calculable, predictable and, in effect, simply represented a scaled-up version of controlled laboratory conditions.

Compared with this relative bedrock of certainty and arsenal of precisely defined measurements, the environmental consultant embarks on an EIA (while clutching a little statue of Tubby) to be confronted with a maelstrom of uncertainty, in which the majority of elements are uncertain or unknown and are anyway constantly fluctuating. Often, the only concrete facts are those which relate to the actual fabric of the proposal—the engineering details of the dam, factory, barrage, wind turbine, road, quarry or whatever. Virtually *every* other factor which must be measured or modeled is instead something which lies outside the predictable world of the controlled environment. Few elements of the environment have given up their secrets to definitive laboratory analysis. Yet the job of the consultant is not merely to understand how the ecosystem works initially, but then to determine the impact of a potentially profound change on this real and 'unpredictable' environment. The EIA consultant, in other words, is very much at the opposite end of the certainty spectrum from the bridge-designer.

The unregulated environment

Another important difference between the bridge-designer and the EIA consultant is that bridge design is heavily regulated. A whole range of safety codes must be followed, otherwise the designer faces prosecution, particularly if disaster strikes. The world of EIA is, in contrast, regulated in only the most general way. For example, under the

Commission for the European Communities (CEC) Directive 85/337/EEC, member states of the European Union are required to ensure that EIAs are carried out under particular circumstances, but the regulations provide little in the way of practical guidelines relating to either content or quality. Within the UK, relevant regulations were generally enacted in the late 1980s and early 1990s e.g. The Environmental Assessment (Scotland) Regulations 1988, and the official country conservation agencies have together arranged for the production of joint guidance relating to their functions within the EIA process, this guidance being in the form of the *Environmental Assessment Handbook*. Then again, though providing a usefully detailed analysis of the steps required to carry out and evaluate an EIA, the *Handbook* is not part of the legislation, and is thus not legally binding.

As far as the regulations themselves go, although, in the UK at least, the greater bulk of the legislation is concerned with determining whether an environmental assessment is required in the first place. In describing the practical (as opposed to the broad) nature of any environmental assessment (EA) and the environmental statement (ES) which emerges from that, the legislation is remarkably coy.

The intention of the CEC Directive is that developers should have considered the possible impacts of any proposed development at the earliest possible stage in their plans. Encouraging the developer to carry out the EA studies is thought to be one means by which a direct interest in environmental issues can be engendered more widely. Unfortunately, the translation of this philosophy into UK legislation embraces the concept to a greater degree than is perhaps helpful.

A developer is required to provide to the planning authority a statement which includes: (1) a description of the physical nature of the development; (2) data with which to assess the *main* environmental effects; and (3) an analysis of likely *significant* effects (both direct and indirect) on

- humans
- flora
- fauna
- soil
- water
- air
- climate
- the landscape
- any interactions of the foregoing
- material assets
- the cultural heritage;

(4) measures envisaged for avoiding, reducing or remedying effects; and (5) a non-technical summary.

An ES may, but is not legally obliged to, include amplification and explanation about: (1) land-use requirements during construction and operation; (2) the main environmental characteristics of the production process; (3) the expected type and quantity of residues; (4) alternative approaches examined; (5) direct and indirect effects of using natural resources and of the creation of wastes; (6) the forecasting methods used for (5); and (7) difficulties caused by technical deficiencies and information gaps. It is recognized that the concept of 'effect' can include those of a secondary, cumulative, short/long term, permanent/temporary or positive/negative nature.

This list of items for investigation is undoubtedly comprehensive, but it's rather like saying to a randomly picked person, a dog-owner perhaps, 'Here's some fish plates, girders and tarmac—now build me a bridge'. No statutory guidance is given as to the form which an ES must take; how the developer goes about answering these questions is left entirely open. The developer is simply told to provide sufficient information on all the listed issues for the planning authority to be able to make a judgment. If the information is not considered adequate by the planning authority the developer can be requested to provide more data until the authority is satisfied. In the absence of a set framework by which an authority can be expected to judge an EA, this represents something of an open-ended commitment on the part of the developer because planning, scheduling and budgeting is very difficult for something which may, ultimately, and at the authority's request, turn into a major ecosystem analysis. Even the consistently informative *Environmental Assessment Handbook* is sketchy in its treatment of the subject, stating blandly that no standard methods can usefully be provided.

This lack of formal provision to ensure that common methods are used between different EAs also means that planning authorities, faced with two successive applications which are concerned with largely similar proposals, may not be able to transfer the knowledge and experience gained from one study over into the process of judging the second proposal. Methods adopted in the two EAs may be so different that comparison of the results between the two may not be valid. Nor will the planning authorities be able to benefit from what should be an accumulating knowledge pool as more EAs are carried out. Similarly, developers are not easily able to draw on the experience and results of previous studies when carrying out their own investigations.

The other major, and possibly more important, problem with the EA philosophy, as practiced, is that the entire process is concerned only with the stages *prior* to the granting of planning consent. This arises from the laudable desire to ensure that environmental considerations are included at the earliest planning stages of a proposed development. This is translated into UK legislation in the form of, as we have seen, a potentially exhaustive review of *likely* effects *prior* to a development being given approval, but nothing in the legislation provides for post hoc monitoring and alterations. The *Handbook* notes that monitoring after planning consent has been granted is possible through the provisions of planning conditions under, for example in England and Wales, Section 106 of the Town & Country Planning Act. However, the *Handbook* also observes that such actions are 'seldom undertaken in the British context', nor indeed is it common practice elsewhere in the world.

The present system therefore has three crucial short-comings:

1. the system fails to encourage any consistency of approach between developers and is thus a recipe for anarchy;
2. consequently, neither developer nor planning authority can easily draw on the results of previous studies, nor is there any provision for the collation of such accumulating knowledge—each EA is a study unto itself;
3. the system is entirely predictive, concerned only with *possible* events in the future and, in practice at least, fails to continue impact assessment into the future to note *actual* effects—not being responsible for the subsequent outcome, EA teams thus have no direct incentive to make accurate predictions.

These flaws in the EIA system itself are then compounded by another, more potentially serious problem, more serious in that, with a simple change in the legislation all three failings listed above can be overcome, whereas this additional complication arises from something more deeply ingrained. It is an aspect of scientific culture which has given rise to many remarkable examples of scientific conduct in relation to EIA work and Public Inquiry advocacy in Britain. At its very worst, it can be described as scientific *hubris*, an arrogant assertion that science has all the answers. Its more normal expression is found either in the belief that, as Robert Earll of the Marine Conservation Society describes it, 'absence of evidence' is synonymous with 'evidence of absence', or as a scientific caution which demands that proof of harm be obtained before action be taken, whether or not that harm can be reversed.

The list of superficial, slap-dash, negligent and in some cases frankly laughable EIA studies or statements which arise from this dangerous cocktail is long and not very edifying. Far too many EIA studies are in reality no more than a cosmetic treatment of the issue, merely providing an environmental gloss to a proposal, a smooth and politically soothing lustre whose foundation is more worthy of Helena Rubenstein or Yves Saint-Laurent than of the Royal Society or the National Academy of Sciences.

Such studies claim to be professionally executed scientific assessments of the proposed development, yet many would be viewed with horror by the engineering profession if applied to the relatively predictable construction of bridges. Applying them instead to the much more complex problem of the environment requires both greater caution and broader vision—caution to avoid over-confidence, and vision to see possible connections, the evidence for which may not, as yet, be available.

Finally, EIA scientists must also be prepared to overcome a particular philosophy which now seems to dominate much of the scientific community, as a result of which too many are reluctant to admit knowledge-gaps in their data and uncertainties in their predictions. Oddly enough, although portrayed in popular myth as an evil ogre plotting to push a scheme through by guile or subterfuge, the developer is often largely blameless for the poor quality of an inadequate EIA. Nor does the problem necessarily lie with the planning authority or the Secretary of State, because many of these poorly-executed EIAs are subsequently rejected. These particular problems arise instead as the result of a particular scientific culture which has been allowed to grow up and in some circumstances almost stifle the spirit of scientific enquiry. This culture could be called 'The Fear of Ignorance' and is also discussed in Tom Wakeford's chapter.

EIA and scientific peer pressure

One normal prerequisite for publication in a respected scientific journal is proof that an experiment has been carried out in such a way as to ensure that all possible variables have been accounted for. Such an approach is designed for science carried out under laboratory conditions. It is a philosophy unsuited to investigations, no matter how objectively rigorous, in an open, 'uncontrolled' environment. Once an experiment moves outside the laboratory environment it becomes impossible to control all variables. Rather than expending useless effort on trying to do so, it therefore becomes more important to identify those elements which can be measured, and those elements which cannot. In general, those which cannot be measured or controlled will outnumber those which can, given the time and cost constraints under which a developer is usually operating.

Many of these unregulated and unmeasured factors may have only a minor impact on the results obtained; such is the assumption of many studies. However, it is quite possible that hitherto unsuspected influences are also affecting the data obtained. For example, it is only with the development of the 'groundwater mound theory' by Hugh Ingram of Dundee University that it is now possible to explain changes in the vegetation of a peat bog some considerable distance from an afforestation scheme on that same bog. These observed changes are now understood to occur as a result of alterations in the overall shape of the bog water-table caused by water removal beneath the trees. Previously, such changes were attributed solely to the effects of grazing or lack of regular burning.

It is impossible to measure every aspect within, and every connection to, an ecosystem. Papers which are concerned with environmental issues and which also aim to provide scientific illumination to a problem should in principle provide a list of *all* those factors which might possibly have a bearing on the results, but which were not investigated, together with an assessment of the possible implications of these omissions. This represents a type of scientific writing which is very different in kind from those papers which describe the more traditional type of controlled condition experiment. Such disarming honesty would make interesting reading and would probably provide a rich vein for further scientific discussion and research. Unfortunately, such documents are currently rare animals.

The reason for this rarity, at least in part, is that scientists are reluctant to admit that they might have missed something, that their experimental method is not as comprehensive as they would like, or that funding and time constraints have simply rendered a proper analysis impossible. Indeed, the scientific community at large, and funding bodies in particular, do not welcome such admissions of omission. Papers have less chance of finding their way into print if they clearly state that certain aspects remain unstudied even though these may have a material bearing on the issue at hand, than those papers which simply do not acknowledge such gaps in the experimental method. Even academic reviewers will often be unaware of the full suite of features and connections which might have a significant bearing on a particular study. It appears that being 'economical with the truth' is a better strategy than 'the truth, the *whole* truth, and nothing but the truth'. The derision with which scientists treat their colleagues in the 'social sciences' seems to intensify with the passing years. At least most social scientists *admit* how complex their subject matter is. This may seem harsh, but look at a range of scientific papers which describe an investigation into the natural world and consider what *other* factors may also have contributed to the observed effects—it is by no means unusual to come up with several which are not mentioned by the authors. Although not quite the level of scientific fraud described in Broad and Wade's classic book *The Betrayers of the Truth*, some papers come pretty close.

The pressures facing environmental scientists over the issue of experimental uncertainty and incompleteness, especially when attempting to carry out scientific investigations which resolve real-life dilemmas, can be judged from some of the recent and occasionally quite heated discussions which have surrounded the concept of the 'precautionary principle'.

The precautionary principle

The unpredictability of many natural phenomena, and the undoubtedly limited level of understanding which ecological science is able to apply to most natural systems, has increasingly obliged politicians and administrators to recognize that even the very best advice provided by the scientific community must be leavened with a significant degree of caution. Such acceptance of uncertainty has increasingly become formalized through intergovernmental action. In particular, according to the UK Biodiversity Action Plan, the principle of 'precaution' will now form one of the primary mechanisms by which the UK Government intends to meet its obligations under the United Nations Conference on Environment and Development Convention on Biological Diversity, signed in June 1992.

Such international commitments explicitly recognize the need to apply precaution when coming to decisions which may affect the natural biodiversity of a region or influence the natural sustainability of an area. The *precautionary principle* is described by the government thus: 'interactions [of natural systems] are complex [and] where there is a significant chance of damage to our diversity occurring, conservation measures are appropriate even in the absence of *conclusive* [my emphasis] scientific evidence that the damage will occur'.

This concept has attracted a lively response from certain scientific quarters. A particularly illuminating set of papers published between 1990 and 1992 in the *Marine Pollution Bulletin* explores the various implications of such an approach, while Alex Milne has launched a vigorous attack on the precautionary principle in *New Scientist*, in response to previous articles from Mary Midgley, Bryan Wynne and Sue Mayer.

Milne argues that the burden of proof which the precautionary principle places on industry is not merely an excessively onerous obligation, but one with which it is impossible to comply. He argues that the precautionary principle is unsound and unscientific because:

1. the definition, derived originally from a German concept, states that action should be taken even before the definitive scientific proof of causal links between emission and effect has been obtained;
2. the principle recommends that action be taken *prior* to complete determination of 'harmful limits';
3. that the proof of 'no-harm' is impossible to demonstrate;
4. that the precautionary principle is a form of moral philosophy, rather than any rigorous scientific principle.

The precautionary principle as moral philosophy

Taking Milne's last point first, most conservationists and scientists would agree with this. The precautionary principle is indeed a philosophical approach, but this is because mankind's relationship with the outside world is generally a 'subjective', moral issue, rather than something which can be defined by science. Science, of course, has no value judgments, and therefore the concept of 'harm', and the desire to avoid such harm, can have no place in a world, ordered strictly by scientific principles. In Milne's world, scientists who have devoted their entire working lives to the study of a single species ought not to regard the extinction of their chosen species with anything but cool, scientific detachment. From an objectively scientific platform, extinction provides an opportunity to investigate the impact which the loss of this species would have on the surrounding ecosystem. It also provides an empty niche for exploitation by other species or even for the evolution of new species and thus the scientist is provided with as rich a vein of research as was provided by the now-extinct species. Few scientists would, however, propose that a species be driven to the brink of extinction in order to study ecosystem interactions.

The anthropocentric view of environmental care states that we should maintain a stable set of conditions, minimizing such extinctions and marked perturbations, to ensure that we, and succeeding generations, can continue to survive and harvest the Earth's resources sustainably. This is not justifiable through any scientific principle, but is a widespread view, even amongst scientists, because we as a species value our continued survival. The world of Lovelock's Gaia hypothesis might easily take a rather different view.

Milne suggests that the kind of moral philosophy enshrined in the precautionary principle is somehow unusual, but scientists are subject to just such moral restraint all the time. Quite simply, some things are acceptable to society and others are not. The recent past contains chilling examples of the extreme and grotesque scientific practices which can result when such moral restraint is lifted. The memory of experiments carried out in the name of science by Dr Joseph Mengele on his concentration camp victims blows like a bleak wind through the halls of 'objective science'.

The simple fact of the matter is that society puts subjective constraints on scientists and their work because society is based largely on values and value judgments. In environmental matters, society has declared that scientists should be *sure* before they do something, just as they expect engineers to be sure when they build a bridge, because a proposal to alter the environment is not the same as some controlled condition laboratory experiment. A bridge which turns into a Galloping Gertie is dangerous or inconvenient only for those wishing to cross the river, but we all have to live with the consequences when an 'objective' scientist inadvertently opens an environmental Pandora's box. Winston Churchill expressed this mistrust when he observed 'Scientists should be on tap, not on top'.

The precautionary principle and the 'proof of harm'

It is probably true that it is not possible to prove conclusively whether or not a substance or action is 'harmless'. This is because virtually everything ultimately has some impact. Obviously, chemical tests which prove the extremely insoluble nature of a substance are, nevertheless, irrelevant if such large quantities of the material are to be dumped that it will smother existing marine ecosystems. Alternatively, construction of a roadway across a hydrologically sensitive peatland site may involve the use of an inert substance. If it requires deep marginal drains to prevent it being washed away, the presence of the inert material may not be a problem *per se* (other than for the immediate area of habitat buried beneath the material); the necessary drainage infrastructure to keep it in place certainly would be.

The real-world context in which a substance or action may ultimately feature is thus a vital part of judging potential harm, but anticipating all possible contexts and evaluating their effects will often prove to be beyond even the most sophisticated environmental model. In his book *The Dammed*, writer Fred Pearce has provided a catalogue of consequences which have followed from the construction of the Aswan Dam in Egypt. These relate to such diverse aspects as loss of the Mediterranean sardine which once bred in the Nile delta, the spread of bilharzia and schistosomiasis, loss of annual silt deposits on farmland in the Nile valley, the lack of fresh clay for the brick-making industry, widespread erosion of the Nile delta and its farmlands, the overwhelming of coastal defenses and the accumulation of salt in agricultural land, this last problem to be tackled by a scheme which will cost more than the original construction of the dam. The complications imposed here by the real-life context are clearly overwhelming in their complexity.

What is 'harm'?

Milne states that the concept of 'harm' is scientifically worthless because it cannot be defined by any rigorous scientific method. Despite this, the brick-makers of the Nile valley, or the inhabitants of Borg-el-Borellos, now submerged two kilometers out to sea because coastal defenses on the Nile delta have collapsed, would doubtless have a very clear opinion of what constitutes 'harm'. Their views may, nevertheless, be disputed by fishermen harvesting fish in these new shallow waters, because 'harm' is indeed a subjective, rather than objective, concept. The degree of change regarded as a threshold beyond which something is regarded as 'harmful' must ultimately be a subjective decision because science puts no values on one sequence of events compared with another.

Just because something is 'scientifically worthless' does not mean it is worthless in the real world, however. If society defines its values, as it has done in, for example, the UK Biodiversity Action Plan, it is then possible to use the best science available to provide data which can be set against these values, and balancing judgments made accordingly. The precautionary principle may be based on the value judgments of society, and not, as Milne would like, on 'objective' scientific proof, but judgments about 'harm' can be informed, rather than defined, by rigorously objective, scientific evidence. The principles of biodiversity and sustainable use, as outlined in the UK Biodiversity Action Plan, make it possible to begin the development of rational, pragmatic guidelines for the definition of 'harm'.

To act before 'harmful' limits have been identified is not scientific

It may be true that, in the strict sense of the term, such actions are not 'scientific' according to Milne, but to what 'action' does he refer? It is actually a decision preventing change from existing conditions. More accurately, it represents the imposition of *no* action until such time as a new proposal has proved itself free of 'harm' within the pragmatic guidelines provided by society.

Milne's approach virtually endorses the instigation and continuation of an activity until it has been proved, beyond any doubt, to be 'harmful'. It is difficult to believe that Milne seriously believes that this applies to all other scientific disciplines. The pharmaceutical world is prevented by society from releasing new drugs until such time as they have been exhaustively and independently tested for evidence of 'harm'. The 'action' of preventing the release of a drug even before the testing for 'harm' begins is standard practice in pharmacology, but is this unscientific? Logically, one approaches with more caution a problem for which one has little data than one does another problem for which the data are largely complete.

Without imperfect knowledge there would be no science

Those, like Milne, opposed to the precautionary principle say that uncertainty is unacceptable and unscientific. Yet if everything in the universe were revealed to us there would be little need for science, because all research feeds only on the unknown. Today, the practice and application of science appears to be so anxious to deny this intimate link, this dependence on the unknown, that a popular perception has developed of the scientist as someone concerned only with concrete facts and absolute certainties. The philosophy of scientific certainty and the fear of ignorance have brought about a general belief, not least in the minds of developers and politicians, that the scientist merely has to wave a magic wand over the problem for all the answers to pop out with the absolute precision of Ammann's Brooklyn Bridge project. Of course, this is rarely the case with the environment. What society gets, all too often, is a Galloping Gertie.

Nevertheless, people continue to believe in the science of certainty and the certainty of science. Consequently, a developer, having paid a seemingly considerable sum for an EIA does not want a consultant's report which lists page upon page of topics not investigated, followed by further pages of cautionary caveats in the impact assessment. Nor does a politician or planning officer, faced with a difficult and potentially costly decision, welcome such uncertainty and lack of definitive guidance.

This belief in the essential certainty of science is encouraged by scientists who make confident statements to the effect that no evidence of harm has been detected using the available methods and therefore it is inconceivable that any harm could occur. This represents a fine example of scientific hubris, especially if such comments are based on limited survey and are thus a clear case of 'being economical with the truth'.

More worrying still, perhaps, are confident predictions that Nature is robust enough to bounce back unchanged, or better than ever, after such events. In the Marine Pollution Bulletin debate, John Gray, for example, confidently predicts that, if ilmenite dumping off the Norwegian coast is halted at some point in the future, the marine ecosystem 'will be restored within 10 years'. Restored? Ten years?

Has Gray studied *all* aspects of the marine ecosystem in the area currently affected by such dumping, or is he talking only of the more evident components of the ecosystem? Such confident statements about recovery and restoration (and such statements are much less rare in EIAs than are frank and detailed admissions of information gaps) should always be very carefully and critically examined.

What is required is a subtle shift in the present scientific ethos, one which welcomes open acknowledgement of ignorance and encourages the limitations of any particular study to be fully explored. If scientists were more up-front, enthusiastic, even, about the true limits to our understanding of an issue, this could, in time, engender a recognition within society as a whole of just how enormous are the environmental uncertainties which currently face us. It would also make EIAs more honest in terms of the answers they can provide.

Building bridges between developers and the environment

The current state of affairs could at least be improved if those involved with EIAs, and perhaps the community of ecological scientists at large, were to adopt the philosophy of the bridge-designer. The key factor in a bridge-designer's mind during the whole process is a constant searching for the unexpected, the unplanned-for discovery, which can then receive immediate attention before disaster sets in. This philosophy, in other words, positively encourages the identification of knowledge gaps because the alternative of hiding such gaps under the carpet, pretending they are not relevant, could lead to collapse, catastrophe and perhaps appalling loss of life. Other chapters in this book suggest that this may have already happened.

The sequence of events involved in building a bridge is not so very different from carrying out an EIA, at least during the early stages, although the bridge-designer is committed to a much longer relationship with the final outcome than is the EIA scientist.

Before exploring this comparison further, however, it is worth turning aside briefly to consider four difficulties which are a chronic problem for EIA studies, and which add significant complexity to any such program of work.

The small extent of existing knowledge

Unlike many of the traditional sciences, which have a formal pedigree going back many centuries, ecology is a very young science. Indeed, the term itself was not coined until 1869 by Ernst Haeckel, and university courses have only been turning out graduates formally trained in the subject since the 1960s. A discipline which has only received significant attention for the last 40–50 years, when some of the natural cycles already identified span 20–30 years, is obviously only going to be able to offer a limited baseline of existing data.

Funding bodies prefer 'pure' and 'big' science to practical dilemmas

Unfortunately, the difficulties of being a recent arrival on the scientific scene has been compounded by the problem that research into the everyday, practical problems of environmental impact has been starved of research funding for decades. Even today, with the upsurge of green awareness and intergovernmental concern about environmental issues, the main projects funded by the UK's Natural Environment Research Council (NERC) are the global issues such as greenhouse gas emissions, or oceanic current movements, or broad pollution mapping of the North Sea. Ask any professional nature conservationist or planning authority what environmental issues require urgent research for the day to day operation of environmental legislation, and the topics will rarely feature prominently in the NERC research budget. The only other significant source of environmental research funding comes through the statutory conservation agencies, but these research budgets have been steadily reduced in recent years to such an extent that only a fraction of the priority projects can now be funded.

The short time-scales available

The lack of existing data will often pose significant problems for the EIA team, but such difficulties will generally be seriously compounded by the short time-scales normally provided for such a study. The team is rarely given the time required to gather sufficiently meaningful sets of measurements. A five-year lead time for the construction of a factory, from initial concept to final completion, is not unreasonable in construction terms. For many environmental problems five years is too short a time in which to measure, understand and model the existing ecosystem, never mind to judge the impact of disrupting this system. A hydrological budget alone requires the accumulation of data over several years to balance out the variability introduced by wet or dry years, and such a budget represents only a small part of what generally requires investigation. Such environmental measures must normally, however, be carried out well within the period of preparation and construction for the proposal. It is not unusual to have an EIA based on only one season's data, and in some cases on only one or two site visits, and even the normally excellent *Environmental Assessment Handbook* suggests that sampling might need to be carried out for as much as a whole year.

The balance of time constraints, cost to the developer and the need to obtain meaningful data is one of the central dilemmas of EIA work. Millions of pounds have been spent on the underground deep storage caverns at the Sellafield nuclear reprocessing plant in Cumbria, UK, yet only now has it been established that the water-table of the underground caverns is connected to the regional groundwater system. Such aquifer links are a common and expensive feature of regional groundwater regimes, yet how often will a developer be prepared to carry out extensive borehole tests to develop a working model of the relevant area of the groundwater and its behavior? Experience suggests that few can even afford to do so. And groundwater behavior is just one aspect. Unraveling the causes behind the steady loss of Norfolk's spring-fen sites poses a problem of labyrinthine proportions. Any development proposed for the environs of these fens has a stark choice—become embroiled in an in-depth multi-disciplinary study, or ride roughshod over fears of further environmental impact.

Natural systems are unpredictable or 'chaotic'

Scientific investigation and modeling has been based for centuries on the assumption that all things are deterministic Newtonian systems, on the assumption that, provided everything is measured carefully enough, it is possible to predict precisely and consistently the behavior of any system under any conditions. Increasingly, this fundamental assumption is being revealed as incorrect, particularly for natural processes. The general rule seems to be that non-linear processes—'chaotic systems'—predominate in Nature.

Weather patterns are coming to be recognized as unpredictably chaotic even by the general public, who accept that it is impossible to predict that a specific shower will fall on a specific place at a particular time, but the weather is just one example of many. This non-linear behavior has profound implications for EIA studies. Measurements taken from such systems provide only one possible set of initial states. In a chaotic system even a fractionally different set of initial conditions will cause any model to spiral away from reality within an alarmingly short space of time. This is why reasonably accurate weather forecasts are only possible for a few days hence, although even then the detail remains unpredictable.

The worlds of the bridge-building engineer and the EIA ecologist should thus be very different in outlook. Bridge building is largely a deterministic exercise in the Newtonian sense, with only a few chaotic elements to cause the odd surprise; ecosystem analysis is quite the reverse, involving a turbulent sea of chaotic systems which swirl around a few isolated rocks of Newtonian certainty. Oddly enough, welly-booted ecologists stomping round in sometimes uncomfortably close proximity to Nature appear to have been slow to recognize the significance of this new understanding of natural systems; it is perhaps ironic that such insight has instead come from mathematicians and physicists sitting in darkened rooms, bathed only by the glow of computer screens. Meanwhile, the ecologist still struggles to fit observed behavior into inappropriate deterministic patterns. The result is a dangerously simplistic set of EIA predictions.

The burden of proof

Although many failures of EIA analysis are not the fault of the developer, but rather of the desire of the scientific community to paper over gaps in the scientific basis of predictions, the developer is not entirely innocent, however.

Until the introduction of the precautionary principle as part of government policy, the burden of proof on environmental issues had been laid firmly on the shoulders of the environmental scientist and the conservationist. Indeed, the desire to prove, scientifically, that damage occurs before taking preventative action is very attractive to certain types of scientific philosophy. In the *Marine Pollution Bulletin* debate, John Gray argues forcefully for this approach to avoid accusations of 'crying wolf' about environmental issues. The counter argument, presented by Robert Earll, points out that the 'dump–monitor–act' approach is all very well, but assumes that monitoring will tell us when to act and that we will know how to cure the problem once we have let it develop to the point of being recognizable. In support of this, Alf Josefson argues that it is not wrong to provide cautionary warnings, even if the scientific evidence is not statistically significant, provided that a clear statement accompanies the warning to the effect that the issue is not yet proved.

As regards industry's demand that the environmental scientist, rather than industry, should bear the burden of proof, Alex Milne makes the following revealing observation

> One of the practical costs of these unscientific and impossible requirements is time and effort wasted by scientists in industry and government. I was not reading the House of Lords Report HI 23 or the European Commission's Marketing and Use Directive for fun, but because they were trying to put manufacturing industry out of business.

Here we have the rub. Neither of the two reports he was reading, nor the sentiments behind them, sought to 'put [Milne's anti-fouling paint] manufacturing industry out of business', any more than the Montreal Protocol sought to send the refrigeration industry to the wall. They are instead examples of national or international efforts designed to encourage industry to adopt new methods which, for whatever reasons, are considered to be less harmful.

Milne's attitude reflects the impatience of industry reluctantly facing the burden of considering its impact on the 'downstream' environment. Such a sentiment is in stark contrast with the demands of industry for the 'upstream' part of the manufacturing process. Materials coming into most industries must be of a consistently high and predictable quality. Thus particular water supplies, or rock types, or gravel deposits, or peat types are described as 'essential' for the continued survival of the industry. Industry demands predictability in its raw materials and is quite happy to apply the precautionary principle with some vigor at the supply end, therefore, but is often keen to avoid being bound by this same principle in its outputs—or at least in certain outputs.

A manufacturing or production industry—take the antifouling paint industry as an example–will already have carried out exhaustive tests on its paint product for the effect on a boat's underside (no point in producing a paint which dissolves the gel of a glass-reinforced plastic hull), as well as tests to ensure that the paint will not eat its way through the storage tins while on the retailers' shelves and presumably also have exhaustively tested the paint's toxicity to humans. A manufacturer's nightmare is the release of a product which must subsequently be withdrawn because of a defect in these, or any number of other aspects. We can therefore be reasonably confident that testing for such features is rigorous, thorough and reliable; the same approach, indeed, as a bridge-designer would employ when preparing a new design. The difference with these outputs is that the customer can sue. The environment cannot sue anyone, it can only suffer in silence.

Even this high level of caution is, as we have already seen, still not sufficient to ensure that even the basic functions of the finished product can be guaranteed. Galloping Gerties will always be with us, popping up unpredictably in even the most rigorously controlled environments. Yet compared with the care lavished by industry on the relatively straightforward processes of raw materials acquisition and subsequent product manufacturing, the level of attention usually devoted to the environmental 'downstream' aspects of production is extraordinarily meagre. Milne seems to express a lofty sense of world-weary contempt for the idea that the manufacturer should devote any significant effort to evaluating such 'downstream' aspects of production, even if it is only to identify those areas where uncertainty exists—this is time and effort wasted by scientists in industry and government.

Improving Galloping Gertie's current form

There are a number of ways in which the present unsatisfactory and haphazard situation could be improved. Achieving these improvements would require a willingness on the part of industry and developers generally, and perhaps most importantly, environmental consultants, to embrace the philosophy of long-term 'downstream' monitoring, together with all its implications and responsibilities. Like a puppy, an EIA is not just for Christmas, it is for life. Both developer and consultant must be prepared to adopt the sense of responsibility and long-term commitment to their EIA that has been felt by designers of bridges probably since the first tree-trunk was felled across a river.

Establish a single authority responsible for overseeing EIAs

An improvement on the current EIA free-for-all would be to have a recognized authority to whom both developer and planning authority can turn when an EIA is required. The EIA Authority would then be able to define for the developer those environmental parameters which should be investigated, and in what way, to provide the best evaluation possible. If the developer's resources are limited, this authority would be capable of guiding the developer to the most critical issues. It can then assist the developer in drawing on the accumulated archive of similar studies and scientific publications to assist the ES make best-possible predictions. It can subsequently guide the planning authority in assessing the degree of certainty which can be placed on what has been achieved within the developer's available resources.

One of the advantages of such an authority for scientists involved in EIA work is that the authority can take responsibility for identifying those aspects which have not been or cannot be investigated. It can endorse the practical decisions not to investigate certain aspects, while at the same time explaining to the developer and politician the implications of this for the certainty or otherwise of any final predictions. The EIA scientist is thus not left in what is often perceived as the exposed position of having to chose which aspects not to investigate. Such choices can be shown instead to have been made in consultation with the EIA Authority.

The Authority would also be responsible for accumulating the data archive from EIA studies, as well as pulling together information from published scientific data. In this way it can establish best-practice methods for investigating particular aspects. It can also enable EIA studies to maximize the use of resources available by avoiding work which merely repeats what is already known and instead identifying the key areas which cannot yet be resolved using existing knowledge.

Finally, the Authority would provide the long-term link required to ensure that, even if individuals in the company or consultancy change, post hoc monitoring is carried out in a manner which is consistent with the requirements for monitoring change, that the results are collated and reviewed on a regular basis, and that this information is conveyed to the planning authority.

The EIA legislation needs to be changed to incorporate after the event (post hoc) monitoring

It would seem sensible to incorporate such a system into the existing planning legislation, with perhaps a three- or five-year review period for any scheme. On the review date, the need for additional safeguards in the light of either evidence of change, or of improved scientific understanding, can then be assessed. The EIA Authority would be responsible for coordinating the efforts of developer and EIA team to ensure that the best possible advice is provided for this review period, but the decision would remain with the planning authority.

Ecological science needs to become more chaotic

Despite the increasing enthusiasm of the mathematical world for the non-linear behavior of Nature, the number of ecological and environmental scientists making the effort to link up with non-linear mathematicians is very small. There is undoubtedly a rich seam of understanding to be gained from such a cross-disciplinary collaboration, but it so far lies almost completely untapped.

Edward Lorenz's paper about chaotic weather patterns lay unnoticed in an obscure meteorological journal for almost 15 years before it was finally re-discovered, to much amazement and excitement, by mathematicians and physicists. The same is now in danger of happening in reverse; ideas from this new mathematics are filling entire mathematical journals, but few of these ideas are filtering through into ecological and environmental journals.

Funding is needed for research to protect the environment

There is no question that funding is available for environmental research, but only a tiny fraction of this is used to address practical environmental questions. The major part of environmental funding goes towards big, fashionable topics which have little practical relevance to everyday conservation. The global picture is thus being studied intensively, but meanwhile things in our own backyard are quietly going to blazes.

The UK's NERC, ironically, regards the giving of research grants to study practical conservation issues as too applied, by which it presumably means 'too close to the environment'? It is a revealing reflection on the scientific community's view of the environment that funding for large particle accelerators runs into multimillions of pounds, but most practical conservation research survives on sums of a few thousand pounds, if, indeed *any* funding is available. This is despite the fact that, in many ways, resolving some of the practical environmental problems in our own backyard can involve working on a system as complex as, and probably more unpredictable than, some of the largest atomic physics programs. Funding for environmental protection science is still stuck in the days of 'bucket ecology', although today some of the answers being demanded are beyond the long-term predictive ability of even the most powerful computers.

Scientists need to be more explicit about information gaps and uncertainties

Precisely because much of our understanding of, and modeling capability about, the natural world is currently so limited, it is important that those reading assessments and predictions fully understand the degree of uncertainty which exists.

Greater willingness to identify such limitations can produce two benefits. Firstly, decisions can be made about development proposals on the basis of a full understanding of the risks and benefits. Secondly, regular and consistent identification of gaps will generate a rich seam of potential research projects, as well as revealing and emphasizing those areas of environmental research which urgently need to be addressed by environmental scientists.

Closing thoughts

At one time, the engineer faced a world which was filled with mystery and uncertainty. History is rich in examples of edifices such as the Tower of Babylon, many early cathedrals, the first aeroplanes, and 'unsinkable' ocean liners, which all produced rude and bewildering shocks because they ended in catastrophe. After 7000–8000 years of experimentation and trial and error, however, the engineer can now expect at least the majority of projects to behave as planned. As Furnas and McCarthy observe in Time/Life's celebration of *The Engineer*

> . . . *the engineer has changed over the years from an ingenious improviser who worked by trial and error, to a skilled and systematic specialist who brings a wealth of scientific knowledge to bear on the increasingly complex problems of today and tomorrow.*

Scientists, in their interaction with environmental problems, are still at the trial and error stage.

In adopting the strategies outlined above, we have the potential to bring the work of EIA analysis from its current state of error and anarchy closer to the structured approach of the engineer. We should aim to be able to say, if decline or disaster should occur—'Well, yes, we knew that was a gap in our knowledge-base. Let's learn from this to fill the gap and add to the knowledge-pool'. At the moment, the system doesn't even help us to learn from our mistakes.

Volcanologists can sympathize with the present plight of the environmental scientist and the EIA consultant. A sobering observation made after the catastrophic eruption of Mount St Helens in Washington State, USA (thereby ending in the state where we began), and which could apply to all who struggle to understand the natural world, expresses it thus[2]

> . . . *perhaps the most important lesson of the past 30 years has been the virtue of scientific humility: who knows which ideas that now appear untenable will turn out to be right, and which of those ideas that we currently accept on the basis of available evidence will seem hopelessly naive 2000 years from now?*

Galloping Gertie was born because Leon Moitseief, in attempting to bridge the Tacoma Narrows, accidentally strayed from the relatively calm and safe waters of established bridge engineering into the uncharted reefs of untested predictions. Those reefs cost Moitseief his reputation and Tubby Coatsworth his life.

There are currently no clear open seas for the environmental consultant embarking on an EIA; the study begins amidst reefs, beyond which are only bigger reefs. The prudent professional acknowledges every reef and makes allowance accordingly. When things become difficult, the little statue of Tubby should act as a reminder that insufficient attention to detail can destroy part of the natural world as surely as the final design of Galloping Gertie sealed the fate of the Coatsworth's dog. A little caution and a ready, unabashed acknowledgement of scientific limitations would, under the circumstances, seem very little to ask.

Notes

1. Quotes from the 1993 Channel 4 TV programme *Bridging the Future*, written and produced by Chris Haws.
2. Quote from *Volcanoes*, R. Decker and B. Decker, New York: W. Freeman and Co., 1989.

Annotated List of Further Reading

Betrayers of the Truth, William Broad and Nicholas Wade, London: Century, 1983.
   Sociologist Deena Weinstein argued in a classic study in the 1970s that there is no reason to expect any less fraud in science than in any other area of society. Broad and Wade graphically describe some of the most famous cases, but most scientists would find the fuzzy distinction between truth and invention all too familiar.

Environmental Assessment Handbook, London: Environmental Resources Ltd, 1992 (versions for England, Scotland and Wales).

The bible of the official UK conservation agencies when guiding and evaluating environmental assessments. A lucid handbook which gives much helpful advice, though rather glossing over some of the more fundamental problems of EIA work as it is necessarily practiced.

Biodiversity: The UK Action Plan, Cm 2428, London: HMSO, 1994.

The official UK Government response to the Biodiversity Convention signed in Rio. There is much that is very useful in this document for all aspects of nature conservation and environmental protection. It contains some very clear statements indicating the need to recognize uncertainty and act with caution when carrying out activities which may affect the environment.

Can Science Save its Soul?, Mary Midgley, *New Scientist*, 1 August, 1992. *How Science Fails the Environment*, Brian Wynne and Sue Mayer, *New Scientist*, 5 June, 1993. *The Perils of Green Pessimism*, Alex Milne, *New Scientist*, 12 June, 1993.

An entertaining and sometimes illuminating set of articles about environmental precaution and responsibility. Midgley is a philosopher, Wynne a sociologist, Mayer an environmentalist and Milne an industrial scientist.

Marine Pollution Bulletin, 1990–1992.

Contains a series of articles and letters about the precautionary principle, sparked off by Professor John Gray's short paper in the 1990 volume, *Statistics and the Precautionary Principle*. Various means of approaching the precautionary principle are discussed, and although the issue is not resolved, a number of useful points are brought out.

Darrell Addison Posey.
Credit: Oliver Tickell

Author biography

Originally trained as a biologist, Darrell Posey studied anthropology and became one of the founders of the subject of ethnobiology, which he researched and developed during 15 years of work with the Kayapó people of Amazonia, recently winning a United Nations Global 500 Award. Author of numerous articles and books, he is at the Brazilian National Council for Science and Technology and is a Visiting Scholar at the Institute for Social and Cultural Anthropology, University of Oxford.

Chapter 11

Darrell Addison Posey

Indigenous Knowledge and Green Consumerism: Cooperation or Conflict?

A SERIES of meetings in London in May 1990, signaled a new wave of economic activity to establish a greener road towards saving the planet. Opened by HRH the Prince Charles, the international gathering called The Rainforest Harvest, was sponsored by the Royal Geographical Society, the British Overseas Development Administration and the Body Shop. The sponsorship sounds like a strange mixture of science, government and private enterprise—and the participants represented an even stranger mixture of Amazonian Indian leaders, ethnobiologists, human rights activists, environmentalists, economists, Members of Parliament, New Age thinkers, international lawyers, business entrepreneurs and royalty.

The meetings attempted to show that the *living* rainforest and its *living* inhabitants hold countless secrets about new, natural and sustainably produced products that are practically bursting out of the trees to reach concerned and enlightened consumers in the developed world. Just imagine, a new generation of soaps, oils, insect repellents, food colorings, clothes softeners, perfumes, foods and medicines which are produced in ways that preserve the biological and ecological diversity of the planet's endangered rainforests, while at the same time actually benefiting the people who teach us about them and conserve the plants from which they are produced.

In this way, consumers of the world can unite to 'vote' through their individual consumption for the way they want the future of their planet. An international 'consumer democracy' seems a possible pragmatic response to the new world order that depends more upon international economic links than geopolitical alliances.

Miraculous? Perhaps, but miracles are needed to save the rainforest and the peoples of the rainforest—and many think even bigger miracles are needed to halt the destruction of the planet. In recent years, an area of tropical rainforest the size of Belgium has been annually destroyed in the Brazilian Amazon alone. No-one knows how many cultures have become extinct in the wake of this habitat destruction—and even the most sophisticated scientific studies cannot measure knowledge loss due to cultural degradation.

For many years there have been warnings of the impending destruction of the Amazon and the implications of those losses for all of humanity. As Michael Irwin has pointed out for the Amazonian region: 'Scientists are competing with extinction in their race to inventory what the world contains. Amerindians are the only societies with the necessary knowledge, expertise, and tradition to prosper in the Amazon jungle. Amerindians not only profoundly appreciate what exists, but also understand ecological interrelations of the various components of the Amazonian ecosystem better than do modern ecologists. Indians perceive specific relationships which biologists are only now discovering to be accurate'.

Traditional knowledge of medicinal plants, natural insecticides and repellents, fertility-regulating drugs, edible plants, animal behavior, climatic and ecological seasonality, soils, forest and savannah management, skin and body treatments attest to but a few of the categories of knowledge that can contribute to new strategies for ecologically and socially sound sustained development. However, as work by Richard and Michael McNeil has pointed out: 'knowledge has sometimes been extracted from rainforest people . . . in transactions which may be characterized as unjust and illegal. From both moral and legal standpoints we may have obligations to compensate people of these tribal societies for the immensely valuable intellectual property which we obtained from them'.

Yet native peoples and their knowledge systems are threatened with imminent destruction. Eighty-five Brazilian Indian groups became extinct in the first half of this century. In the Amazonian region a conservative estimate would be that, on average, one Amerindian group has disappeared for each year of this century. Unfortunately, we have no calculations showing the worldwide extent of cultural extinction.

In many cases, indigenous societies are becoming extinct at an even faster rate than the regions they have traditionally inhabited. Culture change is so rapid for many groups that young people no longer learn the methods by which their ancestors maintained fragile regions. This is a global tragedy, for with the disappearance of each indigenous group the world loses an accumulated wealth of millennia of human experience and adaptation. One should not be too hasty in the pronouncement that native peoples are all becoming extinct. Demographically, native groups, with guarantees of land rights as well as political and economic independence, have some of the fastest growing populations in the world.

Indigenous communities and the need for economic options

Indigenous leaders frequently voice concerns about the lack of economic options that allow them to avoid the ecologically destructive ways of the industrialized world. How can traditional knowledge be defended and valued within a native society when, in fact, such knowledge offers little economic benefit to indigenous groups caught in the maze of consumerism and basic survival?

Kayapó chief, Paiakan, has often spoken of how warriors from his people traveled to the Brazilian capital during the Constitution Convention to defend native peoples against proposals that, if included in the new constitution, would have stripped many groups of their protective status as Indians. Had the physical presence of the Kayapó lobby not been evident during the Convention, Indians would not have achieved the new laws which guarantee to them in the new Constitution the right to independent legal representation, and decisions regarding their lands would still be signed behind closed doors by government officials.

The Kayapó were in a fortunate position: they are relatively wealthy Indians, whose money comes from mining and lumber extraction. Ironically, with all of the much-heralded biological and ecological richness of Amazonia, the only products which command stable and reasonable prices are cattle, minerals and timber—all of which require the destruction of tropical ecosystems. It was with gold and timber money that the Kayapó sent on many occasions their delegations of 100 or more warriors on the costly 1000 km trip to Brasília. 'If we had not had that money', explained Chief Paiakan, 'Brazilian Indians would have had to sit helplessly on their reserves as the politicians did exactly what they wanted. The government certainly was not interested in funding our journeys to the Capitol. Indians these days must have financial resources too. Our people want radios and batteries for their tape recorders. We need the White Man's clothes when we go to the city— and we must go to the city to defend ourselves against those who would dispossess us of our lands and turn us all into fourth class citizens with no food, medicine, or money.'

Indigenous knowledge and its worth

Industry and business discovered many years ago that indigenous knowledge means money. In the earliest forms of colonialism, extractive products (called 'drogas de sertão' in Brazil) were the basis for colonial wealth. More recently, pharmaceutical industries have become the major exploiters of traditional medicinal knowledge for major products and profits.

Rarely do native peoples benefit from the marketing of traditional knowledge or natural products that were 'discovered' from native peoples. For example, less than 0.001% of profits from drugs that originated from traditional medicine have ever gone to the indigenous peoples who led researchers to them.

Growing interest and catapulting markets in 'natural' food, medicinal, agricultural and body products signals increased research activities into traditional knowledge systems. Now, more than ever, the intellectual property rights of native peoples must be protected, and just compensation for knowledge guaranteed. We cannot simply rely upon the goodwill of companies and institutions to do right by indigenous peoples. If something is not done now, mining of the riches of indigenous knowledge will become the latest—and ultimate—neocolonial form of exploitation of native peoples.

Perhaps what is needed is a re-ordering of priorities and values: a new code of ethno-ethics. The code would not depend upon any international laws or conventions, would not be legislated in congresses or parliaments, nor depend upon enforcement of copyrights or patents.

It would depend upon scientists who explained to the natives they study what they are doing and why it is important for the people themselves. Researchers should voluntarily sign contracts with native groups guaranteeing a percentage of any profits from medicines, films, new plant varieties, books, or whatever. (Appendix 1 shows the efforts of the International Society for Ethnobiology to develop a responsible and ethical relationship as expressed in The Declaration of Belém). Businesses should guarantee excellent prices for natural materials, help local peoples add value to those materials and profit from their activities, help them market the products and return a percentage of the profits to the community. Film and television crews should pay generous prices for filming native peoples and return some of the profits.

But as I realize that, even if this new eco-ethno-ethic were to come to pass, the exceptions would require the rules, then it is important that our ideals be rooted firmly in international laws that juridically protect the intellectual property rights of native peoples.

Consumer education, aided by surveillance by non-governmental organizations, can go a long way to make a new code of ethics work. Informed consumers have made major differences in production patterns in the past, and can do so in the future. Maybe it is time for an international 'consumer democracy' that empowers each consumer to act in a responsible way that directly affects the planet's human and natural resources.

Planetary resources are already stretched due to current levels of consumption: imagine what will happen with all the new demands. In the euphoria of what it has labeled 'victory', Western capitalism will now be put to the ecological and social test.

For 'consumer democracy' to work, alternative products must be developed and the consumers educated to the social and ecological benefits of what may be more costly products. A few successful projects working with native communities to develop their own natural products, markets and distribution contacts would go a long way. Or, alternatively, a few more successful projects utilizing native medicinal or edible plants, or cosmetic preparations that really take care to study the social and ecological impact of management decisions and work with the communities to determine what just compensation should mean, would be more effective than hundreds of national and international laws.

Certainly the mechanisms of what is just compensation and how such benefits would be distributed opens a Pandora's box. But to *not* open this box is to accept the ethical and moral responsibility of paternalism (those from 'advanced societies' know what is good for the 'native' because we have already made the mistakes of squandering our cultural and natural wealth) that has undermined indigenous independence since the first wave of colonialism.

Native peoples must have the right to choose for themselves. Without economic independence, such a choice is not possible. Nonetheless, many will oppose intellectual property rights for indigenous peoples because they know that they too will have to drastically change their working lifestyles. Incomes from published dissertations and other books, slides, magazine articles, phonograph records, films and videos—all will have to include a percentage of the profits to the native subjects. It will probably become normal that such rights be negotiated with native peoples before undertaking initial fieldwork. This kind of behavior has never been considered as part of the professional ethic of scientific research and business, but certainly must become so in the near future.

Linking biodiversity, intellectual property rights and markets

The links between biological and cultural diversity are inherent in the Biodiversity Convention which was signed by 126 Heads of State during The Earth Summit in June 1993. Specifically with regard to indigenous peoples and their rights, the Preamble establishes the 'desirability of sharing equitably benefits arising from the use of traditional knowledge innovations and practices relevant to the conservation of biological diversity and the sustainable use of its components'. Article 8(j) calls for the promotion of a 'wider sharing' of traditional knowledge, as well as an 'equitable sharing of the benefits arising from the utilisation of such knowledge, innovations and practices'. And, finally, in Article 18(4), a call to 'encourage and develop methods of co-operation for the development and use of technologies including indigenous and traditional technologies' can be found.

Although the language of these sections has been harshly criticized by indigenous peoples, the wording nonetheless represents a considerable advancement in international language. If nothing else, the Convention frees up—and gives a clear mandate to—the relevant UN agencies and programs to do something about indigenous knowledge and its protection.

Chapter 26 of 'Agenda 21' deals specifically with indigenous peoples' traditional knowledge and sustainable development. This list of 'priorities for action' is more than adequate to direct major global resources into the use, application (and protection) of indigenous peoples, their cultures, physical and intellectual resources. The importance of doing such is summarized in Principle 22 of the Rio Declaration

> *Indigenous people and their communities, and other local communities, have a vital role in environmental management and development because of their knowledge and traditional practices. States should recognize and duly support their identity, culture and interests and enable their effective participation in the achievement of sustainable development.*

Some kinks in the model

Ecologists are justifiably concerned with the ecological impact of production of 'natural products' that become too successful. The tendency is always toward monocultures of cash crops. Many worry that international demands may spell the end of biodiversity, rather than encourage conservation of natural resources as initially desired. As Michael Soulé and Kathryn Kohm have put it

> *Increased pressure on biological resources arises because of increasing human populations, changing consumption patterns, and new technologies. Although agricultural intensification will continue to be necessary, its impact on biological resources is not predetermined. Conservation poses important research questions relevant to the design of new production technologies and land use systems: Can biologically diverse and low energy technologies be*

extended and/or intensified? Can production systems be differentially intensified so as to maintain biological diversity in other parts of a system? How does increased exploitation of specific species affect other species and general system properties?

Anthony Anderson has drawn attention to the relatively low productivity of some traditional models of economic exploitation, including, most specifically, the 'extractive reserves'. He shows how reliance on only Brazil nuts and rubber is not only economically impoverishing, but decreases biodiversity as well. 'Before we can work to improve extractive reserves', he argues, 'we need a critical vision of their limitations. While it is necessary to clear the air of some of the romantic myths associated with extraction, I would disagree with the contention that extractivists are marginal elements in the process of frontier expansion in Amazonia and that we should, therefore, concentrate our efforts in improving land-uses among the numerous colonists'. 'In a practical sense', says Anderson, 'the forces struggling against deforestation in Amazonia are vanishingly small, and it is imperative that allies and battleground be chosen carefully.'

John Browder is yet another persistent voice in pointing out the over-rated productivity of traditional Amazonian models of exploitation. He expounds the somewhat politically incorrect position that Chico Mendès and 'his rubber tappers', for example, were a political movement and not an environmental one. Quite to the contrary, says he, rubber tappers will deplete their resource base as any other group will when given the chance. He maintains that too many funds have gone to 'help one small segment of the rural poor hold onto their cultural heritage and economic way of life', while what is needed are 'solutions for millions of other poor inhabitants of tropical forests'.

Thus too many resources have gone towards supporting the limited 'extractive reserve' model, while abandoning the 'landless peasants, small farmers and even big ranchers to find financially profitable uses for tropical forests'.

Likewise, Kent Redford has warned that many 'traditional societies' heavily exploit the fauna of their reserves and provoke reduction, even local extinction of heavily hunted species. This process of 'defaunation' can also lead to 'ecological extinction', defined as 'the reduction of a species' abundance, so that, although it is still present in the community, it no longer interacts significantly with other species'. Indigenous peoples, says he, are not the 'ecological noble savages' we have made them out to be. The degree of ecosystem destruction on the global level may mean that, in some cases, the only way to conserve biodiversity is to abolish all types of human behavior—from road-building and timber extraction to indigenous hunting and extractivism.

Provocations of cultural changes can be equally concerning. By establishing mechanisms for just compensation of native peoples, are we not also establishing mechanisms for the destruction of their societies through the subversion of materialism and consumerism?

Stephen Cory, Director General of Survival International, one of the major indigenous rights groups, is one of the most radical opponents to 'the harvest'. He points out that, historically, indigenous peoples and local communities have never fared well with the vastly more powerful outside economic system. He has even gone so far as to suggest that in the famous rape case of Kayapó chief Paiakan, it was the Kayapó's relationship with The Body Shop that was ultimately to blame for the chief's alleged disastrous behavior.

The 'harvest ideology', charges Cory, 'reveals itself to be essentially an integrationist argument dressed in snazzy, green clothes; a retrograde philosophy which, if allowed to gain momentum, could set the campaign for tribal peoples back 25 years or more by playing right into the hands of those who want to *oppose* the movement for land rights.' He continues, 'If allowed to take hold, this new integrationist ethic masquerading as environmentalism will be deeply corrosive to the struggle which so many indigenous peoples' organisations are waging to teach the outside world that their land is not for sale and that they will not put a cash value on it any more than they would sell their own mother.'

In a recent attack on Cultural Survival and The Body Shop, Cory describes all trading with indigenous peoples as 'slow poison' and those involved in such activities as 'not rainforest traders, but rainforest raiders, squeezing what they can out of the public's goodwill and the latest forest fashion.'

Indigenous societies and their natural environments are being destroyed by the dramatic expansion of industrialized society *now*. Good or bad, pharmaceutical companies and 'natural products' companies have tasted success in their efforts: they will not go away. It is also fairly obvious that, like it or not, an ecosystem that has no value will be leveled to make way for whatever system has value—even if only on a limited scale and for only short-term profits in its place.

Besides, says Jason Clay of Cultural Survival, 'Even the most isolated peoples in the rainforests, with few exceptions, have needs that only the market place can meet . . . We might leave such groups alone, but others won't. We could even think about building a fence around them, or around the whole Amazon, but these options aren't workable. And if the destruction of their land continues at its present pace, all will be over for them soon.'

'For this reason', Clay continues, 'we must act quickly. This is where the links between human-rights violations and poverty on the one hand and environmental degradation on the other enter in. It turns out that the most successful strategies for conserving rainforests maintain their natural biodiversity *and* meet the economic needs of the forest peoples . . . Cultural Survival hasn't abandoned its work on land rights, political organising, and sustainable development; we have added a dimension to it. Simply put, we seek markets for sustainably harvested rainforest products that can help support those who live in the rain forest.'

The 'turf war' between the Body Shop, Cultural Survival and Survival International has received extensive press coverage. More than any other issue in recent memory, 'the harvest' has put researchers, biologists, human and indigenous rights groups, and average citizens in a state of perplexity. It is not a question of the 'the good, the bad and the ugly' versus the 'right, the saintly, and the true heroes'. The real tragedy may be that the concern for the rainforest and its peoples gets harshly and unceremoniously divided between patron groups.

In my opinion, the current conflict will result in the ultimate move by indigenous peoples to divest themselves of all intermediaries, taking the opportunity to exert their independence and global consciousness that has been emerging for 30 years—and exploding in the last decade. Thus, in the long run, the whole ordeal will have a positive outcome.

The future

The current devastation of native peoples and the ecological systems that they have conserved, managed and intimately known for millennia, requires that new and drastic steps be taken to reorient world priorities. All channels and organizations—governmental, nongovernmental, professional, business—must work together to reverse the current momentum in the loss of cultural, ecological and biological diversity of this planet.

Three major changes would at least be a move in the right direction are:

1. recognition that native peoples hold the key to understanding the rational use and management of these living natural areas, and probably others;
2. giving economic value to the *living* forest and natural habitats by giving increased value to natural products based on traditional knowledge and produced by local communities;
3. developing legal and practical mechanisms for the just compensation of native peoples for their knowledge through the guarantees of intellectual property rights for traditional knowledge.

Appendix: Declaration of Belém

Leading anthropologists, biologists, chemists, sociologists and representatives of several indigenous populations met in Belém, Brazil to discuss common concerns at the First International Congress of Ethnobiology and to found the International Society of Ethnobiology. The major concerns outlined by conference contributors were the study of the ways that indigenous and peasant populations uniquely perceive, utilize and manage their natural resources and the development of programs that will guarantee the preservation of vital biological and cultural diversity. This declaration was articulated.

As ethnobiologists we are alarmed that since

• tropical forests and other fragile ecosystems are disappearing

- many species, both plant and animal, are threatened with extinction
- indigenous cultures around the world are being disrupted and destroyed

and given

- that economic, agricultural and health conditions of people are dependent on these resources
- that native peoples have been stewards of 99% of the world's genetic resources
- that there is an inextricable link between cultural and biological diversity

we, members of the International Society of Ethnobiology, strongly urge action as follows

1. Henceforth, a substantial proportion of development aid be devoted to efforts aimed at ethnobiological inventory, conservation and management programs
2. Mechanisms be established by which indigenous specialists are recognized as proper authorities and are consulted in all programs affecting them, their resources and their environment
3. All other alienable human rights be recognized and guaranteed, including cultural and linguistic identity
4. Procedures be developed to compensate native peoples for the utilization of their knowledge and their biological resources
5. Educational programs be implemented to alert the global community to the value of ethnobiological knowledge for human wellbeing
6. All medical programs include the recognition of and respect for traditional healers and the incorporation of traditional health practices that enhance the status of these populations
7. Ethnobiologists make available the results of their research to the native peoples with whom they have worked, especially including dissemination in the native language
8. Exchange of information be promoted among indigenous and peasant peoples regarding conservation, management and sustained utilization of resources.

Annotated List of Further Reading

Ethnobotany: A People and Plants Conservation Manual, Gary Martin, London: Chapman & Hall, 1994.

An authoritative guide to the practical study and conservation of plant resources in their social and ecological context.

Alternatives to Deforestation: Steps Towards Sustainable Use of the Amazon Rain Forest, Anthony B. Anderson, Boston: Island Press, 1990.

A book with a rich collection of papers by Amazonian researchers working to find ways of utilizing, while conserving, natural resources.

Indigenous Peoples and Tropical Forests: Models of Land Use and Management from Latin America, Jason W. Clay, Boston: Cultural Survival, 1988.

A brief survey of indigenous natural resource management projects in Latin America that shows the relevance of indigenous knowledge to biodiversity conservation.

Plants for People, Anna Lewington, London: Natural History Museum Publications, 1989.

A popular and colorful glimpse of the importance of plants to people and vice versa.

Intellectual Property Rights and Just Compensation for Indigenous Knowledge, Darrell A. Posey, *Anthropology Today*, 6 (4), pp. 13–16, 1990. The first publication to link the concept of intellectual property rights with indigenous peoples and their rights, calling attention to the role of anthropologists and other scientists in addressing a growing issue.

Stephen Tomkins

Author biography

Stephen Tomkins has taught biology in schools, and written texts for students, in both the industrialized and non-industrialized world. He played an early part in developing East Africa's science curriculum, and has taught in Cambridgeshire community colleges and a large sixth form college in Cambridge. He has developed the new school subject of natural economy and is well aware, as an examiner, of how the examined curriculum drives what is taught in the classroom. He is now concerned principally with teacher education, as Head of Science at Homerton College, University of Cambridge. He is devoted to keeping brine shrimps in 'Gaia bottles' on his windowsill and in thus encouraging children to experiment in the design of sustainable ecosystems.

Chapter 12

Stephen Tomkins

Science for the Earth Starts at School

In the end we will conserve only what we love, we will love only what we understand, we will understand only what we are taught.

Baba Dioum, Senegal poet

THE aim of this chapter is to examine school science teaching in the context of the wider question of how to steer a large proportion of the human species away from its abuse of the global environment. Teachers are challenged to find the most effective way of conveying to their pupils the urgency of the action that seems to be needed. It is important to understand what teachers are trying to do and the context within which they operate. There are many significant and exciting things going on in schools. I conclude that working scientists should regard it as a duty to involve themselves more with children's education.

For teachers in their day to day work, the sentiment expressed by Baba Dioum is more pragmatic and hopeful than some of the siren voices elsewhere in this book, however pertinent. It expresses well the challenge to all those concerned with science and education. Even if we have only been successful, so far, in formulating that very simple goal, the concept of *sustainability*, we have begun to make change a reality.

I want to follow two lines of thought: one examines the place of schools in bringing about social change and the other looks at the place of science in schools as agents of education for change. Although I draw largely on the English, European and Western tradition, much the same may apply to other areas of the world.

Environmental abuse is not new; it goes way-back into prehistory. Lyn White, 25 years ago, laid some of the blame for our environmental ills on the Judaeo-Christian tradition. Even if guilty, out of that dominating culture undoubtedly emerged much of our science and our contemporary worldview. For our own survival there is only one option: to be assertively positive about our capability and very forward-looking. This is what education is all about.

Schools in society

Changing the way people think is a major social as well as educational enterprise. It is important to ask, first of all, how effective schools are in giving impetus to the direction of social change. Emile Durkheim, the founding father of sociology, saw the function of education as the transmission of society's norms and values. He maintained that a society would only cohere if its individual members were led to see that cooperation and social solidarity were important. Durkheim's views are broadly accepted and are reflected today, for example, in the way that children in the USA, through a common curriculum and despite a diversity of ethnic origins, achieve a national social allegiance. Durkheim saw history as the vehicle for this process of socialization: the American student, beginning each day with a national oath of allegiance, learns about the Founding Fathers, the Constitution, Abraham Lincoln and the roots of democracy. Clearly, schools are powerful agents of such socialization.

Why can we not then just teach environmentalism and see a rapid change? Anyone training to be a school teacher may be given a rather damning dictum to consider; after more than a quarter of a century in the classroom it is no less poignant to me than it was when I first heard it. It is this: 'If the pupil has not learned, the teacher has not taught'. After all their exposure, then, to environmental thinking, why is it that children, on becoming adults, are so unable to alter the behavior of the society into which they go? Surely, in some respect, the teachers have let the children down, for are not schools the social milieu in which our children develop their skills and formulate their own ideas and attitudes? Most people outside the world of sociology probably see education in schools as highly formative and powerful in its effect on the ability of a society to change. It certainly feels that way to those who have achieved academic success, and indeed it is often the hope of young teachers entering the profession that it may be so. Perhaps schools are a reflection of the society within which they lie to a far greater extent than they are able to operate as agents of its social transformation. Durkheim, although in the end an optimist for the power of schooling to generate social change, saw that Education '. . . is only the image and reflection of society. It imitates and reproduces the latter in abbreviated form; it does not create it. Education is healthy only when peoples themselves are in a healthy state; but it becomes corrupt with them, being unable to modify itself. If the moral environment is affected, since the teachers dwell in it they cannot avoid being influenced . . . Education, therefore, can be reformed only if society itself is reformed'.

Are schools not then the place to begin? Adopting the quest to achieve a more sustainable human ecology may well involve a huge change in societal values, and in this schools have a long record of assisting change. In this respect it is worth looking over our shoulder and examining some transformations in social and educational history from the recent past. In Britain, in the 19th century, there was a great debate (amongst the educated elite) as to whether the proposed development of mass education would serve the forthcoming industrial revolution by providing a minimally educated workforce alone or whether, in addition, the resulting enlightenment of the underclass might not also sow the seeds of revolution and destruction of the ruling elite's control of power. The former argument that the mass of the people should be educated to fulfill the industrial need won the day. What followed in the schools, however, was a gradual shift away from the original emphasis on the societal goal of training for the task, which was undoubtedly realized, towards the enlightenment view of education, emanating originally from Rousseau, of empowering each individual through their education to better themselves. Society has changed hugely as a result and the original elite's forebodings over their loss of power has also been amply fulfilled.

In Britain and in the USA in particular, the self-reliance and hard work ethic has enabled many of those with talent and industry to break through social barriers. In Britain, that initial tension over the aims of mass education is still very much here today. Schooling is seen to consist both of a training that is given to suit a social and economic purpose, and as a truly liberating education that empowers individuals to change themselves for their own good, to perhaps challenge ruling elites and vault social barriers. Government, which controls funding of state education, not surprisingly, sees education in terms of training. Most teachers are very hostile to too great an emphasis on training alone and are very committed to the widest education for their children. As a consequence, much of the quality of our Western educational system resides in what David Hargreaves has described as its *culture of individualism*, standing as it does for creativity, freedom and autonomy.

The freedom that most of us espouse has a huge demand for responsibility attached to it. Durkheim saw, in the late 19th century, the negative side of the liberation of the individual and it worried him to see the decline of commitment by individuals to corporate social goals. He disliked the excessive individualism (egoism) and the lack of social obligation (anomie) that he saw it produce. The very individual freedom which education brings may also corrupt and undermine commitment to social structures. Certainly, our industrialized societies are now experiencing a more massive culture of individualism than ever before, and much societal breakdown. We urgently need to understand the interplay between these societal and attitudinal changes and our own behavior as a species. This has a great bearing on environmental issues. Today we find governments, often not a little unsure of where they are going, over-centralizing their power. It is interesting that Durkheim saw the best social control of egoism and anomie in the decentralizing of power. He came to recognize that societies were most able to steer away from such destructive forces where there was a broad base of different social groups working to influence the wider society, each of which exercised real effect. Thus governments which, in centralizing their power, deride and undercut such institutions as trade unions, professional associations, teachers, or the voice of local communities or religious groups, may do so in a way that often makes a constructive social change more difficult.

Where does this leave schools? Clearly schools and universities are socially formative institutions, but what they contribute to the way a society behaves is only a small part of the whole. Environmental lobbies, such as the World Wide Fund for Nature (WWF), Greenpeace, Friends of the Earth and the Royal Society for the Protection of Birds (RSPB), in the UK, well recognize the importance of influence in the various social power groups and legitimately try to permeate them with their thinking. For example, a particularly powerful and persuasive document has been produced by the RSPB seeking to influence the whole of Further and Higher Education curricula with sustainable development thinking.

Those wishing to press for a change in environmental thought must openly acknowledge that they are engaged in a socializing process and must not overdramatize situations for the short-term benefit. Typically, teachers are very wary of proselytizing organizations and children may well be very hostile to what may become perceived as 'establishment' pro-environment pressure in the curriculum—'Oh no, not *Saving the Rainforest* again!'. On the credit side, human freedom to protest and organize campaigns for the environment are a product of this culture of individualism. We would do well to remember that adolescent children are the most assertive individualists and not without power in lobbying for social and environmental change.

Within schools, it is often the vociferous and isolated teacher who will fight for an environmental perspective being part of the curriculum. Once it is established there are undoubted benefits in having a social milieu of school training in which environmental thinking becomes more second nature. Much is currently achieved in schools, for example, by a quiet insistence on patterns of behavior which respect wildlife, engender compassion for endangered environments and stimulate environmentally caring behavior. Thus the management of nature areas, or the practice of tree planting or of paper and aluminum can recycling are important. But, unsurprisingly, to most environmentally concerned teachers these feel woefully inadequate, and many teachers are spurred to proselytize for those causes that they feel most passionately about. I have recent memories of opposing, at a full meeting of a Governing Body, the siting of a staff car park on a meadow patch of cowslips in a school grounds. Classrooms had been built on the old car park, yet the 'nature area', arguably an open-air classroom in itself, despite protest, eventually went under the tarmac. It is a fine line for teachers to tread, surrounded as they are by self-doubt as to their perceived eccentricity on the one side, and cynicism as to the point of trying to stop 'the inevitable' on the other. Environmental leadership is essential to provide an ambience that gently challenges prevailing social attitudes. To their credit, most schools aim to challenge both children and society. The seemingly mad ecology lecturer who announced to his students that he would not mark, read or even accept a written assignment that was not written on the back of already once-used sheets of paper is making a public statement of environmental commitment. Such a teacher's stand is certainly one that will make students sit up and think again; they may even need to go and find some paper from a waste bin to recycle.

To conclude, the environmental ethic which we seek will require a large element of social engineering to be successful. It is right that we should promote our cause and fully acknowledge what we are doing. We need to embrace a gentle subversion. However, we also need to stand up for the culture of individualism at the same time and to curb its selfish vices into a more collaborative, communal, altruistic and committed frame. At the heart of doing this, in schools, lies a discipline in simple living, even an asceticism, an honesty with children and an openness to their needs and questions. We need to follow with them in their personal discovery of Nature. We need to value and praise their work and skills. Such adult behavior with the young builds equilibrial societies that may be able to work out a more sustainable future.

Science for the Earth in schools

How much science is now taught in schools? How do children learn science and what is meant by 'science', in this school context? Is the science that is taught sufficiently integrated, scientifically and culturally, to address the needs of both the general populace and the few who will need specialist training in environmental matters?

Science is being taught in schools to an increasing extent. In the UK the changes have been dramatic. In 1950, science was only taught to a minority of the most academically inclined children at secondary level. It was easy to pass through the elite education system with barely any science or maths courses. Comprehensive schools widened the access to science and made all manner of course combinations possible for children. Such schools have also fostered specialism, perhaps at the expense of a broader grounding in humanities subjects for those keen to pursue their science. Awareness of equal opportunities has expanded the access to science for women. The National Curriculum was introduced, in part, to marshal this diversity of opportunity into a more coherent and common frame and to raise standards. Science, with maths and English, is today a National Curriculum foundation subject and is compulsory within the school curriculum for all students to the age of 16, occupying for most approximately 20% of class time. The way in which the National Curriculum is delivered is not prescribed. Certain learning outcomes are required, but the teaching approaches and precise nature of the content within the subjects will be left up to the teachers. Soon there should be no reason why any intelligent student at 16 +, in the UK, should not be able to read and understand articles in popular science.

What is meant by 'science', in a school context? There are, as amply demonstrated elsewhere in this book, different perceptions of what it means to scientists. Perhaps two different expressions of science find a place in schools. Firstly, science describes the framework of thinking and knowing, the paradigms, in which one operates in attempting to solve the puzzles that the world presents. This is what T. S. Kuhn called 'normal science' and is what, for children, delivers 'the facts'. Learning about the world we live in proceeds upon assumptions, and Kuhn has described how a science with a firm set of agreed ideas and procedures develops a confidence and maturity in its field. Taking a paradigm for granted enables one to make speedy progress in puzzle-solving and one thing builds certainly upon another in one's picture of the way the world appears to be. Most of what goes on in schools, as science, is firmly set within this rather *unquestioning* frame. Uncritically presented, it leads to what teachers call 'subject content'. Secondly, science is widely seen as a process of application and testing of knowledge, through observation and experiment, where conjectures are ruthlessly criticized. Both the encouragement of a free and creative imagination and a skeptical and disciplined criticism is vital. In schools, this is encouraged as much as possible through experimental and investigative science and most particularly through individual student investigations. For the best teachers and their pupils it means that the process of getting to the answer is a most important part of the enterprise. This emphasis on 'process' is firmly enshrined in the National Curriculum also.

Good teachers keep content and process in balance. School experimental science can often ring a bit hollow for able students, for they often perceive that what looks like an open-ended experiment at first sight is merely a ritual investigation to assert the authority of the paradigm within which they are operating. 'What is supposed to happen?', they ask, 'Why did my experiment go wrong?'. This is a serious difficulty in science teaching and it fails to produce an adequate climate of thinking. It has been aptly put that, in the last analysis, we need young scientists who question the answers, not just answer the questions. However, to say this in school can be rather trite, for students know only too well that they have 'got to know the facts' and teachers are judged by the quality of their students' exam results as well. In school science, therefore, the quest is always on for investigations that allow the experimenter to ask questions simply and get answers relatively quickly.

In ecology this is difficult because things work so slowly. We therefore need to work on the small scale, which is also cheaper. You can ask microorganisms questions about how they like to live in a Petri dish. You can ask a duckweed (the scientific name of which is *Lemna*) what light and nutrient regime it prefers, and what pollutants it will tolerate, employing a series of tiny vessels (like discarded film canisters). We can have students play with very small model ecosystems, like *Artemia salina* (brine shrimp) ponds in bottles, in which the environmental parameters may be manipulated to test hypotheses about environmental effects. In such a scenario, one student's bottle community will certainly behave differently from another, even if all the bottles were set up together with as many variables as possible controlled. In such a small ecosystem many relationships may be observed. Changes in temperature, oxygen and pH may be monitored by datalogging with a computer. There is here an educational challenge, to build little ecosystems, 'Gaia bottles', that model what happens in the larger world (see Figure 12.1). A small group of us have developed the 'Gaia bottle' idea over the past few years and taken it to several international science education festivals, such as Edinburgh. We think that it represents one of the best ways of demonstrating that humans must live, like the shrimp, with limited resources and that without other organisms to recycle our waste, and hence grow our food, we could not exist at all.

An education in science should ideally initiate students into a tradition of putting concepts at their disposal and in teaching them how to use them to good effect. Much of the teaching about science has been in that older mold where emphasis was on content and the acquisition of a body of 'correct' information. Such teaching tended to come from a relatively rigid and prescribed curriculum. The newer paradigms of education (see Table 12.1) contain more that chimes well with better science. As Marilyn Ferguson has made clear, the purpose of education, in an age of change, is to learn how to learn, for our minds need to be flexible and adaptable. We need to let go theories that no longer explain things adequately and set to and seek new explanations and methods. Teachers have a huge responsibility for helping young people to find these new horizons.

In looking at the way in which children come to an understanding of the world it is vital that children's sensory

Figure 12.1. A sustainable closed ecosystem model, a Gaia bottle, for observation and experiment. Brine shrimps in a marine microbial ecosystem may be kept in a discarded plastic bottle. Provided with full light, the ecosystem establishes a permanence that will endure for months even when the bottle is sealed. Such 'bottled planets' are highly suitable for investigation by young scientists. Further details from Shrimp World Watchers, Homerton College, Cambridge, UK

and observational experiences are paramount. The emphasis in junior school science is rightly upon touching, seeing, feeling, tasting and smelling. Urban living has destroyed a freshness in personal discovery and produced an alienation from the plants and animals that feed and clothe us. Perhaps the start of good school science is the rediscovery of that young hunter-gatherer within each of

Table 12.1. Two paradigms of education (after Marilyn Ferguson)

Old	New
Emphasis on *content*, acquiring a body of 'correct' information, once and for all.	Emphasis on learning how to learn, ask good questions, pay attention to the right things, be open to and evaluate new concepts, gain access to information. What is now 'known' may change.
Learning as a product.	Learning as a process.
Hierarchical and authoritarian structure. Rewards conformity, discourages dissent.	Egalitarian. Candour and dissent permitted. Students and teachers see each other as people, not roles. Encourages autonomy.
Relatively rigid structure, prescribed curriculum.	Relatively flexible structure. Belief that there are many ways to teach a given subject.
Priority on performance.	Priority on self-image as the generator of performance.

us. The marvellous *Naturalists' Handbooks* series (see Figure 12.2 and reading list) have pioneered this approach, allowing children to make real and valuable discoveries of the natural world for themselves. Once imagination is fired and reasoning capacity enlarges, most children become devoted to environmental exploration and discovery.

There are real problems with space and time that, initially, young minds cannot grapple with easily. It is worth thinking hard about what we are asking children to cope with in the full extent of Nature's size and scale. Children know about atoms and they have seen stars. At one extreme, the diameter of an atomic nucleus is about

Figure 12.2. The *Naturalists' Handbooks* series, edited by Henry Disney and Sarah Corbet of the University of Cambridge. They combine easy to use identification keys that allow everyone to 'make discoveries' with authoritative descriptions of plant and animal ecology

1×10^{-15} m wide, at the other extreme the nearest star to us (after the Sun) is about 1×10^{15} m away. Thirty places of decimals are a lot to cope with. We may try to simplify these matters of scale by saying, for example, that the ratio of size between a virus and a human is in the same proportion as that between a human and

Figure 12.3. Perceiving size and scale in science. The ratio between the size of a virus and a child is the same as that between the child and the whole world

the whole Earth (see Figure 12.3). This helps, but this is only a factor of 10^7 each way. From the virus to planet Earth spans just 10^{14} out of the 10^{30} dimensional scale that we expect children's imaginations to encompass.

Getting human evolution in perspective, which is hard for most people, is much easier with such figurative processes, not in space, but in time. Geneticist Steve Jones has pointed out that if you can visualize a long line of ancestrally related humans, all holding hands, one may translate it into a picture of evolutionary time. If each individual is holding hands along a line of time, each with their own child on the one side and one parent on the other, you have a line running from yourself at one end, in the present, back in time to your ape-like ancestor. The intriguing thing is that this line is only a few hundred kilometers in length. Such a hand-holding from London to York will span five million years. This line of both DNA transmission and cultural Chinese-whispers is intriguing to contemplate. Novel mutation and cultural innovation mark the path of history. Our recent animal origin is certainly well illustrated on that older analogy of the 'clock-day'. Even in setting the whole of the Earth's time-scale into a single day, our time-line of anthropoids will only appear in that last minute to midnight. Such analogies help children too.

In the science teaching classroom there needs to be a fluidity of roles as well as modes of activity. Some activities are teacher-centered, others have a pupil focus, some are necessarily didactic (telling) whilst others are more heuristic (involving questioning), some must be theoretical, others will be practical. The learning of science in the classroom should be a rehearsal for living life itself.

Science in schools has been very formally regimented into the classical disciplines of physics, chemistry and biology. Elements of what is now seen as Earth system science, referred to in Nigel Woodcock's chapter, have for a long time been part of geography. Many of the formal barriers are now disappearing with more integrated and modular courses. We need to perceive that the past divisions of classical science subjects reflect little more than the previous specialisms of teachers.

Occasionally, new syntheses are attempted, but many are so resisted by vested interests that teachers feel their work, careers and prospects may be threatened by them. If curricular reorganization is to take place, it undoubtedly works best when the individual teacher's enthusiasm is harnessed to the curriculum development in question. Public examination boards can move, on a four or five year lead-time, to a new public examination. The publishers of school science books perhaps need less time. All recent syllabuses have a far higher content of material on the social, technological, economic and environmental aspects of science. These have been well supported by extensive publications to promote student learning. The WWF has provided welcome help for environmental teaching through its data support service for teacher–authors and examiners.

'Environmentalism' (with 'citizenship') is a cross-curricular theme that is required within the new (England and Wales) National Curriculum. Organizations such as English Nature, the WWF and the RSPB have produced excellent materials in support of these requirements and have indeed played no small part in establishing the dictat that environmental awareness should have a thematic primacy.

One noteworthy curriculum development of a totally cross-curricular type is 'natural economy'. It was presented as an exemplar at the Earth Summit in June 1992. This secondary school subject is a direct educational response to the Brundtland Report and it aims to highlight the dynamic nature of the interaction between people and the world environment. At present it is serviced by a syllabus from the University of Cambridge Local Examinations Syndicate (Overseas Examinations Division). It is a very small initiative, but children between 14 and 16 in English medium secondary schools that enter children at 16 for the International General Certificate of Secondary Education (IGCSE) are studying this subject all around the world. Natural economy has a subject content some parts of which are at home in classical geography and biology, but its frame is very different (see Table 12.2 and reading list).

Running across the four spheres of the Earth's inter-connected structure (lithosphere, hydrosphere, atmosphere and biosphere) are four different aspects of the environment in relation to people. 'Resources' addresses the way in which the natural systems work, 'development' looks at the human uses of the resources, 'impact' seeks to discover how development changes the environment and 'management' examines the question of sustainability. The

Table 12.2. The matrix of the new school subject natural economy

	1. The natural environment (Resources)	2. The human environment (Development)	3. Environmental change (Impact)	4. Sustainable development (Management)
Lithosphere	→ Structure of the Earth	→ Rocks and Minerals: Exploration, Exploitation, Trade	→ Rocks and Minerals: Development Consequences Responses to Natural Disasters	→ Rocks and Minerals: Conservation and Management
	Geological Dynamics	The Limits on Human Activity		
Hydrosphere	→ The Water Cycle	→ Intervention in the Water Cycle	→ Water Hazards	→ Clean, Safe, Water Strategies
	The Oceans	→ Exploitation of the Oceans	→ Threat to the Oceans	→ Managing the Oceans
Atmosphere	→ The Atmosphere at Work	→ Human Activity and Climate	→ Atmosphere at Risk	→ Action on the Atmosphere
	Elements of Climate			
	The Ecosystem	→ The Changing Role of People in the Environment	→ Ecosystem under Threat	→ Conservation of the Ecosystem
Biosphere	→ Elements of Vegetation	→ Population Growth	→ People under Threat	→ Population Management
	Elements of Soil	→ Modification of Vegetation and Soils	Land under Threat	Managing the Land
			→ Agriculture under Threat	→ Managing Agriculture

greatest examined component is biosphere management, making it a uniquely different school subject. Children studying natural economy need a rudimentary knowledge of science only. It takes a holistic view and emphasizes the understanding of environmental processes as the basis for analyzing and discussing future human impacts and future options. It is very skills-oriented at this level and raises the profile of children's personal development in the context of their involvement with environment and development issues.

To conclude, where does this leave our *angst* about science and the world? We need confidence in the human species, not techno-fixes, as being the solution to the problem it has seemingly created for itself. We need to develop a new process of societal learning in which humankind is viewed much more in its evolutionary and ecological context. We need to enrich our scientific culture and seek a new holism with social sciences and the arts. This means investing greatly in all those means that will allow individuals to act more freely and informedly in their own perceived best long-term interests. Much can spring from work in schools.

Annotated List of Further Reading

Natural Economy Syllabus 0670, University of Cambridge Local Examinations Syndicate, 1 Hills Road, Cambridge, UK.
> Perhaps the first secondary syllabus to take an interdisciplinary overview of human ecology as its starting point.

Naturalists' Handbooks, Sarah Corbet and Henry Disney (Scientific Editors), Slough: Richmond Publishing.
> Based on the principle that anyone interested in natural history can make original discoveries, at home or at college, in the back garden or in the countryside. These unique books aim to provide what

investigators without specialized training or facilities need to contribute knowledge about local plants and animals, and have fun. Each book contains a clear introduction to what is already known about the natural history of each group, highlighting topics on which further research is needed. Accurate and attractive colored illustrations and line drawings make for user-friendly keys for identification. As well as being widely used in schools and colleges, the 25 books in the series are valued by anglers, farmers, gardeners and other naturalists.

Part III

SYNTHESIS

Wangari Maathai.
Credit: Jim Dallas/Edinburgh District Council

Author biography

Trained as a biologist in the USA and her native Kenya, Wangari Maathai spent her early career teaching micro-anatomy and histology in the Faculty of Veterinary Medicine at the University of Nairobi. But increasingly she saw that soil erosion and deforestation were brought about, not by local people themselves, but by national and international political and economic policies and corruption. She has played a key role in the establishment and development of the Green Belt Movement, which has involved 50 000 women in the planting and subsequent maintenance of 10 million trees. She has also consistently campaigned for the protection of the environment, against corruption, for human rights and for the building of an open, civil society. Although persecuted by her own government, Maathai has received many honours, including the Africa Leadership Prize for Sustained End of Hunger, the Goldman Environmental Award and the Edinburgh Medal.

Chapter 13

Wangari Maathai

A View from the Grassroots

I HAVE spent the last 20 years of my life at the grassroots, with thousands of women, men and children, in a partnership intended to utilize my education and experience to better the quality of life of my family and my community in particular, and my country and the world in general. The partners represent the people at the bottom of a pyramid which local and international political and economic systems have created on both sides of the equator. At the bottom of the pyramid are people of all shades, races, religions and gender, but by far the majority at the bottom are citizens of the world south of the equator.

Upon birth, we begin a journey which should lead to happiness and fulfilment. That is the purpose of all our efforts. Between birth and death, however, there are many obstacles which separate us from that goal. Some are natural, but most are made by humans. The fulfilment and happiness we crave on this planet should be possible, and there should be enough for everyone's needs. Believing it to be so, we wake up every morning to toil on the resources available to us so that we can realize these goals of happiness and fulfilment. For many of us, however, and especially for those at the bottom of that pyramid, there are not enough resources to meet even our basic needs.

The greater awareness we now have of the systems of our planet makes us appreciate the dilemma which Rachel Carson described in her book *Silent Spring* before it became fashionable to appear green. The air we breathe, the water we drink and the soil in which crops and other vegetation grow are limited resources. They are available to us to use as others before us have done and those who will follow us will need to do. It was Mahatma Gandhi who gave the world the often-quoted words of wisdom, 'the world has enough for everyone's need but not for everyone's greed'. These words become even more meaningful the more we appreciate that this planet is a closed system, and therefore what there is on the Earth is all we've got. How then do we achieve our goals if we feel the need to satisfy not only our needs but also our greed? How can we make this journey and realize our goals despite our limited resources? After all, in some countries, and for the majority of people at the bottom of the pyramid, the journey comes to an end even as it begins and just as most of us turn 35 or thereabouts.

Some of us believe that perhaps we are not the only ones making this journey? Perhaps all creation has a purpose, and this has nothing to do with our own happiness and fulfilment? Perhaps it is not our business to decide which species should be allowed to exist and which should be denied this right, just because they are no use to us just now?

To understand our position in relation to other forms of creation, we should seek knowledge and inspiration from science and from creation itself. The message coming to more and more people now strongly suggests that we are one species which needs to be less arrogant and exploitative against our brothers and sisters in the wide spectrum of creation. Every other species has a right to exist and to pursue its own happiness and fulfilment and has no obligation to *Homo sapiens*.

Science and technology now dominate, and have greatly changed almost all aspects of our lives on both sides of the equator. This is especially true at the bottom of the pyramid, where applied modern science is a new experience, and scientific and technological know-how is lacking. Indeed, the bottom of the pyramid associates science and technology with magic and miracles of the glittering industrialized world. And with good reason: commercialized science has greatly enriched societies which have made scientific discoveries and have been able to apply them and create new and more efficient tools. This miracle appears well beyond the reach of the bottom of the pyramid, and may even be perceived as magic or a gift from God. Even though science and technology impacts on the world at the bottom of the pyramid, that world hardly understands them or how the impact comes about. The people toil nonetheless, and search for their own happiness and fulfilment. But is it possible for them to realize their goal with so few resources? And will those who have know-how be willing to share it, when such knowledge gives them the advantage over those at the bottom? How can they when, with that advantage, they (the top) can exploit not only their own resources, but also the untapped resources belonging to those at the bottom of the pyramid?

The world I work in is concerned about the environment. The resources on this planet are not only limited, they are also being degraded. Many people at the bottom of the pyramid do not understand 'limits to growth' and they do not appreciate that, as they seek their own happiness and fulfilment, they could adversely affect the same resources and jeopardize the capacity of future generations to meet their own needs. The top is blinded by an insatiable appetite, backed by scientific knowledge, industrial advancement, the need to acquire, accumulate and over-consume. The revolution in information dissemination worldwide plays on the ignorance and the fear of those at the bottom of the pyramid. It promotes the lifestyle of those at the top of the pyramid and sells it as the ultimate in fulfilment and happiness.

In my part of the world, environmental degradation is brought about by soil erosion, deforestation, pollution and loss of biological diversity in our Earth systems. These in turn are brought about by political and economic policies and activities which are dictated by greed, corruption, incompetence and an insatiable desire to satisfy the inflated egos and ambitions of those who wield political and economic power. They are exacerbated by population pressure, international debts and interest rates, low prices for export goods, commodity protectionism and inevitable and debilitating poverty.

Many governments, aid agencies and charitable organizations invest heavily in the symptoms of environmental degradation as they mop up the world. Less effort and enthusiasm is demonstrated in dealing with the causes of the garbage they are so willing to mop up. This is not to say that people are not appreciative of aid and charity. But the majority of the people at the bottom of the pyramid are both the causes and the symptoms of environmental degradation. They are caught in a vicious circle of poverty and underdevelopment. The Green Belt Movement endeavors to assist them to break that cycle and liberate themselves from the bonds which block their paths and separate them from their goal of happiness and fulfilment. Lifting them may be a noble and fulfilling challenge, but it is also very demanding because the bottom of the pyramid, especially south of the equator, is very heavy.

Many of us at the bottom make our children believe that education is the key to a good job, a good salary and good quality of life. They believe that education will get them out of the bottom of the pyramid and provide comfort without effort. It seems easy enough, because passing examinations and moving to the next grade may come easily. As they struggle through school they console themselves with the promised success which will ensure them a place at the top of the pyramid. If that depended on good grades and certificates many of us would have little to worry about. We would be at the top!

Between reality and childhood dreams are many hurdles made by humans which the people at the bottom fight against all their lives as they try to overcome them and to achieve meaningful development, improve their quality of life and realize their full potential. These obstacles prevent them from utilizing much of the knowledge, expertise and the experience they have acquired in their studies and in the course of their lives. This knowledge and experience is supposed to make the journey surer and easier, but there is a big difference between childhood dreams and the reality of the pyramid. At the bottom of the pyramid, sooner or later, we all learn that.

Take me for example. I am basically a biologist. However, in the course of my postgraduate work I acquired experience in histological preparations of laboratory specimens and basic principles of embryology. With that background I was hired by Professor Dr R. R. Hofmann, who became my academic adviser and friend, to teach micro- and developmental anatomy in the Faculty of Veterinary Medicine at the University of Nairobi. I felt satisfied with playing an important role in educating future veterinarians who would supervise the livestock industry in my country. Such experts were expected to ensure that there would be adequate and healthy animal production provision for our society, to control animal diseases and ensure that our livestock industry was successful.

Part of the university assignment is to do research and publish results in scientific journals so that higher academic promotions can be achieved. Eager to make my mark in the scientific world, and of course also earn my academic credentials, I commenced on a research project immediately. I decided to work on a problem which was adversely affecting the livestock industry and especially the dairy section. To improve our indigenous dairy cattle we had imported exotic breeds from Europe and were cross-breeding them with local stock. The project was very successful, except for one problem: east coast fever. This parasitic disease proved 100% fatal to the imported exotic breeds and their progeny.

The parasite is transmitted from one animal to another by brown ear ticks, so called because the ticks love to congregate particularly on the ears of the victim. The parasite is ingested by the tick from an infected animal during feeding and eventually finds its way into the salivary glands of the ticks. From here, the parasite is passed onto the next victim during the next feed. I decided to work on the microscopic anatomy of this parasite because I was keen to make a contribution towards the research of its lifecycle. I started with its anatomy in the salivary glands of the infected ticks.

Anxious to be a good career woman and to set a good example to fellow members of my gender, students and colleagues who had not worked with women professionals before, I did what I thought mattered: I reported to work on time and was both industrious and productive. Upward mobility seemed assured if the university authority would respect what they had written in the letters of my appointment. But the inevitable happened: there was a hurdle which nobody articulated. It was not an academic hurdle, but a hurdle nevertheless. Mobility upwards was too slow. It was as if I did not matter as much as the others. There was something I did not have and I could not have. The hurdle had nothing to do with passing examinations, having certificates or being a good teacher. It had everything to do with my gender. What a discovery!

I had just returned from the USA where I spent the first part of the 1960s. Those years are partly remembered as the years of the Civil Rights Movement which was led by Martin Luther King Jr. At least in the street battles the issues were clear: color was the problem. Several years later I was in the village of my birth and childhood and I was at home with people who were black like me. I was still not OK. This time though, it was my gender that was the problem. I have since learnt that at the bottom of the pyramid there are very strict cultural and religious norms which govern the birth, life and death of women in society. These age-old traditions make the bottom quite heavy.

By now I had married. To do everything right we followed all the proper religious and traditional requirements. He promised happiness and fulfillment. He was a good Christian like me, had also been educated abroad, had been exposed to Western ideas and values and we shared our traditional wisdom. I never would have thought that all the things I had worked so hard for in school and at home would become a burden, an obstacle to my domestic peace. Apparently, those academic certificates and letters of appointment to high offices were secretly emasculating the man in my life. What a catastrophe! I should have known that ambition and success were not expected to be a dominant character in, especially, an African woman. An African woman should be a good African woman whose dominant qualities should include coyness, shyness, submissiveness, incompetence (feigned if necessary) and crippling dependency even if they have the opportunity to be economically independent. A highly educated, independent African woman is bound to be dominant, aggressive, uncontrollable, a bad influence on other African women. She is unmarriageable. Such qualities are attributes expected in men only. I lamented that nobody warned me about such hurdles! (I fell deep inside the pyramid and a large part of those at the bottom still struggle to keep me there.) In the meantime, I struggled for freedom so that I could realize my full potential, but so many opportunities to improve the bottom had been lost, much energy wasted and a lot of mileage lost on the journey. The bottom is especially heavy for women.

Figure 13.1. Soil erosion in Central Province, Kenya

To go back to my research project, in the early 1970s I spent much time collecting ticks which should have been infected with the east coast fever parasites. The cows which carried the ticks were often so skinny that I could count their ribs. This was because there was inadequate grass for them and they obviously did not have enough supplements. This observation eventually led me to appreciate the relationship between the wellbeing of domestic animals, a degraded environment and the carrying capacity of any resource. A degraded environment (Figure 13.1) could not sustain our domestic animals. Indeed, the livestock industry was threatened more by environmental degradation than by either the ticks on the ears of the animals or the east coast fever parasites in the salivary glands of ticks.

That was one of the many experiences which led me into environmental activism. I henceforth sought to understand and appreciate not only the symptoms but the causes of environmental degradation. This, and other concerns, inspired me to initiate the Green Belt Movement (Figure 13.2). The overall objective of the Movement was to raise awareness of symptoms of environmental degradation and raise the consciousness of people to a level that would move them to participate in the restoration and the healing of the environment. The majority of the people at the bottom of the pyramid would rather deal with the symptoms because their objectives are short term and are directed towards immediate survival. The Green Belt Movement encourages them to understand the need to get to the root causes and to act.

But the women of the Green Belt Movement try. To begin with they are mostly rural women who can hardly read or write their mother tongues, let alone the official and national languages of Kenya, namely English and Kiswahili. And there are about 42 different mother tongues in Kenya. Communication is therefore a big barrier and

Figure 13.2. The author with sign in Kiambu, Central Province

although practical teaching (by demonstration) is applied, there is not enough time and personnel to go around. Our program does not incorporate adult education, but there are many groups which plant trees and also participate in the adult education program conducted by the Ministry of Education. Fortunately, forestry techniques are simple and are similar to the practices applied by the farmers. With basic demonstrations groups of women are able to adapt the various forestry techniques and to overcome many

Figure 13.3. Mama Kayahwe with a fruit tree and seedling

Figure 13.4. Mama Kayahwe and other women working in Muranga, Central Province

problems which could be a nightmare to a professional forester (Figures 13.3 and 13.4).

The Green Belt Movement is basically an environmental campaign for tree planting. The objectives are many and varied, but the overall concern is to raise the awareness of ordinary men and women of the need to take care of the environment so that it in turn can take care of at least their basic needs. The initiators are groups of women who mainly come forward because they experience the direct impact of an environment which is degraded. They lack wood fuel, water, food and fodder. They are poor, have no cash income and are confined to rural life. They work very hard. For example, in sub-Saharan Africa women produce 80% of the food, provide the manual labor on farms and homes, raise their many children and serve as heads of households for their absent husbands. Yet they form the bulk of the bottom of the pyramid. Without education, capital, or political and economic policies to support them they find themselves engulfed in vicious circles of debilitating poverty, lost self-confidence and a never-ending struggle to meet their most basic needs.

For the past 15 years the Movement has been trying to break that cycle. The greatest obstacles have been the very systems which are created by the people at the top. These systems are designed to disempower those at the bottom, to deny them basic freedoms and rights. This is done so that those at the top can more easily rule over and continue to exploit them. Because of trying to uplift the bottom of the pyramid, the Movement has been portrayed as anti-government, and the organizers and partners as dissidents. I have been the subject of unsavory and even uncouth commentary, and have been threatened with bodily harm by the political leaders who swear to protect a constitution in which are enshrined the right to freedom of movement, information, expression and association. The rights of those at the bottom of the pyramid are violated every day by those at the top.

The sheer number of those at the bottom of the pyramid creates the weight. This is compounded by all the problems enumerated above. And the numbers are getting bigger. The economic and political systems are designed to create more numbers, and thus deforestation and desertification and other aspects of environmental degradation continue. The signs are everywhere to be seen.

Science and technology can sometimes lighten the burden, but do not seem to be doing so. Perhaps part of the answer lies with people themselves. Humans have to reassess their roles on this planet, reassess their values, reassess their understanding of the universe and perception of what constitutes their happiness and fulfillment. We may have to reassess systems of governance and seek security and peace not in a pyramid but in a balanced and harmonious whole. For as long as we sustain a pyramid, the bottom will continue to gather momentum and may take all of us with it where it is always going, to the abyss of the bottom.

Annotated List of Further Reading

The Reality of Aid: an Independent Review of International Aid, Judith Randel and Tony German (eds), London: Action Aid.

Each person in the industrialized countries spends just over US$70 a year on government overseas aid. Who does it go to? What is it spent on? Does it result in reduced poverty and sustainable development? Twenty non-governmental organizations work together to produce this annual report, which draws attention to the current realities of aid. Recent editions have charted the increasing diversion of aid from long-term development to emergency assistance and the continuing use of aid to promote exports from the rich countries.

The Myth of Wild Africa: Conservation without Illusion, Jonathan S. Adams and Thomas O. Mc Shane, New York: Norton, 1992.

Two respected conservationists show that it is both immoral and pointless to try to conserve wildlife without involving local people. However, for decades the industrialized countries have made the mistake of trying to cut Africans off from their environment, rather than helping restore the balance they had maintained before colonization.

Camping with the Prince and Other Tales of Science in Africa, Thomas A. Buss, Cambridge: Lutterworth Press, 1992.

A fascinating first-hand account of a journey through Africa demonstrating the difficulties of imposing foreign ideas on a people, many of whom can find their own, much more successful answers.

The Critical Villager: Beyond Community Participation, Eric Dudley, London: Routledge, 1993.

A considered account of the problems related to aid intervention which makes 'development' look more suspect than ever. He suggests that the hazy principle that the people are not always right is not only patronizing, but irrational. Respect for villagers is best shown by treating them as consenting adults with whom one can argue, disagree and negotiate. 'A booklet which is ostensibly aimed at semi-literate villagers is likely to find its way instead onto desks in Washington D.C.' says Dudley.

Brian Moss

Author biography

HAVING worked in universities in Africa, North America and Europe, Brian Moss, presently Professor and Head of the Department of Environmental and Evolutionary Biology at the University of Liverpool, has an overview of how academic science operates, especially concerning environmental projects. His own work helped produce a methodology for the restoration of degraded lakes that use biological manipulations where hard technology is inappropriate or ineffective. He is currently encouraging the use of 'value-changed' approaches to monitoring water quality, which are more transparent in interpretation, and hence less politically manipulable, than are existing schemes. He is author of *Ecology of Freshwaters: Man and Medium*, as well as numerous scientific and popular articles.

Chapter 14

Brian Moss

The Emperor's Clothes of Knowledge and the Seamless Cloth of Wisdom

Naturam expellas furca, tamen usque recurret
(Though you drive Nature out with a pitchfork, she will still find her way back)

Horace, *Epistles*, I.x.24

The flight from science

I remember the 1950s as a time of considerable optimism. Attempts were being made in Britain to solve the problems of slum housing, insecurity, lack of access to the country-side for recreation and the injustices of privileged education. In secondary schools, the opportunities to study the sciences were enthusiastically welcomed. A whole new world of physics, chemistry and biology was being opened up. We had a picture of the atom, we had new concepts of the genetic material, DNA, and could approach the complexities of the properties of elements in a systematic way that was starting to make sense.

Forty years later, when our appreciation of the phenomena of nature, from the quarks to the stars and from the gene to the biosphere, is little short of astounding, there is a major drift of pupils away from the physical science subjects taught in English secondary schools. In turn this is reflected in declining applications to study engineering and physical sciences at many universities. Both the UK Government and the universities inevitably see this trend as undesirable, for the former sees it as unhelpful to the development of industry and the production of wealth, and the universities see it as a waste of opportunities to pass on the immensely interesting advances of their research. Several reasons have been put forward. A lack of suitably qualified and scientifically motivated teachers is one and this is attributed to a movement of physical scientists towards better paid jobs in industry or the finance markets. The trend is not paralleled in much of the biological and environmental sciences.

Attempts to reverse the trend through the teaching of technology in primary schools, and financial incentives paid to trainee teachers in the physical sciences, show few significant impacts. I cannot help but feel that such measures attempt to treat only the symptoms without investigating the ultimate causes. What has never been confronted is that the strong movement towards the biological and environmental sciences (and also the humanities) may have much deeper reasons than the size of a pay check. To seek these out requires a use of judgment based on what students say once they reach the universities and an appraisal of the present state of the planet.

The result of such introspection is a proposition that the rejection is not of science *per se*, but of the manipulation which science has suffered. This is through its application, in both material and social technology, in support of a way of organizing society which benefits a minority of people to the ultimate detriment of most. Despite an increasing degree of cynicism, many young (and some older) people react against this on moral grounds.

Science is perceived by many young people as the way through which the planet's resources have been exploited, rather than as a means of understanding them and using them wisely. They believe that the harnessing of science has created environmental problems, the solution of which is cynically avoided by those who create them. They see gross injustice to many of the world's peoples and they react against this, for may not they themselves be, indeed are they not already being, similarly abused?

Increasingly, they see the present technological world as failing to support the values that they would wish to hold. Hence they vote with their feet in their choice of studies and they also often turn to mysticism or fantasy to cope with the huge gap that they see between the reality around them and the sort of world they would like to see, but about whose likelihood they have become increasingly despairing.

There are thus two issues to be dealt with. Firstly, how to change the status of science to a broader context and, secondly, a much more fundamental look at what might be the most appropriate ways of organizing society in the future.

The nature of science

Science is not truly the compartmented areas of physics, chemistry, biology, geology and the rest, which represent the convenient territorial claims of particular groups of people. None of these areas, designated in the 19th and early 20th centuries, has any boundaries that are relevant to the 21st. Nor is there any dividing line which inevitably separates them from such equally artificially designated areas such as psychology, sociology, history, philosophy or ethics. In the past there have been hierarchies of perceptions of value that have ranked subject areas. Indeed, immense prejudices still exist. What can be apparently dispassionately established is valued above that in which there may have to be strong human involvement.

Such rankings, and the conceit that science is value-free, have diverted more complete understanding. They have also supported the exploitation of physical and biological science by fortifying the rankings on the basis of a subject's value in wealth creation. This is also, of course, roughly a measure of the degree of its exploitation of the environment.

What does exist, however, is a distinctive scientific approach which values, in the creation of opinion, a rigorous cross-checking of information, where possible the confirmation of prediction by deliberate experiment, and the discarding of beliefs when they have been shown to be wrong. This approach is used by all sorts of people in investigating natural and human phenomena and who might conventionally be designated historian, anthropologist or chemist. Richard Feynman, categorized by others solely as a physicist, encapsulated the nature of the truly scientific process very well

Science is a way to teach how something gets to be known, what is not known, to what extent things are *known (for nothing is known absolutely), how to handle doubt and uncertainty, what the rules of evidence are, how to think about things so that judgements can be made, how to distinguish truth from fraud, and from show.*

If science is then taken to be all that can be examined by such an approach there is no drift away from it at all. Indeed, in the questioning now applied by young people, there may even be a drift towards it. Young people are as keen as ever to discover the reality of things and do it through a range of conventional subject areas. Ultimately, like us all, they wish to understand themselves and their relationship with the world around them. Many, however, may feel that the compartmentalism of conventional science stands in the way when it appears to take no heed of the impacts which its discoveries have had and the ways in which they have been used. Weapons technology, intensive agriculture, particularly in animal husbandry, the development of toxic substances such as biocides, and psychological exploitation through advertising are all germane in this respect.

The many positive uses of technology are not necessarily rejected, but the impact of technology is perceived negatively overall because of what many see as its exploitative use in the maintenance of existing power structures. It will not be until these structures are re-examined, and perhaps rejected, that conventional science and technology will be seen in a more favorable and balanced light.

Western technological society

How does our society operate? By 'our society' I mean the high technology-based system found in most of Europe, North America, Japan and the newly industrializing countries of eastern Asia. Increasingly, it is also found in less developed countries that are currently being tempted and edged into this system.

Western technological society is not the only possible model. Although presently declining in number, there is a vast array of other sorts of ways of organizing human societies on this planet, many with longer histories of persistence than the one the Europeans created, with its roots only two to three hundred years old. Our present society is ultimately based on a biological view of human beings. It rests on the principle that individuals who are capable of taking resources are free to do so and gain advantage from this ability. Resources are treated as there for the taking and the process has no recognition of future needs. It is like that of natural selection, in that those individuals best able to acquire resources in a given situation at a particular time will be likely to breed most successfully and proliferate.

Such a system works powerfully to match exploitative abilities to resources available to be exploited. In organisms controlled by natural selection, turnover of individuals and species is generally rapid and cooperation with others is promoted, so long as its pay-offs are positive. This biological system has characteristics that are immaterial to the individual concerned but which are collectively crucial in human terms. These are such that present exploitation may lead to a failure of future resources, and thence to extinction. There is no provision for a future, merely a reaction to the present.

Our present biologically determinist Western technological society benefits its members *vis-à-vis* the rest of the world and it benefits particular individuals much more than others. It achieves and maintains this imbalance of power in many ways that tend to stabilize it against contrary questioning, and thence potential change. These are ways that favor the acquisition of resources by particular individuals. They include: emphasis on competition; maintenance of numerous hierarchies of status, from prefectorial systems in schools to political honors; manipulation of school curricula; weakening of institutions like universities and research institutes, whose research might, as they should, question the status quo; organization into lobbies and interest groups such as political parties, professional associations and organized religions; centralization of decision-making; manipulation of the media through commercial ownership, political and advertising propaganda.

The mechanisms operate overtly, and less obviously in small ways. One common device is to corrupt the phraseology of alternative systems as in the emerging use of the oxymoron 'sustainable growth'. Another is the hidden agenda of such apparently sensible assertions as 'preparing pupils for the world of work', which really means ensuring that a lot of very variedly cross-sectioned pegs fit neatly into the pre-shaped holes most convenient to the needs of the existing power bases.

Our present system is thus one in which, in the divide and rule philosophy, the conventional divisions of science can be conveniently harnessed. The characteristics of such mechanistic systems have been drawn together in Table 14.1. It is not hard to recognize the features of western technological society as mechanistic and to deduce from them the fragmentationist world view (Table 14.2) which underlies such systems. The emphasis is on separation and exploitation. We see ourselves as superior, dominant, masters of the world's resources. All activity can be analyzed and explained objectively and rationally or else is rejected. We do not stop to analyze our behavior, to take an introspective view. We achieve by acquisition rather than by understanding.

Conventional science can underpin such a system because its reductionist approaches fit well into a system that places humans outside the global support system, as users rather than as parts of it. Conventional science itself is presently deeply immured in this system. The only ways in which

Table 14.1. Characteristics of mechanistic and non-mechanistic organizations. Modified from S. Greig *et al.* (1989) *Greenprints for Changing Schools*, Kogan Page/World Wide Fund For Nature

Feature	Mechanistic	Non-mechanistic
Structure	Hierarchy; unequal status; delegation downwards	Heterarchy; equal status; reciprocal delegation
Policy making and control	Authoritarian; change discouraged	Consensual; change initiated throughout and welcomed
Purpose	Wealth production for selected castes; suppression of personal potentials; extrinsic rewards through product orientation	Common good; encouragement of individual potential; intrinsic reward through personal satisfaction
Communication	Inhibited, factional	Open and communal

most scientists can carry out their research is by participating in its mores. Funds for research come mostly from bodies that are inherently self-preservationist—industry, government departments and many quangos, themselves inextricably linked in our exploitative system. Meanwhile, only a token sum comes to support genuinely fundamental research—that which alone may question and threaten the existing system. The recent White Paper on Science produced by the UK Government has taken as its text that science is for the creation of wealth, with only a minor subtext allowing research to contribute to the quality of life. Research institutes, formerly supported to carry out fundamental work, have increasingly been required to find support from sources with sectional interests. The heads of UK Research Councils, formerly distinguished scientists, are now to be part-time industrialists.

Analogies in other systems

Characteristics, like the buffer mechanisms listed above for Western technological society, which tend to preserve systems against displacement, are well known in ecological systems. These provide useful analogies. For example (Moss 1989), in shallow lakes, extensive beds of aquatic plants may be threatened by competition for light from overlying single-celled algae (called protists) as inputs of nutrients such as nitrogen and phosphorus compounds increase from human activities. The plankton can begin growth earlier in the season and can grow rapidly because all the cells are photosynthetic and the organism does not support structures that are energy-demanding without being energy-fixing, such as roots and rhizomes.

Despite all this, however, the plant beds can prosper for long periods as nutrients increase and ostensibly should favor the plankton. This persistence is because the plant system has developed buffering mechanisms (Figure 14.1). The labyrinthine structure of the plant beds provides a physical habitat for huge populations of a whole range of small animals (such as the 'water fleas') which move out into the open water to graze on the plankton. Within the plant beds such animals find refuge in daylight against fish predators, which would otherwise decimate their populations. The plants may also secrete chemical inhibitors against phytoplankton growth.

Several alternatives of such buffered systems can exist equally stably under the same set of imposed external conditions, but the alternatives can be switched from one to another. Once established, the new alternative is equally stable and maintained by its own buffers. Thus the plant-dominated system can be converted to a plankton-dominated system (Figure 14.1) without any plants at all. The plankton is maintained by a buffer which guarantees

Table 14.2 Comparison of fragmentationist and holistic world views. Modified from Grieg *et al.* (1989)

Fragmentationist	Holistic
Emphasis on separateness and disconnectedness. Wholes are made up of the sum of their parts and are neither more nor less than this sum. Separateness from other peoples and the global environment	Emphasis on connectedness. Wholes have properties additional to the sum of the parts. We are profoundly connected with other peoples and the global environment
Preference for analysis and reduction	Preference for synthesis, integration and the synoptic
Observer is separate from what (s)he observes. Complete objectivity is achievable	Observer and observed are intimately connected. Interpretation is influenced by observer's priorities and values. The observer is to some degree observing his or herself and cannot be outside, neutral or objective
The rational and cerebral are separate from and superior to the emotional, the intuitive and the spiritual	Full potential is only realized through the acknowledgement of the emotional, intuitive and spiritual and their interplay with the rational and cerebral
Egocentrism. Identity has its source only in self	Individuality. Identity arises from an interaction between self and the whole. We achieve the highest level of individuality when we reflect the whole

Outer-directedness; we look out on the world and seek to understand it. The focus is on change external to the person	Outer- and inner-directedness. A 'journey outwards' to understand the world requires a reciprocal 'journey inwards' to understand self and self in the world. The focus is on personal growth and transformation as much as social/environmental change
Patriarchal values; masculine behaviors and qualities are prized; feminine qualities and behaviors are devalued	Post-patriarchal values. A merging of both masculine and feminine behaviors and qualities
Emphasis on hierarchical, centralized, inegalitarian structures, competitive relationships, authority and experts. A 'control' mindset	Emphasis on non-hierarchical, decentralized, egalitarian structures, cooperative relationships, participation and involvement. A 'liberationist' mindset
Anthropocentric; humankind seen as the principal actor on the planet; other organisms and inorganic matter accorded value only in terms of human priorities and needs	Biocentric; humankind seen as but one element in the planet's system; other organisms and inorganic matter have their own intrinsic value
Separateness from, domination and control over nature; an exploitative ruthlessness towards the environment	Oneness with nature; reverence towards the environment

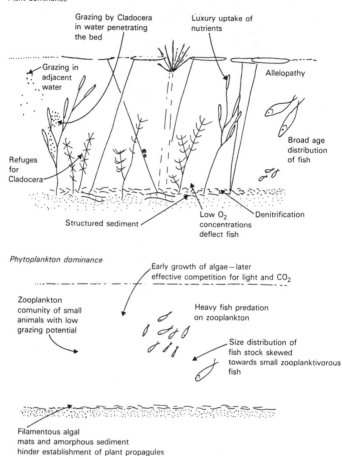

Plant dominance

Grazing by Cladocera
in water penetrating
the bed

Luxury uptake of
nutrients

Grazing in
adjacent
water

Allelopathy

Broad age
distribution
of fish

Refuges
for
Cladocera

Low O$_2$
concentrations
deflect fish

Denitrification

Structured sediment

Phytoplankton dominance

Early growth of algae — later
effective competition for light and CO$_2$

Zooplankton
comunity of small
animals with low
grazing potential

Heavy fish predation
on zooplankton

Size distribution of
fish stock skewed
towards small zooplanktivorous
fish

Filamentous algal
mats and amorphous sediment
hinder establishment of plant propagules

Figure 14.1. Buffering mechanisms that stabilize different ecological communities in shallow lakes. Reproduced from Moss (1989) with permission from Blackwell Science Ltd, Oxford

that the grazing animals are in short supply. In the structureless open water there are no refuges for them against fish predation and the algal plankton, once established, has all the advantages adduced above. The principle of alternative stable states or systems is important in considering human societies.

Ecologically sophisticated systems

Thus it is possible by analogy to conceive of very different human systems from that of the Western technological society we have come to accept as normal and inevitable. Indeed, the world is replete with alternatives, though all are threatened by pressures from ours, which is yet another example of the ways in which the preservative buffers of our own society act. We derogate the alternatives as tribal, primitive, undeveloped and backward, but in truth they have sets of values which might offer much more secure futures than does our own society. They all have the characteristic that humans are not regarded as masters of the Earth, but that people are a part of a greater system on which they depend and which must be properly looked after. There is nothing mystical in this—it is plain common sense. These are ecologically sophisticated societies, whereas ours is ecologically primitive.

The San people of the Kalahari, for example, have an extensive knowledge of the properties of the hundreds of plants and animals on which they depend. They use, for instance, ostrich eggs in which to cache water along their migration routes across the desert, but are careful never completely to empty an ostrich nest. The Haida Indians of British Columbia evolved a wonderful system which allowed careful exploitation of resources, coped with a food supply variable from year to year and allowed a degree of hierarchy within the society. They lived in a coastal forested area with abundant wood and several species of migratory salmon in their local rivers. The salmon were their main food resource, for fish can be dried and stored. Individual families 'owned' land and stretches of river and regarded their resources as available for personal disposal. However, there was a system of constraint, called the potlach, which limited the exploitation.

A family maintained its position in the hierarchy by giving gifts of fish, and other products fashioned from natural resources, to those lower in the hierarchy. The arrangement was that the gift had later to be reciprocated with interest and then again returned and so on. Failure to reciprocate on either side led to a severe fall in status. The size of the initial gift was thus constrained by its future consequences and, so long as the gifts originated directly from local natural resources, a constraint was imposed on their exploitation. The system served to share food in times of local scarcity or surplus and, importantly, only broke down when it was corrupted by the import of goods from elsewhere following European contact. Metal axes and knives and blankets traded for sea otter pelts led to an inflation of the system, followed by the near-extinction both of the sea otter and the Haida. The potential parallels with our own system, which is now totally uncoupled from the sustainable use of resources, is startling. Perhaps we too are corrupted by the likes of the electric toothbrush, the pornographic video, and the pizza I once observed in a North American supermarket, whose list of components read like a chemical catalog and included nothing that could immediately be linked with a plant or an animal.

Other, potentially equally stable, systems are very different. Rice-growing families in Bali, for example, have developed ways of cultivation and of using water so efficiently that very high population densities can be supported with no intervention at all by the agricultural technologies of chemical fertilization and pest control. Bali is mountainous, and water cascades rapidly to the sea if unchecked. The Balinese have a system of conserving the water (and the fertile silt it carries) in terraces on the mountain slopes, allowing the water to be released in an orderly way from the upper to the middle to the lower terraces in a sequence which supports waves of rice growth in the alternately flooded and drained terraces. Organization of such water use depends on complete cooperation of all the growers in an area and this has been developed through the use of a religious calendar, which ordains auspicious times for the opening of water gates, coinciding rather closely with the needs of the rice crop. It is a system which requires a degree of conformity, but which seems to have produced a society with no greater social problems than our diametrically opposite one, indeed it appears to have far fewer. Cooperation in food production in this way does not inevitably mean loss of the independence of thought which we prize, though it must constrain independence of certain actions, to the common good.

A not dissimilar system (Figure 14.2) pertains in the Dombe region of southern France, where ancient laws govern the movement of water through fields which, over a sequence of years, are used for alternate carp culture in the flooded phase and maize growing when the water has been passed on downstream. The debris from the maize crop provides an energy source for the food webs supporting the carp, and the silt in the flood provides nutrients for the maize. Here, cooperation is legally controlled rather than religiously enshrined, but the difference is trivial. Ultimately, there is common agreement for the good of all. None of these examples should be seen through rose-tinted spectacles. All undoubtedly operate in less ideal ways than a superficial description might suggest. There will be or have been individuals in them who cheat the system and

Figure 14.2. La Dombe, France. The upper photograph shows a shallow lake area that has been drained temporarily for its crop of common carp, *Cyprinus carpio*, to be removed. The area will then be further drained and maize (lower photograph) grown on the accumulated fertile sediments. A year or two later the area will be reflooded and stocked with carp again, which will benefit from the organic matter left as maize stubble

to some extent their relatively low impact on the rest of the ecosystem has been fostered (except in the case of the Balinese) by low population densities. However, they differ from our own society in that their arrangements do not contain the assumptions that exploitation of resources is desirable for its own sake, nor that the accumulation of resources in a competitive way is something to be glorified. These are our particular myths.

Alternative systems for us

What alternative system, therefore, might we conceive for our own society? Firstly, there must be acceptance that all is presently not well, and I believe the evidence for this to be obvious and that most of us would recognize this. Nonetheless, let me categorize some of it, beginning at the global level with increasing changes in atmospheric composition leading to increases in harmful ultraviolet radiation reaching the ground and changes in global temperatures and moisture deficits at an unprecedentedly high rate. Then there is the alarming rate of increase in the world population, with the greatest rates of increase in those areas where the only way to counteract material insecurity is through additional pairs of hands, and where the women's education is often suppressed. We may add widespread deforestation, soil erosion and desertification, often linked with the destruction of traditional systems through commercial influence. Then there is large-scale overfishing, the near-extinction of several species of whale and increasing numbers of species of land mammals and birds, and the repercussions of modern intensive agriculture on the countryside. At the level of society, there is an increasing number of small wars (the former Yugoslavia, Yemen, Rwanda, Sudan, Russia and Kurdistan come immediately to mind); a preoccupation with defense and weapons production (the international arms trade, which vastly benefits our technological society, makes all of these more intensive and prolonged than they might otherwise be); and widespread political repression. Sometimes this is overt (Amnesty International has never had so prominent a set of problems to confront); sometimes it is subtle and operates through the buffers described earlier.

The reactions of Western technological society to all of these problems are either to deny their existence or to attempt patchwork solutions. Perhaps some of the problems will prove to be less intractable than they seem. But there is no lack of candidates to be considered and it would be very surprising if a large body of considered opinion was wrong about everything. It is notable that in his recent analysis of the nature of our future, *Towards the 21st Century*, Paul Kennedy offers fascinating predictions but very little in the way of solution. His prognosis is that there will continue to be winners and losers and that the gaps will indeed widen. He sees increasing tensions, including mass movements of peoples from the less favored areas to the greater, and suffuses his text with the sense that the greater part of the world will not cope well, if at all, with the impositions of climate change, increasing automation in industry and biotechnology in food production.

What may be needed is a rather fundamental set of changes. We need a recognition that it is ultimately not possible to maintain a society which conceives that resources are infinitely exploitable, or, failing that, that technology will always find a substitute, and one which contemplates indefinite economic growth. These very ideas lack common sense, especially as the world population doubles from about 5.5 billion to 11 billion in the next

Figure 14.3. A contrast in resource use. The upper panel shows a waste collection station at Southport, England; the lower, part of the market stall in Rwanda, Central Africa, where metal cans are on sale either as such or modified into oil lamps

313

40 years or so. The technological world has been limited by resources for some time, but has avoided having to cope with this fact essentially by parasitic exploitation of the resources of the rest of the world, either in labor or in materials. Figure 14.3 gives an ironic contrast. The upper panel shows Sunday afternoon in the English suburbs, when queues of cars line up at municipal collection stations to dump enormous quantities of waste destined to fill yet more rubbish tips. In the lower panel, from central Africa, the humblest old cans are being resold, converted to paraffin burners to provide light for huts in a region where electricity is unaffordable.

The time must come when even the resources presently purloinable from the less developed world are used up or, more quickly, when the rest of the world will refuse to cooperate any longer in its own exploitation. Witness the present widespread increases in nationalism and religious fundamentalism as the first indications of this.

A new paradigm for society?

You took away all the oceans and all the room.
You gave me my shoe-size in earth with bars around it
Where did it get you? Nowhere.
You left me my lips, and they shape words, even in silence.

Osip Mandelstam (1891–1938) (following his exile in 1934 on account of his authorship of a bitter satire on Stalin)

What sort of society is likely to be an indefinitely sustainable one, what might be necessary to achieve it, and what role might science, in the conventional sense and in the wider sense, have in achieving it? The latter question is perhaps the easiest to answer. Conventional science in its boundaried form has little to contribute. For the moment it is undermined by the role technology has played in establishing the current situation. On the other hand, science, in the sense of a methodological approach to complex, many-faceted problems, has the central role.

There can be no future place for approaches that are harnessed to the prejudices and advantages of particular interest groups, and to the service of establishments at the expense of humanity in general. Uncovering the real *raisons d'être* in as comprehensive and honest a way as possible can be the only way to proceed if a great deal of present human misery is to be curtailed and, in future, avoided. Non-partisan scientific investigation is the only way to achieve this.

We might begin by learning from the examples we already have of ecologically more sustainable societies, before they disappear altogether under the weight of our ignorance. The key to them is that they do not regard humans as separate from the natural systems on which they depend. They see themselves as a part. It follows that they do not prize particular interest groups among themselves. They have organization, but power is not concentrated very much in individuals. Devices have been created to regulate the use of resources and to guarantee their renewal. We may have lost our sense of connectedness with our environment, but ultimately we are no less dependent on rates of photosynthesis and the availability of primary minerals than the Amazonian Indians or Kalahari bushmen.

Table 14.1 outlines some of the characteristics that such a non-mechanistic society needs to have and Table 14.2 the world view that it would need to take. It is a holistic sort of organization, as opposed to a fragmentationist one. It would maximize the ability of individuals to cater for the overall benefit rather than themselves alone, would recognize our participation in the biosphere rather than assuming a dominance of it and would call for a much more introspective examination of our motives for particular actions. It would be a society where ultimately the provision of goods and services is pegged to the renewable availability of materials. Economic features not linked to the sustainable availability of natural resources—currency speculation, planned obsolescence, disposable articles, for example, would have to disappear. It would be a society that so valued the individual that it organized its taxation systems to give emphasis to labor and skills and the production of quality goods. It would perhaps discourage, by high taxes, goods that had high ratios of energy and scarce materials to labor costs. The taxes would escalate with increasing scarcity of material and with decreasing renewability. Negligible taxes would be placed on goods that favored the use of human talents at the expense of resource use. It could be a much more interesting and fulfilling world for all of us.

Of course, such a system will be vigorously opposed by the minority groups who presently hold power in the technological world. The buffers which preserve systems will come into play in increasingly powerful ways the more the system is challenged. There will be attempts at suppression of such ideas; there already are. But in the end the attempts will fail. There can be no ultimate suppression of ideas that are inherently supportive of the majority rather than the minority good, as Cooper and Meyer point out in their chapter. The details that would need to be worked out are many, and the idea of a sustainable society will be attacked from the point of view of individual details. But, if the principle is correct, the details will inevitably follow.

The facilitation of change

What might be done to help bring about change? The problem is analogous to those in the ecological systems I have described above (Figure 14.1). It is that of determining the nature of the mechanisms that cause the switches between alternative states. In the example of the shallow lakes alternatively dominated by plants or plankton, there is first of all a whole series of possible switches from the plant state to the plankton state. Some are violent and unsubtle—the mechanical removal of the plants, on a devastating scale, by harvesting or damage by boat propellers. Others more subtly lead to greater losses of plants than their growth can sustain—declines in water level which allow greater access of grazing birds to the plants or the introduction of new grazers such as exotic birds or mammals which rapidly achieve high population densities. Yet another involves the temporary loss of the small animals (the zooplankton) that graze on the phytoplankton, and which the plant beds shelter, by the effects of pesticide runoff or increased salinity following penetration of relatively small amounts of sea water. More subtly, a switch may follow a change in the balance of piscivorous fish to zooplanktivorous fish, caused by the differential effects on the piscivores of deoxygenation under prolonged winter ice.

The lesson is that the switches can be various and in themselves apparently small, yet their ultimate effects are completely to change the system. Another characteristic is that because the systems are complex, the list of possible switch mechanisms is indefinite; the unexpected can happen and be as effective as that for which there is a well understood precedent. In forecasting the likely mechanisms that will switch our human organizations from the present, ecologically primitive ones to the future, ecologically sophisticated ones, we have less understanding than we have for the shallow lakes. What is likely is that the switch will arise from a small change, perhaps intended to have some other effect, but which sets off a chain of more fundamental consequences. This is perhaps the one situation where ignorance is a virtue, for what cannot easily be predicted cannot be intercepted and annulled by those whose interests might be served by its suppression.

The problem for human societies, however, is that the unexpected can often also be the chaotic. It would be much better to decide on the need for change and systematically to bring it about in a planned way. The first step has to be the acceptance that an indefinite growth in the local or global economy is a nonsense. It is here that the conventional scientific community can use its influence, if it can retrieve its independence. It must take a wider view of its own understanding of natural phenomena and accept that the chain of response of technological fix to technological fix ties a Gordian knot whose eventual and inevitable cutting will be by the forces of chaos and violence.

Many individual scientists do realize the serious state into which the biosphere is gravitating. It has, after all, been their work which has demonstrated and documented the changes. A joint publication of the US National Academy of Sciences and the UK Royal Society perhaps somewhat belatedly acknowledges this, but the collective tone of the document is still that of science as a separate agent whose talents might be called upon to solve the problems in conventional ways. It is not a convincing document for it nowhere explores the ultimate causes of the problems, but contents itself only with the proximate ones, the symptoms alone.

If science is to be part of the solution and not to be perceived as part of the problem then it must not stand apart, as we humans in the Western technological mode see ourselves as standing apart, from the rest of the biosphere. The compartmented attitudes of conventional science embrace masses of information; but used in sectional ways this knowledge has the value only of the

Emperor's clothes. Perhaps our young people are the children in Hans Christian Andersen's story and have seen the Emperor to be naked. Perhaps it is time for conventional science to regain an independent role and, with other areas of knowledge, to form the seamless interdisciplinary cloth that converts mere information to wisdom. Only then may young people cease their current drift away from conventional science.

Annotated List of Further Reading

Water Pollution and the Management of Ecosystems: a Case Study of Science and Scientist, Brian Moss, pp. 401–422 in *Toward a More Exact Ecology*, P.J. Grubb and J.B. Whittaker (eds), Oxford: Blackwell Science Ltd, 1989.

This paper, from a symposium of the British Ecological Society, gives more detail on the ecological example of alternative stable states discussed here and traces the research and thinking that lead to it. It focuses on the problems posed by attempts to restore a polluted area of the Norfolk Broads in eastern England.

Millennium. Tribal Wisdom and the Modern World, D. Maybury-Lewis, London: Viking Penguin, 1992.

A glimpse of the new anthropology where the former perspective of study by a superior Western culture of the curiosities of the rest of the world is replaced by one in which it appears that we have much to learn and comparatively little to teach.

Man on Earth, J. Reader, London: Collins, 1988.

A series of accounts of the diversity of human societies, from the hunter gatherers to the urban dwellers of Western cities. The writing is superb, the detail fascinating.

The Family of Man, Edward Steichen, New York: Museum of Modern Art, 1983.

A collection of photographs created by Edward Steichen, first published in 1955. When you tire of the endless words and arguments, look only at this and reflect.

Harmke Kamminga

Author biography

Coming from a background in pharmacology and biochemistry, Harmke Kamminga has worked for nearly 20 years in the history and philosophy of science. Her research topics have ranged from theories of the origin of life on Earth to the history of X-ray crystallography, from the philosophy of biology to the cultural history of nutrition. She oversees the modern biomedicine program in the Wellcome Unit for the History of Medicine at the University of Cambridge. Her current interests lie in the reciprocal interactions between science, epistemology and social/political culture, especially in relation to the biomedical sciences.

Chapter 15

Harmke Kamminga

Interpreting the World, Changing the World, and Living in the World: Is a 'Science for the People' Possible?

'There must be some way out of here,' said the joker to the thief . . .
> (Bob Dylan, *All Along the Watchtower*)

What I propose, therefore, is very simple: it is nothing more than to think what we are doing.
> (Hannah Arendt, *The Human Condition*)

IT is a common perception today that we are living in a world in crisis. War, starvation, environmental disaster, mass poverty, social unrest and fragmentation, gross exploitation of people and of nature, unbridled consumerism, post-modern intellectual nihilism—these are just some of the visible elements that seem to be intrinsic to our much heralded 'New World Order' (not all of them new, of course). At the same time, scientific and technological expertise are available globally on an unprecedented scale. Is there a role for scientists in rescuing the world from catastrophe, in making it a place fit to live in for all its inhabitants? The answer is by no means straightforward.

In this chapter, I aim to examine the role that science and technology have played in producing the world we live in today, and to suggest tentatively some ways in which scientists themselves might work towards a more benign impact of their collective endeavors. No quick fixes are in the offing in this respect, but the issues need to be confronted if we are not to surrender to a cynical technocracy on the one hand, or to an anti-intellectual movement in principle hostile to any form of science on the other hand.

The central thesis from which I start is that modern science is both a product of modern (Western) culture and, in turn, has helped to shape modern (global) culture. Science is, after all, a human activity, and it is human beings who produce and apply scientific knowledge, in interaction with the material world—whether it be in a natural setting, in an experimental setup in the laboratory, or in the pages of scientific journals. Not even the most monomanic scientists are products solely of their scientific education and their immediate scientific environment—they, too, are members of the society in which they live and which inculcates them with a set of cultural values more or less specific to that society. I shall argue that these values are incorporated in the scientific work in which scientists engage, and by bringing their scientific knowledge and its products out into the world, scientists help to reinforce the values that they have internalized.

In the following pages, I shall sketch briefly how science came to have some of the characteristics that it has today, in terms of its methodology, its social role and its political uses. I shall consider the implications of a science that is above all interventive in its dealings with nature, within a framework of 'progress thinking'. I shall point to the strong coupling between modern science and established power structures, and the consequences of that coupling for the exploitation of nature and of human beings. I shall claim that a constructive science will require the subversion of existing links between science and power, and shall offer some preliminary suggestions for what it will take to set in motion such a process of subversion, and what role scientists can play in this respect.

Radicalism, conservatism and the origins of modern science

Taking my cue from recent scholarship in the history of science, I shall take 'modern science' to mean the scientific practices and institutional organization which developed, initially in Europe, in the era from the French Revolution and the Industrial Revolution onwards. It is in this era that scientists moved into the laboratory *en masse*, became supported by the state, established strong links with industry and began to have a significant influence on social and state policy. Of all forms of knowledge, scientific knowledge acquired the highest status, science became prominent in the rapidly expanding university system and science became secularized.

Before then, science (or, more accurately, natural philosophy) was above all about the workings of God's universe: natural philosophers investigated nature as God's creation and as being regulated by laws written by God. Humans might contemplate nature and exploit the fruits of nature, but only God had the freedom to set the terms

323

on which nature operates and yields her fruits to humans. In the 19th century, science came to be about the understanding and manipulation of nature in its own right: whether they were believers or not, scientists no longer wrote about God in their scientific publications, but about the natural world and about experimental systems whose intentional manipulation revealed the fundamental properties of nature.

Intervention and manipulation are fundamental characteristics of modern science. It is primarily by intervention through experiment that modern science produces its representations of reality. Theoretical concepts and models are given content by making them work under specific sets of initial and boundary conditions selected by the investigator; thus electrons, microbes, DNA, etc., are made visible and become real for us. Moreover, the knowledge produced by science is taken out of the laboratory, into the world and is transformed into specific practices of applied science and technology. Although technology has a very long history in its own right, the notion of applied science was only given content in the course of the 19th century. Witness the rise of the chemical industry, the agribusiness with its chemical fertilizers, the beginnings of the pharmaceutical and the food industries, telegraphy, electrification and so on. Since then, science and technology have become increasingly intertwined, to produce increasingly powerful impacts on nature and on society, which are changed, for better or for worse, in the process.

Of course, using the resources of nature for human ends is as old as humanity itself. The wearing of clothes, the building of shelters, the use of tools, growing crops, lighting fires, fermenting grapes, making cheese—these are just some of the ways in which human beings have long tried to make their lives and their environments comfortable and pleasurable for themselves. The novelty of modern science, and its marriage to technology, lies in the use of scientific theories as instruments of prediction, control and change of natural states. In the process, human society has moved from exploiting nature to manipulating nature and, indeed, changing nature. In an ever-increasing number of scientific domains, the 'natural' has become just one among many producible states. It is the choices that have been made about which of these realizable states to produce that have helped to create the world we live in today.

These developments did not occur in isolation, but in specific sociopolitical settings. Modern science was born and spent its infancy amidst revolutions: the French Revolution, the Industrial Revolution and the 1848 revolutions in France and in the German states. It grew up within the unificatory nationalist movements in the 19th century which created the modern nation state. In the same period, economic and political power began to shift from the land-owning classes to the new industrialists and an expanding, newly professionalized middle class. The new scientists belonged overwhelmingly to the professional middle class, which is reflected in the values they adopted. It is suggestive, moreover, that the move into the laboratory by the new experimental scientists happened in parallel with the move into the factory by the new industrialists—the production of knowledge and the production of goods were both transformed.

One of the values which was placed at center stage in this period was the ethos of progress, which, it should be stressed, was new. Where there had been natural balance before, in the 19th century everything came to be seen as being in progressive development: society, the economy, knowledge, science, life on Earth, the universe itself. A new notion of indefinitely evolving knowledge and indefinitely evolving human wellbeing became central to social and political theory, to philosophy and to science. Progress thinking was built into the very foundations of modern science *and* of the modern nation state. It was also at the root of a whole spectrum of political movements spawned in the 19th (and indeed the 20th) century, from liberal democracy to communism, from socialism to social Darwinism.

In addition, empirical science inspired, and served as a model for, political and social theory. Science, being regarded as the most progressive form of knowledge, was adopted as a model and as a tool for social change by the most influential political theorists of all complexions. And the visions of social progress offered by political theorists of different kinds were, in turn, adopted by different scientists. Together with these political perspectives, they adopted specific sets of values, which they brought into their scientific work.

The German situation is an influential case in point. A significant number of young scientists and medical men were politically active around the time of the 1848 revolutions against the autocratic Prussian monarchy. They were mostly liberal democrats or socialists, atheists and philosophical materialists, and they saw their science as an integral part of their social and political ideals: being a scientist *meant* being in the vanguard of intellectual, social and political progress. The conservative backlash after 1848, resulting in the consolidation of Prussian hegemony (and eventually in the 'iron' rule of Bismarck over a unified, centralized Germany), caused a large proportion of these radicals to abandon political activism. Many of these retreating activists stuck to their scientific ideals, however, and tried to use their scientific authority to effect social change, through the application of scientific knowledge. But, in so doing, they almost invariably found themselves cooperating, willingly or unwillingly, with an authoritarian state machinery which used the scientists' expertise for its own ends: under Bismarck's rule, the building of a strong, expansionist nation went hand in hand with the building of state institutions for scientific research which served the nation.

State support for science and the appointment of scientists to socially, economically or politically influential positions were instrumental in forging the links between science and ruling power structures. This happened not only in Germany, of course, but quite generally in the industrialized nations, albeit at different rates and times. (The German model was certainly much admired and emulated.) Moreover, through colonialism and imperialism, science was exported throughout the world and, at the instigation of the colonial powers, began to transform the colonized world. Upon decolonization, newly independent governments of all political persuasions made it a priority to harness Western-style science and technology as an essential route towards economic and political autonomy. (In practice, such development usually led to new dependencies and to compromises with the very powers of imperialism which had been challenged in struggles for independence, as described in Claude Alvares' chapter.)

Regardless of the political system within which they worked, scientists had a great deal to offer the state, industry and multinational organizations—and still do. It is precisely the interventive power of modern science that has, in practice, been of enormous economic, social and political use. The term interventive is used here to refer to the act of intervening in a morally neutral sense. In enlisting science, politically and economically powerful groupings have also steered science along the route towards ever-increasing intervention and control (see, for example, the study by Kay, for a discussion of the objectives of the Rockefeller Foundation in the shaping of 20th century biology). Looking at the world today, one does not need to be a Luddite to ask whether the price paid for the marriage between science and political power may have been too high.

The main point I have tried to make so far is that modern science, from its beginnings, has been seen as a prime instrument for effecting social change, both by political radicals and by those concerned with conserving or enhancing their economic or political power. I also maintain that it is the promotion of the interventive capacity of modern science that has made it into an instrument that is progressive by the criteria of a whole spectrum of political ideologies, from left to right. The politically schizoid roots of modern science, in radical materialism and in an expansionist free enterprise industrialism, need to be recognized if we are to understand how science has changed our conception of reality and the world itself, and how this cuts through conventional political divides.

One of the *Theses on Feuerbach* written by Karl Marx in 1845 states that 'The philosophers have only *interpreted* the world in various ways; the point, however, is to *change* it.' Marx, too, saw science as a pre-eminently progressive force and tool for change, and science has certainly played its part in changing the world—though not generally in the ways that Marx had in mind. I submit that it is pertinent to raise the question to what extent the perceived fundamental characteristics of modern science itself have, in practice, guided the ways in which we interpret the world, change the world, and live in the world.

Science, knowledge and reality

Let us consider some common assumptions about science: (1) while fallible in principle, science progressively approaches truth; (2) by virtue of its method, science is objective—the truths it produces are universally valid and value-neutral; and (3) science provides us with representations of reality which are more reliable than any that can be produced by non-scientific means.

The elusive nature of truth

The truth of scientific theories is notoriously difficult to defend, either historically or philosophically (Cartwright, 1983). All scientific theories of the past have been amended or overthrown altogether because they were subsequently judged to be inadequate (not to be 'true'). And rigorous criteria of truth for scientific theories cannot be offered: how would we recognize truth, in the sense of correspondence to what the world is 'really' like, if we ever reached it? As the most junior students of philosophy of science know, confirmation of predictions deduced from some theoretical formalism (when given a physical interpretation) is no guarantee of the truth of that theory, because false premises can yield true conclusions by logical deduction.

If we use weaker notions of truth, in terms of consensus or of coherence among a network of theories, we cannot escape historical relativism: neither consensus among scientists nor theoretical coherence has maintained stability over time. This observation, however, leaves open the possibility that changes in consensus, or coherence, have conserved the truth content of old theories, and added new truths to these theories while eliminating their failures— that there has been progress overall. Is it possible, perhaps, to measure progress?

Theory-neutral criteria of progress, in the sense of increased truth content, are in fact equally problematic. Certainly, a particular lineage of successively modified theories typically displays increasing explanatory and predictive success and/or greater coherence within a broader theoretical framework. Such measures may indeed indicate that a succession of theories has displayed progress internally, but, beyond that, further progress is by no means guaranteed: such a lineage can still be overthrown, become extinct, in the long run. The intermediary improvements may then, retrospectively, look like scholastic tinkering towards a dead end. Ptolemaic geocentric astronomy is a classic example.

Although absolute truth is elusive, we do not need to become out and out skeptics. We all accept, in our everyday lives, certain 'truths' produced by science, for instance when we take antibiotics against infections, swallow vitamin pills, use fertilizers in the garden, refuse to buy aerosols containing chlorofluorocarbons, and so on. Such accepted truths, however, are invariably the outcome of controversy and of contests for authority in the production of knowledge. As historians and sociologists have been demonstrating, the outcome of most scientific controversies is unpredictable *at the time*: all sides engaged in a controversy tend to muster convincing arguments and experimental demonstrations and to show up inadequacies in those of their opponents. As Bruno Latour has argued, nature only becomes the arbiter once a controversy has been closed, i.e. when one side's 'truth' has become accepted. In a winners' history, the victors may in retrospect seem to have had right on their side all along, but multiple elements are involved in the closure of controversies: quite often closer study reveals that, in some form or another, it was *might* the victors had on their side.

This may be an uncomfortable conclusion for defenders of the verisimilitude and objectivity of science, but it also opens up new freedoms: collectively, we make *choices* in the attribution of truth. That does not mean that we can have a vote on whether, say, the second law of thermo-dynamics holds or not. By committing ourselves to some 'truths', we have to take others on board. In that sense, science has displayed a strong internal dynamic; once the nature of the enterprise has been accepted, we are not free to invent anything we like.

Nevertheless, nature offers many degrees of freedom in the ways in which we represent and understand natural states. Which kinds of representations and understandings we accept as true (in practice) depends crucially on collective attributions of expertise. With respect to our understanding of nature, it is modern science that, by social consensus, has become the pre-eminent provider of expertise. The forging of that consensus was not inevitable or predetermined–it was a social process, driven by social choices. In theory at least, we can still make a collective choice to steer that process in a different direction. In practice, the strong alliance between science and economic and political power has provided established power structures with the technological means to uphold their power. It is these power relations, not simply nature itself, which constrain our choices in practice, also with respect to attributions of truth and expertise. On a more optimistic note, power relations have never remained permanently stable in human history, and it is up to us, collectively, to challenge them if that seems necessary to create a better world.

How objective is scientific knowledge?

Are the assumptions of objectivity and universality of science grounded any more firmly than the notion of scientific truth? In fact, criteria of objectivity and universality are just as difficult to maintain with rigor as are criteria of truth. We cannot stand above and outside scientific practice to judge whether its principles are objective or universal. At best, we can have inter-subjective agreement (consensus) about the validity of scientific knowledge. Generally, such judgments are made by those already initiated in the practices and culture of science, whether directly or indirectly. To us the knowledge gaining (what philosophers more precisely term 'epistemological') and pragmatic successes of modern science are indeed impressive and persuasive, but that observation provides insufficient justification for the claim that science produces forms of knowledge which are objective and universally valid for all time.

It may be instructive to examine where the notions of universality and objectivity come from and why so many people, including most practicing scientists, have faith in them. I propose that part of the answer lies in the transformation of natural philosophy into modern science. Natural philosophy was fundamentally about God, about nature as God's creation and as being regulated by laws written by God. The workings of nature could be made visible to humans, but were themselves above and beyond human activity and control. In this sense, the workings of nature were transcendent, and the principles underlying natural phenomena, being God's, not human's, invention, were universal and independent of human value systems.

The displacement of God from nature upon the making of modern science was not, however, accompanied by an exclusion of this notion of universality from science. The fundamental workings of nature remained transcendent in the sense of being thought to be beyond human control, and what scientists found out about nature continued to be seen as universally valid knowledge. The successful exploration of scientific theories in a variety of settings was extrapolated to infinity by holding laws of nature to be space and time invariant. In other words, secularized science still had its universal laws of nature, even if it no longer recognized a legislator.

The characterization of science as being objective has an intricate history, complicated by profound changes in meaning of the objective/subjective distinction, as Raymond Williams pointed out in 1976. Very briefly, the traditional distinction in scholastic philosophy saw the 'subjective' as what things are in themselves (their substance), and the 'objective' as those features of things that are presented to consciousness. After various transitional uses, the most radical transformation of these original meanings came with German classical idealist philosophy: the subject became the active mind or thinking agent, and the object that which is other than the active mind or thinking agent, so that the objective is that which belongs to the object of thought. Moreover, in this idealist tradition it is the thinking agent (the subject) which actively shapes the objects of thought. In the (romanticist) scientific form of German classical idealism, *Naturphilosophie*, it was introspection by the thinking subject which created the objects of thought *as* truths about nature.

In the course of the 19th century, the increasingly influential positivist philosophy gave currency to more familiar meanings of the terms: 'subjective' began to mean that which only exists in the mind of the subject, and eventually that which is based on impressions rather than facts and is influenced by personal feelings. 'Objective', on the other hand, began to mean that which is taken from an external object, and eventually that which is factual, neutral, impartial, reliable. It seems that modern science inherited both the idealist and the positivist senses of objectivity: thoughts and statements about nature that are supposedly neutral and impartial are *at the same time* regarded as truths about nature—moreover, they are regarded as *universal* truths of nature.

Unlike the philosophical idealist, the materialist assumes the existence of a mind-independent reality. According to the materialist, the ways in which we acquire knowledge of that mind-independent ('objectively existing') material world depend on the ways in which we, as human beings, interact with the world. Some versions of materialism have traditionally adopted a somewhat naive epistemology, which, in effect, comes very close to an idealist epistemology: it holds that our careful observations of nature bring us directly into contact with the objective features of nature, with truths about nature. This kind of epistemology, linked with positivism, has, implicitly, been very common within science in the last two centuries.

Also during the course of the 19th century, scientists increasingly made attempts to reduce the subjective influence of the individual observer in scientific enquiry: more and more recording instruments were introduced to eliminate the subjectivity of perception, measuring devices were standardized to reduce the variability of observations by different observers, data were tabulated for impartial interpretation. Of course, the design of recording instruments, the means of standardization and the interpretation of data were, and are, theory-laden, and in that sense not neutral or impartial, but such stratagems nevertheless had the effect of making science *seem* reliable in its methods of producing truths in the form of supposedly objective, observer-neutral facts.

Facts and meaning

Modern science, however, is not simply about producing facts—whether we do this by direct observation of nature or by means of experiment. It is also about interpreting facts and organizing them, in the light of or in the form of theories. Concepts and theories are not simple descriptions of 'what is out there'. Concepts and theories are built, by human beings, as a result of their interactions with the world and of their interpretations of the outcome of such interactions. The ways in which human beings interact with the world are a function of opportunities that are created socially, not only in terms of the provision of education, institutional settings, equipment and technical assistance, but also in terms of the setting of objectives for research programs. Once a concept or a theory has been formulated, tested in different settings and accepted, the dimension which typically gets 'abstracted away' retrospectively is the social process that was part of the theory construction. Theories then become 'objectified' and used as instruments for potentially universal use, independently of the specific social processes which helped to generate them. The representations of reality thus produced by science then seem to be socially and culturally transcendent, objective and reliable.

The representations of reality produced by modern science are, as a rule, produced by means of experimentation, intervention and manipulation of some contrived setup in the laboratory (or by examining a pre-selected set of variables in field studies). Such setups (or sets of variables) are not given in nature, but they are selected, designed and constructed by human beings for particular purposes. New instruments, new experimental procedures provide new angles on reality. Such novel perspectives must, first of all, make sense to be of value. The observation of experimental data involves a great deal of interpretation in the light of pre-existing knowledge, and the process of interpretation typically involves an accommodation of new facts within the existing body of knowledge, so as to maintain overall coherence.

Secondly, the attribution of meaning to scientific knowledge produced in the laboratory is made not just by the individual scientist, or even the broader scientific community, but by larger and more diverse social groupings. Specific lines of research are pursued not only because the individuals pursuing them find them scientifically meaningful and of interest, but because they are, or are made to be, meaningful and of interest (not necessarily in the same way!) to funding agencies, technologists, policy-makers, legislators and so on. It is important to realize that the overall intentions of individual scientists and of those promoting their research need not be the same.

For instance, the scientist trying to identify a genetic marker for a particular disease is likely to pursue such research with the ultimate aim of alleviating human suffering. (Of course, scientists, like other people, always have multiple aims; for the sake of argument, I shall here leave out of consideration aims such as making a living, intellectual excitement, impressing one's peers, publishing papers to secure further funding, etc.) On the other hand, health insurance companies may stress the importance of the same research (and even fund it) because the prospect of screening becoming possible for that disease will enable them to increase insurance premiums for carriers of the gene sequence in question (or they may even refuse to insure carriers at all if that would be economically most profitable). In this example, the interests of the scientist and of the health insurance company coincide at the level of means (the identification of a genetic marker), but the ends are quite different.

Most practicing scientists are, of course, well aware of the fact that the ways in which the knowledge they produce is used by society at large do not necessarily conform with their own intentions. Most practicing scientists also feel, however, that they are not responsible for that situation: *they* produce the objective facts and society at large decides what to do with those facts. It is this strict separation between supposedly objective, value-free knowledge and the value-laden social application of that knowledge which gives many scientists their curiously amoral and apolitical self-image as scientists; the results of their work stand above morality and politics, while the application of these results is the concern and responsibility of others.

I propose that *this is a pernicious and profoundly alienating situation*. We all, collectively, help to define social and political values and objectives—even scientists. In that sense, we are all responsible for the ways in which scientific knowledge is produced and applied. If we feel that the profit motive or military power, for example, are unworthy objectives in scientific endeavor, then it is the principles underlying the profit motive or military power we should challenge—not retreat under the 'objective' cloak of the laboratory as if these principles had nothing to do with us.

As a matter of fact, science has not been the only player in the game of controlling and manipulating nature, and scientists have not been the only people to decide how such control and manipulation should be directed. But scientists have (very successfully) created possibilities that have suited the aims of those with the means and power to exploit them. A greater political involvement of scientists is required—not as experts to be consulted, but as *critics* of the established order—so that we can all have a say in the kind of world we are creating.

One practical implication would be that science education, at all levels, needs to be broadened significantly: science should be taught, not as the sole pinnacle of human progress, but as one endeavor among many human endeavors, and it should be critically evaluated and compared with other endeavors in terms of the cultural values which it incorporates. Scientists themselves could most usefully press for such changes in education and training, albeit at the cost of de-emphasizing the technical content of their own specialities. In other words, I am not advocating, as the top priority, that scientists should educate the general public about science, although that, too, is necessary: the most pressing priority is not to take science out into the world, but to bring the world explicitly back into science.

Science as politics

There are, of course, many scientists who are politically aware and active, as witnessed, for example, by environmentalist movements and organizations for the social responsibility of science. From them, we obtain exposures of links between specific research programs and, for example, the military–industrial complex, we are alerted to the potentially sinister implications of, say, the Human Genome Project, we obtain critiques of scientific reductionism, of the separation between humans and nature, and so on. There is, however, a more fundamental issue that needs to be addressed, and that is whether the value system inherent in modern science as a means of understanding the world can be separated in any meaningful way, firstly, from the value systems which direct science as a means of manipulating the world and, secondly, from the value systems of the ruling powers which promote scientific development along specific routes.

I have already referred to the new 'progress thinking' that became so commonplace in the industrialized nations in the 19th century. 'Progress' is built into the very foundations of modern science and, once we think in terms of the category of progress, it is all too easy to see as progressive the enormous growth in scientific knowledge over the past 200 years. Similarly, the social changes brought about by applied science and the social changes brought about by political and economic movements towards democracy and self-determination are commonly interpreted in terms of a progressive development. Without going into the general problematics of progress thinking here, I want to draw attention to what I believe to be one of its elements—that is, the emphasis on predictive power as a criterion of what constitutes knowledge.

The predictive power of a scientific theory is nowadays upheld as one of the central yardsticks of its success. The capacity to yield novel predictions which are then confirmed has become perhaps *the* criterion of what constitutes scientific knowledge (and, by implication, of what constitutes rationality). Predictive power and explanatory power tend to be mentioned in the same breath, the link between the two having been formalized by the Hempel–Oppenheim symmetry thesis, according to which the logical forms of an explanatory and of a predictive argument in science are equivalent. Despite the acknowledged problematic nature of the symmetry thesis, the capacity of science to explain and its capacity to predict continue to be seen as intimately linked.

Historically, however, the emphasis was on the explanatory content of theories of nature, long before the use of theories as instruments for novel prediction became prominent. (There have also been profound historical changes in criteria of what constitutes a good explanation, but I shall here restrict the discussion to prediction.) To my knowledge no-one has yet explored the questions of when and why predictive power became such a potent criterion of what constitutes good science. It was not always used as a criterion: it was *chosen*, and that choice has had far-reaching consequences for the ways in which modern science has developed. Yet the process of choice has become invisible.

Retrospectively, we can see any deduction from some formalism, say Newton's laws of motion, as a prediction, but that may not have been at all how Newton and his contemporaries saw it. For example, Bishop Berkeley, the 18th century philosopher, is nowadays widely interpreted as having regarded Newton's laws as predictive devices. Berkeley himself, however, used the term 'expectation', not prediction. For Berkeley, God was the ultimate explanation of everything, and I would interpret Berkeley's 'expectation' as *anticipation* of what God will present to us—certainly not as a prediction of what will happen when we apply a theory in manipulating a particular experimental system.

What is misleading for us, when we project our categories back into the past, is the perceived link between logical deduction and prediction. Because predictions are made by deducing the logical consequences of some theory's formalism, we are liable to think that *any* exploration of the logical consequences of a theory, present or past, entailed the making of predictions in the modern sense. The deductive ideal, with Euclidean geometry as the prime exemplar, was certainly powerful in the marriage between mathematics and the study of physical phenomena. (Indeed, many developments in mathematics, such as the development of differential calculus, were motivated by problems in natural philosophy.) But deduction is not automatically the same as prediction. For a start, theories and theoretical models are abstractions and idealizations, which must then again be given a physical interpretation to test predictions in practice. Setting up a predictive argument is more than a matter of logic alone. Moreover, although prediction and deduction are regarded as formally equivalent now and although that equivalence can then be projected back into the past, we should recognize that there may not have been any *intention* to predict in the modern sense until laboratory science made prediction relevant in the context of intervention and manipulation.

It seems plausible that the origins of the emphasis on prediction were bound up intimately with thinking in terms of progress, which brought the future into view more forcefully than ever before and, most directly, with the rise of laboratory science. Once scientists systematically began to explore the consequences of their theories in contrived settings in the laboratory, it became pertinent to work out what, according to the theory, *should* happen under the specific initial and boundary conditions of a particular experiment. (I do not wish to imply that the theory is always prior to the empirical investigation; clearly, there are constant interactions between theory and experiment, with modifications being made both to the theory and to the experimental setup to make the two fit.) Successful prediction also opens up possibilities for the controlled production of science-based technology.

As I have suggested earlier, it is precisely this capacity of science to intervene and to manipulate, on the basis of prediction, which made applied science a socially successful enterprise and which coupled science so strongly to technological, social and political intervention. Predictive power, which we now regard as an objective measure of rational scientific knowledge, became meaningful as such because science was steered into the direction of manipulating the world, over and above manipulating contrived settings in the laboratory, and over and above interpreting (explaining) the world. In that sense, the choice of predictive power as a criterion of what constitutes knowledge was fundamentally a political choice, not one that was value-free. And if we accept predictive power as a prime criterion of knowledge then, for better or worse, we accept with it more general values of intervention and manipulation. In any case, an intellectually serious scientific community should be aware that even our seemingly most solid criteria of knowledge were constructed historically and should not simply be taken on trust as perennially objective yardsticks.

The recognition that human beings create not only possibilities for the manipulation and control of nature (the activity which is often, and significantly, referred to as 'playing God'), but also the criteria of success of that endeavor, entail that changing nature is within human control. Of course, there are limits to such control and of course changing nature often has unforeseen consequences (nature 'bites back' in multiple ways). By creating and using antibiotics, we create antibiotic-resistant strains of bacteria; by creating and using chlorofluorocarbons, we create holes in the ozone layer, and so on. What we predict will happen under one set of conditions will typically have unforeseen consequences under more complex sets of conditions. By the predictive criterion itself, the successes of our interventive science in epistemology have often been more limited out in the world than they have been in the laboratory (or the factory), even if other objectives, such as refrigerating perishable foods or making profit, have still been met. Given that there are multiple objectives at play, it is important not to confuse success in terms of some pragmatic criterion, such as making profit, with objective epistemological success.

A new generation of scientists may be willing to shed the ungrounded (and alienating) notion of transcendent objectivity and be prepared to admit that, by acknowledging control over its practices, it has control over the knowledge it produces. To avoid misunderstanding, I stress again that such control does, at any given time, operate under social, cultural and natural constraints—we are not, I hope, Nietzschean supermen. The point is that these constraints are not fixed for all time—they are dynamic: we ourselves help to support them and we ourselves can help to transform them. With any luck, a re-politicized scientific community will question more forcefully than has become the norm what kind of knowledge it is producing, and whose interests are being served by the production of that knowledge.

Conclusions

With the practices of modern science, our interpretations of and interventions in nature have changed the world and do change the world profoundly. Is there any way, then, of enlisting science to change the world in such a way that we can live with it and in it for our mutual wellbeing? I have here tried to uncover some of the political roots and political content of modern science in general terms. I have suggested that the way in which modern science operates is a function of social and political choices made historically by human beings, regardless of the political system within which it is practiced now. That suggestion entails that we cannot simply make a better world by linking science, as it is, to whatever we may regard as a better political system: the capacities of science for intervention and manipulation are liable to be exploited by any sociopolitical power structures that are in place, or come into place. Nor is it simply a matter of persuading scientists that choices between competing scientific methodologies or models are political choices.

The fundamental point is that criteria for what constitutes knowledge have, historically, been contested, and that contests for knowledge are contests for power. For nearly two centuries, that contest has been rigged in favor of scientific knowledge by the established power structures. We should ask *why* scientific knowledge has acquired the privileged status that it enjoys, *why* it is that scientists' endeavors are not seen to be on a par with other cultural endeavors, but have come to be singled out as providing the one and only expert route to knowledge and guide to action. We need to confront the question of what kinds of knowledge we want to produce and recognize that it is at the same time a question about what kinds of power relations we want to support—and what kind of world we want to live in.

A socially responsible science has to be a science that does not allow itself to be set apart from, let alone above, other human endeavors. In our interactions with the world we are all involved in the production of knowledge about the world—in that sense, there is no single group of experts. Experts are defined as such and supported by those in whose interest that form of expertise works. Rejecting the label of 'scientific expert' would be one first step towards the making of a science for the people. Scientists *can* make their pacts with nature and with their fellow human beings, providing that they are prepared to acknowledge, and to transform, their pacts with power.

Annotated List of Further Reading

How the Laws of Physics Lie, Nancy Cartwright, Oxford: Clarendon Press, 1983.

The central claim of this book is that really powerful explanatory laws such as those found in theoretical physics do not state the truth about natural phenomena. Cartwright shows that the fundamental laws of science are abstractions and idealizations which do not govern real objects: they only govern objects in theoretical models. An important implication of this argument is that the application of ideal and abstract laws can mislead scientists into thinking that they can explain and control nature vigorously, when they are in fact explaining and controlling models—with unforeseen consequences in the real world.

De-centring the 'Big Picture', The Origins of Modern Science and the Modern Origins of Science, Andrew Cunningham and Perry Williams, *British Journal for the History of Science* **26** (4), 407–432, 1993.

A radical challenge to the common view that modern science began with 'scientific revolution' in the 17th century. Instead, the authors argue persuasively that it was only in the 19th century that practices, aims and values of science, in a form recognizable to us, were first put into place.

Representing and Intervening, Ian Hacking, Cambridge: Cambridge University Press, 1983.

A pioneering and readable philosophical account of experimental practice in science, which explores the creation, production, refinement and stabilization of phenomena in the course of scientific experimentation. Hacking argues that it is through experimental manipulation, not theorizing, that scientists provide evidence for the reality of hypothetical objects: if a theoretical entity can be manipulated so that it has observable effects in our experimental setups then, says Hacking, it exists.

The Molecular Vision of Life, Lily E. Kay, New York: Oxford University Press, 1993.

A very readable history of American molecular biology, which demonstrates the role which key scientists and private sponsors played in directing biological research towards a shared vision of science and society. Especially informative about the intimate links between political and scientific aspirations in the Rockefeller Foundation's Science of Man agenda—the driving force behind the Foundation's powerful support for the molecularization of biology.

Science in Action, Bruno Latour, Milton Keynes: Open University Press, 1987.

A provocative study of scientific practice which successfully undermines the traditional demarcation between 'external' social context and 'internal' scientific content: Latour shows that both context and content are constitutive of consensual scientific knowledge. Richly and wittily illustrated with real-life case studies mapping the diverse strategies involved in the production of scientific knowledge.

Controlling Life: Jacques Loeb and the Engineering Ideal in Biology, Philip Pauly, Berkeley: University of California Press, 1987.
Much more than a scientific biography of Loeb, this work presents an innovative history of the control of life as a persistent scientific ideal of the 20th century and analyzes its repercussions in subsequent attempts towards the control and artificialization of living organisms. Telling examples range from the production of genetic mutations, via behavioral psychology, to the development of oral contraceptives and the new biotechnologies.

Man and Society: Political and Social Theory from Macchiavelli to Marx, Vol. III: Hegel, Marx, Engels, and the Idea of Progress, John P. Plamenatz, 2nd edn with R. Wokler, London: Longman, 1992.
First published in 1963, this monumental work on the history of political and social theory has become a classic. Volume III discusses the idea of progress as a novel, modern belief in the indefinite increase of man's knowledge of and power over nature, leading to ever increasing human happiness.

Keywords, Raymond Williams, London: Fontana, 1988 (revised edn).
An incisive analysis of how meanings have been shaped, altered, confused, redefined and reinforced as the historical contexts in which they were applied changed. An essential work of reference for anyone tempted to project current meanings back into the past.

Tom Wakeford

Author biography

Tom Wakeford is one of three science students who met at King's College, Cambridge and conceived the idea of bringing together scientists concerned to use their different disciplines to focus on science's potential to benefit and harm the Earth and its inhabitants. Having studied biology, ecology and the history and philosophy of science at Cambridge, his current doctoral research at the Department of Biology, University of York, UK, concerns intracellular symbiosis and microbial ecology.

Chapter 16

Tom Wakeford

Bringing Science Down to Earth

IN contemporary culture 'science' is a potent instrument of persuasion. Many disciplines have associated themselves with those who are seen to follow 'the scientific method', by renaming themselves. Endeavors that had not traditionally been recognized as 'science' have augmented their status by association: for politics read 'political *science*', for physical education, 'sports *science*', while librarianship has become 'information *science*'. Some well-established scientific disciplines thus attempt to enhance their status and authority. Geology is often renamed 'earth *science*', botany 'plant *science*' and neurology 'neuro*science*'.

Despite the authority attributed to science, a recent Nobel conference asked whether today we are instead witnessing the 'end of science?'. The introduction to the conference proceedings described the question as being 'rather tongue in cheek, but also relevant . . . celebrating 25 years of the

Nobel conference, yet questioning the staying power of science as we know it'. Participants sought to discard the standard account for the nature of the scientific process and even declared the death of science in its present form. For these scholars, science can no longer claim to be a 'fortress of objectivity'. Rather, 'what we know is a function of time, place and accidents of communities and their conversation'.

Some contributors to this book have outlined insights that derive from outside what is normally regarded as 'science'. In the second chapter Lynn Margulis describes a tale from the Chewong people of Malaysia that contains important lessons for all those who carry out research. The idea of the 'pollution of time' was developed by John Whitelegg partly from the imaginative insights of a children's fairy tale called *Momo*. The ability to manage land sustainably was present in the Turkana people of East Africa, amongst others, centuries before the arrival of colonial planners, as described by George Monbiot. Claude Alvares, having lived through the rise and fall of scientism in his native India, describes how colonization by science, 'surreptitiously replaced' the ballot and local wisdom, removing people's right to certify knowledge themselves.

The stark contrast of intellectual worth some scientists perceive when comparing their own understandings with those of indigenous peoples, though repudiated in numerous chapters of this volume, is epitomized by the scientist and popularizer Lewis Wolpert in *The Un-Natural Nature of Science*, where he describes such knowledge as 'witchcraft and magic'. He condemns 'relativists' in anthropology and sociology for an unwillingness to 'regard thinking in primitive societies as somehow inferior to that which characterises the West—namely scientific thinking and a passion for rationality'.

Others now see what has been traditionally separated off as 'science' as just part of a continuum of quests and understandings, from studies of the very simple to the highly complex. Parts of laboratory physics can be extremely simple and predictable in their abstract, idealized settings. But, as Richard Lindsay's chapter explains, out in the real world even the physical sciences have proved unpredictable.

Living organisms are inherently complex products of historical processes. Thus ecological, psychological and sociological phenomena are so contingent on other highly variable factors that, as the biologist G.G. Simpson once remarked, the principles of physics and mathematics alone are unlikely to be able to explain much of what is going on. This is to judge the worth of all knowledge by the standards of physics and mathematics. Harmke Kamminga's chapter suggests that not only is the word 'science' of recent origin, but also that, contrary to most scientists' beliefs, predictability is only *one* of the ways in which knowledge has been certified in the past.

Lewis Wolpert believes that all true science 'aspires to be like physics and physics aspires to be like mathematics'. Thus he argues that 'biology has a long way to go', although he counsels, 'biologists can still be full of hope'. Wolpert goes on to ask 'what hope is there for sociology acquiring a physics-like lustre?' and concludes 'at this stage it is premature to expect much progress'. For Claude Alvares, Wolpert's vision of science presents worrying parallels with totalitarian political regimes—monolithic, dogmatic, expansionist.

There are other challenges to Wolpert's vision of a unified objective science. Ironically, one example comes from the 19th century physicist, James Clerk Maxwell, who Wolpert describes as epitomizing what it is to be scientific. Over a century ago, Maxwell wrote

Perhaps the book, as it has been called, of nature is regularly paged; if so, no doubt the introductory parts will explain those that follow, and the methods taught in the first chapters will be taken for granted and used as an illustration in the more advanced parts of the course; but if it is not a book at all, but a magazine, nothing is more foolish than to suppose that one part can throw light on another.

Wolpert's 'regularly paged' mathematical approach has a long history. Almost 400 years ago, Galileo wrote of a single 'author of nature' writing in the 'language of mathematics'. Yet increasingly, philosophers and sociologists of science are turning towards the 'magazine' model of knowledge.

In contrast with the unification envisaged by Wolpert and others, philosophers Richard Rorty and Ian Hacking see the future of science as disunified and diverse. Having cited Maxwell in his contribution to the Nobel conference, Hacking also questions whether unity is really a sensible goal for science. Why must scientific thought be centered around one unifying discipline? Hacking would prefer that researchers in different disciplines should be able to see more clearly the cross-fertilization of ideas between one and the other without one becoming supreme.

This suggestion is echoed in several earlier chapters by the call for a more interdisciplinary approach to research. In the 1980s Rorty speculated that the term 'science', having lost its honorific value, will gradually decrease in usage over the coming decades. There will be physicists, chemists, ecologists and all the individual disciplines, but no single pursuit called 'science' to be distinguished from what have traditionally been 'the humanities', suggests Rorty. There is no single privileged language, nor any one fundamental template with which all phenomena must be shaped.

One reason why an essentially unified image of science has survived so long is that there are at least two powerful forces promoting such a view. Firstly, there is the way in which funding bodies are seen to judge the scientific merit of an application for funds by the ability of the proposed research to contribute to the further unification of scientific knowledge. Secondly, as the popularity of science declined amongst young people in the late 1980s, as measured by the number of people applying to university to read science subjects, organizations such as the British Association for the Advancement of Science and the Royal Society responded by setting up initiatives to promote the 'public understanding of science'.

In principle, perhaps any initiatives to increase the public understanding of science are worthwhile. After all, who could be against increased understanding? That there should be a greater level of communication between scientists of different disciplines and also between all of them and non-scientists is surely a praiseworthy sentiment. But many commentators have added that there is more to the public understanding of science than merely teaching people about the content of science. There must also be a component about science's institutional embedding, the practices of scientists, controversies and the cultural forces affecting their research.

In 1994, the UK Government funded Britain's first National Science Week. All over the country, the public were encouraged to attend interactive exhibits such as 'virtual reality journeys through a sewage system' or 'getting granny bar-coded'. Letting people take part in simple, pre-arranged experiments, finding that 'science is fun', could be seen as a way of increasing the popularity of science rather than allowing a broader awareness to develop. This fits in exactly with the agenda for public understanding set out by Wolpert, which as science journalist Jon Turney has put it, promotes no more than 'understanding the superiority of the scientific mode of investigation'.

On becoming Prime Minister, John Major announced that he wanted a nation 'at ease with itself'. Science popularizers want the public to be 'at ease' with science, but without questioning the powerful forces controlling, amongst other things, the way in which results are interpreted and applied. If we accept the contemporary portrayal of science as progressing by ethereal and individual far-sighted leaps and bounds, historian James Cornell asks 'What role for lesser mortals? To clap from the sidelines?'. Whether the rest of the world applauds or turns away in bewilderment, scientists remain in the driving seat.

Vacating the driving seat for the armchair, distinguished scientists often turn to popularizing their work in the form of books or magazine articles. In doing so they become, like Wolpert, what Dorothy Nelkin calls 'visible scientists' and are perhaps even more important in shaping the view of science held by non-scientists than the professional promoters of science.

With his book, *A Brief History of Time*, meriting a place in the *Guinness Book of Records* for its length of stay on the non-fiction bestseller lists, Stephen Hawking is the most widely read author in the history of science. Hawking makes available to many millions of people more than just a description of the history of their universe. For them, Hawking embodies much of what science represents.

In his most recent book, *Black Holes and Baby Universes*, Hawking has spoken of a passion for popularizing his scientific worldview. Since the scientific revolution of the 17th century, 'we have extended the work of Galileo and Newton to almost every area of the universe. We now have mathematical laws that govern *everything* we normally experience' (my emphasis).

Despite feeling that humans could conceivably be 'masters of the universe', Hawking concedes that 'love, faith, and morality belong to a different category from physics. You cannot deduce how one should behave from physics'. But, he goes on, 'one could hope that the logical thought that physics and mathematics involves would guide one also in one's moral behaviour'.

Stephen Hawking hopes his work has demonstrated 'that some sort of positivist approach . . . is the only way to understand the universe, at least for a theoretical physicist'. Philosophers of science are typified by Hawking as a 'subspecies' of 'failed physicists' who 'found it too difficult to invent new theories and so took to writing about the philosophy of physics instead . . . They are not in touch with the present frontier of physics'.

For a second example of an ambassador for science who promotes the view of science as uniquely valid we need only move from Cambridge, England to Cambridge, Massachusetts. Edward O. Wilson is a Harvard academic who has become one of a handful of influential experts who are able to move freely about the intellectual landscape and enter new domains of debate. Rather like a multinational corporation, he is able to appear in many locales and in many guises, without being clearly under anyone's jurisdiction.

Having established his expertise in the social behavior of insects, Wilson has moved from an intra-disciplinary frame to make supra-disciplinary claims. In his landmark book, *Sociobiology: the New Synthesis*, Wilson sees his new discipline as being 'created by gifted investigators who work primarily in population biology, invertebrate biology, including entomology especially, and vertebrate zoology'. His central theme, expressed in the chapter title 'The Morality of the Gene', is a prophecy of 'a genetically accurate and hence completely fair code of ethics' via

355

sociobiology. John Lyne and Henry Howe have suggested that, with the use of the genetic terminology, Wilson 'has tapped into an age-old longing to provide a scientific, "deep" explanation, and with it some hope of some sense of closure to the confusion and messiness of human conduct'.

Just as Hawking has claimed that 'the end' is 'in sight' for much of physical science, Wilson proposes the resolution of much of the remaining uncertainties in biological and social sciences. Twenty years later, sociobiology has eagerly attempted to colonize research areas as diverse as economics, anthropology and psychology. Here, judgment against rival hypotheses is often carried out by *ad hoc* strategies rather than the standards of any particular discipline.

Like Hawking, Wilson has little time for philosophers who, 'like everyone else . . . measure their personal emotional responses to various alternatives as though consulting a hidden oracle'. Wilson usually uses the term 'ideology' in contrast with nature and reason, especially since, for him, ideology has to bow to 'our hidden masters the genes'. Others have suggested that far from being above it, Wilson's rhetoric is deeply embedded within his own ideology.

Hawking and Wilson are just two examples of the way in which two 'visible scientists' have helped to establish an image of science as 'objective'. Others, such as the geneticist Steve Jones, appear slightly less enchanted, as shown in his book *The Language of the Genes*. Despite displaying the same contempt Hawking and Wilson show for philosophers, once writing that 'philosophy is to science as pornography is to art', Jones has become well known for stating that science does not have all the answers. He points to how earlier generations of geneticists promoted the idea of human improvement by selective breeding of some and enforced sterilization of others.

Eugenics is one of the many powerful illustrations of the dangers of seeing scientific reasoning as superior to that which takes place, for example, in ethics or sociology. Similarly, with a single paper in *Science*, Garrett Hardin helped to give scientific justification to post-colonial land privatization policies. Consequently, not only did thousands, if not millions, of people die, but as George Monbiot's chapter describes, crude privatization proved far inferior to the native systems that had been in place for centuries. Disasters have also befallen native farmers who have been forcibly 'collectivized' by governments coming from the opposite end of the political spectrum to Hardin. Such was the case in Ethiopia, where farmers were separated from the land that they had farmed for generations by being forcibly moved around under the direction of the communist regime in the capital, Addis Ababa, all in the name of the same, albeit Marxist, science. Thus a belief in the superiority of scientific thinking has been amongst the forces that have brought about the crisis of poverty, malnutrition and environmental degradation for a large part of the less developed world, whether the rulers be advocates of centrally controlled Marxism or the free market.

Newspapers unwittingly highlight the contradictions in science. They describe disastrous projects that either co-opted scientists in their formulation, as in the case of the use of environmental impact assessments as described in Lindsay's chapter, or were actually promoted by scientists themselves. Yet by simultaneously describing how science has 'found the answer' or a 'new cure', the media are often a conduit by which the myth of science as salvation is promoted. The following example, drawn from Dorothy Nelkin's book *Selling Science*, illustrates the potential dangers.

In the 1950s scientists investigated 'interferons', proteins manufactured in the body when a virus invades a cell. The isolation of one of the genes coding for one such protein by a biotechnology firm in 1980 raised hopes amongst scientists of a cure for cancer. Accepting promotional information distributed at the company's press conference, many journalists welcomed this new technological development as a miracle. 'Like the genie in the fairy tale', the *Detroit Free Press* told its readers 'science came up with the key to the magic potion, a way to produce interferon in bulk'. The newspaper's phrasing is reminiscent of the following irreverent description of science by Bruno Latour

> *'Science' only gives the impression of existing by turning its experience into permanent miracle. Unable to admit its true allies it is forced to explain one marvel with another, and that one with a third. It goes on until it just looks like a fairy tale.*

The *Detroit Free Press* is no provincial free-sheet, having the fourth highest circulation of any regional newspaper in the USA. Soon *Reader's Digest*, *Newsweek* and *Time* magazine all weighed in with phrases such as 'wonder therapy', 'miracle drug' and 'sure winner'. Meanwhile, at the *New York Times*, science correspondent Harold Schmeck was cautious. He warned that research had not yet produced definitive evidence of interferon's effectiveness.

While other journalists were still hyping the protein, Schmeck reported on its possibly harmful effects, only to be accused of 'qualified reporting' and 'undermining public support for research' by four scientists in a letter to his editor. Within two years, the tone of press reports changed abruptly after four patients treated with interferon died in 1982. 'From wonder drug to wall-flower' and 'Studies cast doubt on cancer cure' became more typical headlines.

Accounts of discrete, often dramatized, events convey little about the social processes within science. Nelkin suggests science in the press becomes more like the sports pages—a race between scientists in different institutes or between different competing nations. Yet unlike most sports writers, science correspondents—especially those with limited experience in science or in reporting scientific issues—are vulnerable to manipulation by their sources of information. Without time to ponder the complexities and controversies surrounding often highly technical issues, it is all too easy to accept certain scientists as being reliable sources.

Those who present a simplistic view of science tailored for public consumption are, in effect, viewing their audience as if they were uncritical recipients of information. Can we be content with a society where the public can cite past scientific triumphs, but are not able to grasp why scientists disagree as to whether their nitrate-polluted water is safe to drink, or whether their food should be irradiated? Historian Patricia Fara suggests that society is currently

> depriving its citizens of their right to participate in decision-making processes about social goals and the allocation of resources. It is preventing them from being able to voice their opinions about what sort of objectives they would like scientists to aim at. Those who promote science as the most desirable type of knowledge are vulnerable to cynical accusations of being engaged in an élitist propaganda exercise to polish up the tarnished image of scientific research, and thus assure their own future employment.

Such accusations may encourage a skeptical, even anti-science attitude amongst people who had long believed that what scientists said was reliable. Meanwhile, yet another generation is being presented with the image of two cultures of 'science' and 'the rest'.

Some scientists question the intellectual rigor of young people who choose not to take science courses. Lewis Wolpert is one of those who believes that science requires a very special and 'un-natural process, quite different from ordinary thinking', which, he conjectures, many students find too difficult. For him, science is not common sense, but a special way of interacting with the natural world. Young people, he suggests, may be cowardly in that they are not willing to put up with the intellectual rigor that science involves. Rather than being degenerate, timid or even 'lazy' as Wolpert has recently suggested, the chapter by Brian Moss suggests that many young people come to realize that the emperor of scientific objectivity wears no clothes.

Coupled with this apathy towards science amongst a high proportion of the young is a burgeoning anti-science movement, whose views are eloquently, if not comprehensively, summed up by a literary historian in Tom Stoppard's recent play, *Arcadia*

> *I can't think of anything more trivial than the speed of light! Quarks, quasars—big bangs, black holes—who gives a shit? How did you people con us out of all that status? All that money? And why are you so pleased with yourselves? . . . I'd push the lot of you over a cliff myself. Except for the one in the wheelchair—I think I might lose the sympathy vote before people had time to think it through.*

Such sentiments seem full of contradictions, as scientists and others have been keen to point out. Are such people against all knowledge, or just the use to which certain scientific knowledge is put? Are its members prepared to shun their mod-cons, or foresee a society that could? Nevertheless, if science had not become separated from other forms of knowledge as described here, there would have been no opportunity for such views to gain currency. Wolpert's views should be seen in the context of those whom he is opposing. In the USA, the power of the anti-intellectual religious right can make even the teaching of orthodox Darwinian evolution in the place of biblical accounts difficult. Wolpert wants to portray his profession as something special and its practitioners as creative geniuses who should be given their freedom. But this chapter is not arguing that science is a 'bad' or reactionary force, or that 'freedom' should be removed from scientists—rather, I argue simply that science is not distinctly different from other areas of knowledge. To help to end the misunderstandings between scientists and the rest of society, scientists need to shed their exclusive image.

One sign of the need for this shift in perspective comes from the very conflicts between environmental issues and science that have been partly explored in this book and form the subject of *The Green Case* by the sociologist Steven Yearley. Viewing scientific knowledge as socially constructed rather than inherently 'true' or 'false', Yearley suggests that science can be an unreliable ally both for environmental groups and for industry and government:

Members of the public may look for authoritative judgements and may be dismayed by factlessness. They may look to the scientific experts in conservation organisations for the answers to questions that concern them personally and be frustrated because the 'experts' do not know.

Bird watchers, even sportsmen, may be concerned about the reasons for fluctuations in bird populations. They see this as a kind of question which conservation scientists should be able to settle, but scientists may well not know or even be sure how to find out.

Science-related public controversies have multiplied. Greens, anti-vivisectionists and other pressure groups recruit scientists to produce acceptable evidence against other scientists employed by government and industry. More than ever before, science is openly contested. Contemporary controversies may yet prove productive if they encourage more people to enter the debate and discourage premature 'closure' of disputes.

The end of the 200 year old demarcation of science from all other human activities may be in sight. But any such de-throning of science would not condemn its participants, or all of its past endeavors. A new 'research' paradigm would merely acknowledge the demise of demarcated 'science', which was never more objective, more true, or more useful than any of the other areas of knowledge. Realizing that we can never find the transcendent 'scientific' answers in the way our century's scientific prophets hoped we could, we can look forward to the sort of diverse cross-fertilizing investigations, and their applications, which can help to bring about our desired goals. Although this book, and projects like it, produce no prescriptive master plan—indeed, many authors suggest that these have been part of the problem—*Science for the Earth* may mark the early steps on a path which will begin, at last, to bring science down to Earth.

Annotated List of Further Reading

Nobel Conference XXV: the End of Science? Attack and Defense, Richard Q. Elvee (Ed.), Lanham: University Press of America, 1992.
  A debate on the future of science. Scientists, including Nobel Laureate Sheldon Lee Glashow, debate a wide range of issues with philosophers, historians and sociologists of science. Subjects such as science's unity or disunity, feminism, objectivity and the social construction of science provoke lively debate.

The Un-Natural Nature of Science, Lewis Wolpert, London: Faber, 1992. Also see reviews by Jon Turney, Paul M. Clark, Harry M. Collins, Simon Schaffer, James Cornell and Michael Shortland, together with reply by Lewis Wolpert, in *Public Understanding Of Science*, Vol. 2, pp. 257–274, 1993.

Wolpert's book gives a rare insight into the philosophy of a practicing scientist and science popularizer. In a later multi-authored review, several distinguished commentators discuss some of Wolpert's claims and arguments and he is also given the chance to reply.

Selling Science: How the Press Covers Science and Technology, Dorothy Nelkin, New York: W.H. Freeman, 1987.

Investigates how science and technology are reported in the press in the USA, revealing how the constraints, biases and myth-making of journalists are accompanied by public relations ploys by scientists, universities, corporations and the government.

The Racial Economy of Science: Toward a Democratic Future, Sandra Harding (Ed.), Bloomington: Indiana University Press, 1993.

A wide-ranging collection of classic and recent essays on science by historians, anthropologists, linguists, biologists, engineers, policy analysts, sociologists, and community activists as well as statements by such institutions as the National Academy of Sciences and *The Black Scholar*.

A Scientific Agenda for Climate Policy, Sonja Boehmer-Christiansen, *Nature*, **75**, 400–402, 1994.

A perceptive summary of the politics behind the global warming debate, including the accusation that scientists have manipulated public concern for their own ends.

The Green Case: A Sociology of Environmental Issues, Arguments and Politics, Steven Yearley, London: Harper Collins, 1991.

A pioneering sociological study of the relationship between environmentalism and science.

Index